The Causes of Structural Unemployment

Work & Society Series

THE CAUSES OF STRUCTURAL UNEMPLOYMENT
Four Factors that Keep People from the Jobs They Deserve

Thomas Janoski,
David Luke, and
Christopher Oliver

polity

First published in 2014 by Polity Press

Polity Press
65 Bridge Street
Cambridge CB2 1UR, UK

Polity Press
350 Main Street
Malden, MA 02148, USA

ISBN-13: 978-0-7456-7027-0
ISBN-13: 978-0-7456-7028-7(pb)

A catalogue record for this book is available from the British Library.

Typeset in 10.5 on 12 pt Sabon
by Toppan Best-set Premedia Limited
Printed in Great Britain by TJ International Ltd, Padstow, Cornwall

The publisher has used its best endeavours to ensure that the URLs for external websites referred to in this book are correct and active at the time of going to press. However, the publisher has no responsibility for the websites and can make no guarantee that a site will remain live or that the content is or will remain appropriate.

Every effort has been made to trace all copyright holders, but if any have been inadvertently overlooked the publisher will be pleased to include any necessary credits in any subsequent reprint or edition.

For further information on Polity, visit our website: www.politybooks.com

Dedication

To the many workers in or previously from Michigan
who have suffered through
structural unemployment for over three decades.
There are reasons for this other than
those that you have generally heard.

Contents

Tables, Figures, and Boxes

Tables

Figures

Boxes

Note: The workers whose cases are presented in the boxes are given their actual names when they have been profiled in articles or books (indicated by a reference at the end of their story). If there is no reference listed, we have disguised the names, locations, and employers of people we have known or interviewed. None of these workers are composites that compound the problems of multiple people.

Abbreviations

AA	Trade Adjustment Assistance job training programs
ABS	asset-backed securities; a form of collateral
AIC	advanced industrialized country
ALMP	active labor market policy
AMTEC	Automotive Manufacturing Training and Education Collaborative
ARPANET	Advanced Research Projects Agency Network
ARRA	American Recovery and Reinvestment Act, which provided funds for job creation
BCG	Boston Consulting Group
CAD/CAM	computer-aided design/computer-aided manufacturing
CBTC	class-biased technological change
CCC	Civilian Conservation Corps
CDO	collateral-debt obligations; a form of collateral to back an investment
CDS	credit default swaps; a form of insurance for financial transactions
CETA	Comprehensive Employment and Training Act
CNC	computerized numerical control
CT	computerized tomography
dot.com	The dot.com bubble, when large numbers of web and high tech companies folded

FBTC	factor-biased technological change
FDI	foreign direct investment
FILM	firm internal labor market
FIRE	financial, insurance, and real estate
FLA	Fair Labor Association
FLM	firm labor market
GATT	General Agreements on Tariffs and Trade
GDP	gross domestic product
HF	hedge funds as a new and relatively lightly regulated financial institutions
HMO	health maintenance organization
ILO	International Labor Office
IMF	International Monetary Fund
JPTA	Job Partnership and Training Act
LDC	less developed country
LMI	labor market intermediary
LP-1	lean production one
LP-2	lean production two
LP-3	lean production three
LTCM	Long-Term Capital Management
M&A	the merger of two corporations, or the acquisition of one by another
MDTA	Manpower Development and Training Act
MRI	magnetic resonance imaging
NAFTA	North American Free Trade Agreement
NAIRU	non-accelerating inflation rate of unemployment
NCRC	National Career Readiness Certificate
NGO	non-governmental organization
NIRB	National Infrastructure Reconstruction Bank
NJTC	New Jobs Tax Credit program for job creation programs after 2008
NSF	National Science Foundation
NTT	new trade theory
OECD	Organization for Economic Cooperation and Development
OEM	original equipment manufacturer
OILM	occupational internal labor market
OLM	occupational labor market
OPEC	Organization of Petroleum Exporting Countries

PWA	Public Works Administration
R&D	research and development
SEC	Securities and Exchange Commission, which governs the stock market and Wall Street
S&L	savings and loan
SLAM	secondary labor market
SPV	special purpose vehicles that transform toxic assets into something mysteriously better
TAA	Trade Adjustment Assistance
TANF	Temporary Assistance for Needy Families
TARP	Troubled Asset Relief Program
TEU	twenty-foot equivalent unit
TPS	Toyota production system
UAW	United Automobile Workers
UEC	unemployment compensation adjustment or extensions
USES	US Employment Service
VaR	value at risk tax
VAT	value-added tax
WB	World Bank
WIA	Workforce Investment Act
WOTC	Work Opportunity Tax Credit
WPA	Works Progress Administration
WTO	World Trade Organization

Acknowledgments

Barry Bluestone and Bennett Harrison (1982) sounded the early warning call on outsourcing, and Ron and Anil Hira (2005) looked at offshoring more closely. But all in all, few scholars concentrate on the recent rise in structural unemployment and the jobless recession with such a wide-angle lens as we do in this book. Part of the reason is that the measure that would seem most helpful – foreign direct investment or FDI – is flawed and too crude to make any definite conclusions about the impact of offshoring. It just mixes up too many different elements of Wall Street and real estate markets. Others, like Thomas Friedman in *The World Is Flat* (2005), are somewhat celebratory about offshoring, though his more recent book with Michael Mandelbaum is much more sobering and almost a dirge – *That Used to Be Us* (2011).

The most frequent approach to structural unemployment is through skill mismatch. We cover this first in this book and then go on to the three larger issues mentioned below. In this area of mismatch, some very good works are going beyond blaming the victim. Peter Cappelli's book *Why Good People Can't Get Jobs* (2012a) takes an important step to reorient the skills mismatch toward employers who want skills but don't want to train employees. Works such as Arne Kalleberg's *Good Jobs, Bad Jobs* (2011), Harry Holzer and colleagues' *Where Are All the Good Jobs Going?* (2011), and Paul Osterman and Beth Shulman's *Good Jobs America*

(2001) provide an excellent picture of the lower and middle rungs of the job ladder. We build especially on some of Althauser and Kalleberg's work about segmented labor markets and trace how workers have flowed from higher to lower segments. In sum, we take a more jaundiced view toward skills mismatch than they do, but we also bring it together with the three structural forces of offshoring, technology and financialization.

We thank Jonathan Skerrett for asking us to give voice to a number of Americans suffering from structural unemployment, and for giving us feedback on the book throughout its development. We would also like to thank Lane Kenworthy from the University of Arizona for his input at the early stages of this project and coming to give one of the keynote talks at the University of Kentucky "Rising Inequalities Conference." The ideas for this project were in a paper in the National Science Foundation (NSF) report on "Rebuilding the Mosaic" by Thomas Janoski and Christopher Oliver. It was one of the 252 white papers in the NSF report, *SBE 2020: Future Research in the Social, Behavioral and Economic Sciences* (http://www.nsf.gov/pubs/2012/nsf11086/nsf11086pdf; webcast http://www.nsf.gov/news/news_summ.jsp?cntn_id=122464&org=NSF&from=news). Parts of this project were presented from 2011 to 2012 by Thomas Janoski at the University of Kentucky Sociology Colloquium, and by Thomas Janoski and David Luke at the organizations section of the American Sociological Association in Denver, the European Sociological Association conference on economic sociology in Moscow, and the Tennessee Employment Relations Association (TERRA) conference on the auto industry. We would like to thank Patricia Thornton at Duke University, Eric Richmond of the Federal Research Bank of Cleveland, William Canak of TERRA and Middle Tennessee State University, Darina Lepadatu of Kennesaw State University, Bruce Carruthers at Northwestern University, and Gerald Davis at the University of Michigan for their valuable comments. We especially thank three anonymous reviewers who provided especially helpful comments. Finally, we thank Patricia E. White and Jan Stets of the NSF for their help on "The Maturing of Lean Production" grant (NSF-ARRA 0940807) that provided the needed resources to do much of this project.

1
Introduction

To somewhat alter a phrase from Karl Marx and Friedrich Engels, "A specter is haunting advanced industrial countries and it is structural unemployment." In Europe, Spain and Greece are facing unemployment rates over 25 percent. The decline in jobs that comes and goes with the economic ups and downs of the business cycle – cyclical unemployment – is being supplanted by more permanent and disrupting unemployment that threatens the working and middle classes. A 2012 Pew survey of 1,297 Americans says that in the preceding fifteen years, the middle class had "shrunk in size, fallen backward in income and wealth, and shed some – but by no means all – of its characteristic faith in the future" (Pew, 2012:1). Michael Gibbs says that the American "middle class is on the verge of extinction" (2010:B8). The economic recovery after 2001 was unusually weak in providing employment, and since 2004, observers have been increasingly talking about "jobless recoveries"– when an economy experiences growth in GDP while employment stagnates. While the stock market has recovered from the "great recession" of 2008, employment has not. This collapse was considered to be cyclical by many, but much of this landslide of unemployment is clearly structural. The recovery of profits and corporate performance has not resurrected the job market.

Structural unemployment and futile job searches are common, and the most recent generation of young job seekers is being called "the Recession Generation" or "Generation R." There are two versions of Generation R: underworked 20-somethings cannot get their first job and live at home, and overworked 20-somethings hang on to their jobs but have to do twice as much work because employers have cut their workforce to the bone (Schott, 2010; Godofsky et al., 2010; Newman, 1999, 2012). In response to these jobless recoveries, this book explains the four causes of structural unemployment and rising inequality, and then proposes policies to alleviate joblessness.

In our view, the four causes of structural unemployment and downward mobility are diverse and not commonly put together in the same breath. First, the most discussed features of unemployment come from "skill mismatches" caused by the shift from manufacturing to service jobs. Blue-collar skills are a poor fit with white-collar or service jobs. But there is more going on here than a simple need for retraining. Second, corporate offshoring in search of lower wages has moved large numbers of jobs to China, India, and other countries, and this has decimated manufacturing and some white-collar jobs. Offshoring requires massive amounts of direct foreign investment and a consulting industry that backs it up. It is especially caused by two corporate forms of lean production. Third, technology in the form of containerships, computers, and automation has replaced many jobs. The web has devastated jobs in newspapers, magazines, the postal service, and travel agencies. The internet also aids offshoring because it allows people to do information-intensive jobs from anywhere in the world. Automation and robotics reduce jobs on assembly lines throughout the world, and create only a few more jobs in designing and maintaining equipment. And although information technology also leads to new jobs, it does not produce enough jobs in the short term to balance the losses. Fourth, instability in global finance creates pressures for offshoring and makes recessions more frequent and longer. This intensifies the previous three factors by causing downturns that become structural as they increase the duration of unemployment. In sum, new jobs emerge in less-developed countries (LDCs), but these four forces destroy jobs in advanced industrialized countries with an instantaneous, worldwide system of communication.

Economic, Political Economy and Institutional Explanations

There are some differences between the way we use the term "structural unemployment" and the way economists generally use it. We take a macro-sociological approach based on a critical view of political economy. The strength of the economic approach is the creation of a tightly linked theory with a narrow focus on a limited number of variables. In a sense, most economic analyses of unemployment are generally limited to job vacancies, inflation, and economic growth, sometimes adding investment (especially when they move to explaining growth rather than jobs) (Daly et al., 2012; Acemoglu, 2009). The results seem to be tightly focused on mismatch – the first of our four explanations. While this explanation has some validity, sole reliance on it often leads to "blaming the victim" – it's the unemployed workers' fault that they have not retrained or chosen a better occupation. As a result, this approach has little to say about outsourcing, offshoring, ancillary technologies, and the detrimental effects of financialization on unemployment.[1]

Our wider view of structural unemployment builds on some of the mismatch analysis, but focuses more on the conflict between denationalized transnational corporations and employees in advanced industrialized countries (AICs). This is partially a class-conflict approach using elite or neo-Marxist theory with offshore-based profit taking, and an institutional or Weberian analysis of multination states struggling to maintain control of corporations and protect their citizens in a global economic environment. As one can see, the economic results of the last few decades have favored transnational corporations, with their high profits, and the upper classes getting a historically high proportion of income and especially wealth (Goldstein, 2012). Former middle-class citizens have suffered greater unemployment and then a downward shift to lower-paid jobs. In some ways a new social contract is in the initial stages of being forged, with the powerful transnational corporations having the upper hand at this point. This is why explanations that do not use a wider lens – focusing on financialization, the declining middle class, growing inequality, and transnational corporations – are quite myopic. We will discuss economic studies that we believe show that a structural shift has occurred, but our explanations will be much broader than most of these analyses. For instance, in the aftermath of the recession of 2008, Daly et al. say that "a better understanding of the determinants of job creation in the aftermath of recession is crucial" (2012:24). Thus, our intent is to explain unemployment with three additional arguments involving a panorama of American workers in a new and complex division of labor.

In the next sections we discuss (1) the definitions, levels, and types of unemployment, with a focus on structural unemployment, including the Beveridge and Phillips curves, the duration of unemployment, and the stigma involved in current increases in the duration of unemployment; (2) the impact of unemployment on inequality, which starts with unemployment and leads to decreasing one's expectations of work to the lower-level segments of the labor market; and (3) the four factors that cause structural unemployment – the shift to service jobs and skill mismatches, outsourcing and offshoring, new technologies, and structural financialization – which is the main focus of this book; and we end with (4) our governmental policy recommendations to alleviate structural unemployment.

Definitions, Levels, and Types of Unemployment

Unemployment is generally defined as the number of persons who are ready and willing to work who cannot find a job. The unemployment rate consists of those persons who are unemployed divided by the total labor force, which includes the unemployed. It is important to note that if a person is not ready and willing to work, which means that they are not actively searching for a job, then that person is considered to be out of the labor force and is therefore *neither* employed *nor* unemployed. These "discouraged workers" are removed from the unemployment figures and the overall labor force.

People can leave the labor force by routes including retiring early, going on disability, working in the underground or illegal economy, or simply living upon the contributions of others (e.g., family, friends, or the government).

There are two methods for collecting unemployment figures. One method uses a sample survey of the population to find out the number of unemployed and those who are working. The other method relies on the administrative records of the employment service or other agency that gives out unemployment compensation payments and often gives job search advice. The survey research method of collecting the data is generally considered to be the most accurate way to determine unemployment rates because the administrative record method can miss people who do not want to receive unemployment compensation (Davis et al., 2010). Often those people who anticipate only a short stay on unemployment fall into this category, although there are a few people who are ideologically opposed to the idea of government and will refuse their unemployment compensation payments and use their retirement or other savings to tide them over during various bouts of unemployment.

The OECD has devised a method to standardize or harmonize these two diverse methods of collecting unemployment data so that countries can be easily compared. Section (a) of table 1.1 shows some of these harmonized rates for a number of countries, and figure 1.1 graphs the US unemployment rate from 1950 to 2012. Clearly, the unemployment rate has increased since 2000. Figure 1.1 shows US unemployment rates going back to 1950 and up to 2012. The latest figures there match the previous post-World War II peak figures during the oil crises of 1973–4 and 1980–2, when a clear structural factor – OPEC raising the price of oil – increased unemployment. This brought about a massive government effort to support training and create jobs through the Comprehensive Employment and Training Act. Since then OPEC has largely disintegrated as a unified force raising gas prices (Carollo, 2011), but new structural forces involving global trade and offshoring have taken OPEC's place from 2000 to the present.

There are three types of unemployment: frictional, cyclical, and structural. Frictional unemployment is short-term in the

Table 1.1: Harmonized unemployment rates and inequality for seven countries, 1991–2013/14

Year	US	Canada	UK	France	Germany	Sweden	Spain
(a) Unemployment rate (percent):							
1991	6.8	10.3	8.6	8.5	5.5	3.1	14.5
1995	5.6	9.5	8.5	10.5	8.2	8.8	20.1
2000	4.0	6.8	5.4	9.0	8.0	5.6	11.7
2001	4.7	7.2	5.0	8.2	7.9	5.9	10.5
2002	5.8	7.7	5.1	8.3	8.7	6.0	11.4
2003	6.0	7.6	5.0	8.9	9.8	6.6	11.2
2004	5.5	7.2	4.7	9.3	10.5	7.4	10.9
2005	5.1	6.8	4.8	9.3	11.3	7.7	9.2
2006	4.6	6.3	5.4	9.2	10.2	7.1	8.5
2007	4.6	6.0	5.3	8.4	8.7	6.1	8.3
2008	5.8	6.1	5.6	7.8	7.5	6.2	11.4
2009	9.3	8.3	7.6	9.5	7.8	8.3	18.0
2010	9.6	8.0	7.8	9.8	7.1	8.4	20.1
2011	9.0	7.4	8.0	9.7	5.9	7.5	21.7
2012	7.8	7.2	7.7	10.5	5.4	8.1	26.1
2013/14	7.5	7.5	7.7	11.0	5.4	8.2	26.6
(b) Employment rate of population (participation rate, percent), 2012:							
	65.1	72.2	70.9	63.9	72.8	73.8	56.2
(c) Gini coefficient of inequality after tax and transfers, 2008 or 2009:							
	.378	.324	.345	.293	.295	.259	.317

Source: Compiled with data from OECD (2011d, 2012a) and press releases.

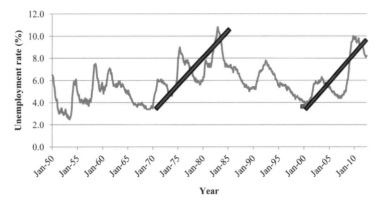

Figure 1.1 Unemployment rates, US, January 1950–June 2012
Source: BLS/CPS (2013).

sense that employers and workers more or less cannot find each other in weeks or months. It presumes that there are no other barriers to employment other than the right employees getting to the job openings that already exist in firms. This is often addressed through the relationship of vacancy rates in firms and unemployment outside of them. Improving information in the economy through better job placement information is often seen as a solution to this problem.

Cyclical unemployment refers to jobs not being available because the economy is in a cyclical downturn that occurs with the generally expected business cycle. This is short-term unemployment of one to two years. Some say that as worker wage rates decline, employers will be more able to hire workers and more interested in doing so. This neo-classical economic theory ran into trouble during the great depression when the jobs took an inordinately long period of time to reappear. It was also accompanied by currency deflation, which exacerbated the problem. With employers engaging in repeated cuts to save money, the economy hit a downward spiral with more and more unemployment. In this sense, cyclical unemployment can become structural. Nonetheless, the post-World War II economy went through a number of business cycles that were somewhat temporary, and unemployment compensation generally tided workers over until the economic cycle reversed and jobs became more available. But in the last recession, this support has not lasted as long as the drought of jobs.

Evidence for Structural Unemployment

When Baily and Lawrence (2004) ask "what happened to the great US job machine?" they are not talking about a short-term blip. Structural unemployment indicates that there is something long-term and even permanent about the nature of unemployment. Jobs are not going to reappear, or they are not going to reappear for the specific unemployed people who are seeking them. Consequently, the duration of unemployment is long-term and workers cannot simply endure until the passing of temporary frictions or the recovery from the business cycle. This does not necessarily mean that unemployment lasts for decades, but it does mean that workers are unemployed and then enter into a process of accepting lower-level jobs, going on disability, or becoming homeless. Structural unemployment indicates that there is something else going on that alters the structure of the labor market, and that is what this book is about – the more enduring changes in the economy that make unemployment and declining social mobility a longer-term problem. And as part of these structures related to unemployment and labor markets, we will use an approach that indicates that there are different types of forces that structure economies through segmented labor markets that influence one's search for employment.

It is often difficult to differentiate between structural and cyclical unemployment. When unemployment first appears it is often labeled cyclical or due to a downturn in business, and when it hangs around, then the term structural unemployment may be used. There is no "label" that comes with unemployment so that one can differentiate these terms. If you ask someone who has lost their job if they are cyclically or structurally unemployed, they will just react with a puzzled look. Much debate goes on about this issue, but we point to five types of evidence that indicate that unemployment is structural: (1) long-term increases in unemployment for more than ten years, (2) the slowdown in the speed that jobs are filled, (3) the lengthening of the time spent in unemployment, (4) the declining participation rate in terms of people actually working, and (5) the increasing financial instability that makes cyclical crises more frequent than in the past.

First, economist J. Bradford DeLong, among others, argues that if unemployment "stays elevated for two or three more years" it "converts cyclical unemployment into structural unemployment" (2010a:1). While this does not pinpoint the actual structures of unemployment, persistently high and climbing unemployment rates above 5 percent over an extended period of time clearly lead to structural unemployment. If we look at Figure 1.1, we can see that from a trough in January 1970 to a peak in January of 1983 (13 years) unemployment rose to over 10 percent. Similarly, from the trough in January of 2000 to a near peak of January of 2013 (another 13-year period), unemployment rose to 10 percent. Each period clearly entailed structural unemployment, using DeLong's definition.

Second, the Beveridge curve measures the relationship of job openings to unemployment over time. Generally, one would expect that the more the job openings or vacancies, the lower the unemployment rate. Hence, the curve with vacancies on the vertical axis and unemployment on the horizontal axis should show a downward slope. Figure 1.2 shows a Beveridge curve from 2001 to 2013. Generally, the curve is relatively straight, but for the most recent period it has shifted to a more sluggish relationship between job vacancies and unemployment. In other words, the jobs are there but people are still unemployed. This shift to more joblessness for the most recent points suggests that the curve has moved to a higher level where unemployment persists even though there are more job openings. This is direct evidence of structural unemployment.

Economists sometimes see this as evidence that the natural rate of unemployment has increased. However, we find "the natural rate of unemployment" a highly loaded concept. One could ask a similar question about "the natural rate of profits" and then accuse CEOs, investment bankers, stockbrokers, and others of increasing not only inequality but inflation. While this is rarely if ever done, it points to the

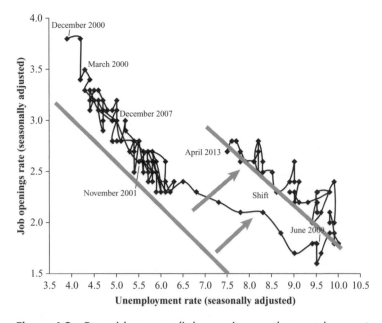

Figure 1.2   Beveridge curve (job openings and unemployment rates), US, 2001–13
Source: Bureau of Labor Statistics, US Department of Labor.

pejorative use of "natural" in these situations. Surely one can be concerned about inflation, but many different countries (e.g., Sweden and Germany) have had very low rates of inflation and high wage levels with low unemployment at different points in history. If Sweden were the example in the 1960s and 1970s, we might declare an unemployment rate of 2.0 percent to be a natural rate when certain policy options are used.[2]

The Beveridge curve tends to be connected to inflation through a form of the natural rate of unemployment or NAIRU (non-accelerating inflation rate of unemployment) and the Phillips curve, which plots the inflation and unemployment rates. This generally shows that as unemployment goes down, inflation will increase. In other words, in helping people get jobs, the overall level of prices will increase and even set off an inflationary spiral (Phelps, 1994). Conservative and monetarist economists are fond of the NAIRU and privilege concerns about inflation since it most often favors the wealthy who invest to create jobs. But recent analysis now sees the Phillips curve as too simplistic. Nonetheless, economists and some policy makers still debate what the natural rate might be. In the modern offshoring period, the Phillips curve is partially reversed in that unemployment or underemployment increases while prices for many goods produced in China and India may go down. In any event, we find the shift in the Beveridge curve, which may be due to many different types of institutional changes, to be solid evidence of structural unemployment (or simple blockages in people not getting the jobs that are actually available).

Third, a more direct measure of the structural nature of unemployment is the long-term unemployment rate. Taking over 27 weeks of unemployment as the measure of long-term unemployment, we can see that the duration of unemployment has generally gone up (Rothstein, 2012; Tasci and Lindner, 2010). From figure 1.3 we can see a structural shift. From 1975 to 2002 the first estimated regression line shows a small increase (i.e., slope) in the percentage of unemployment that is long-term (i.e., over 27 weeks). The second

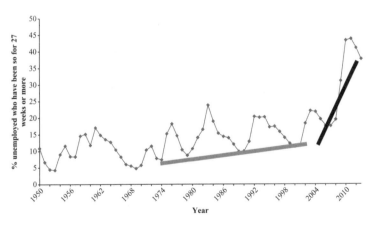

Figure 1.3 Shift in long-term unemployment, US, yearly averages, 1950–2013
Source: BLS/CPS (2013).

estimated regression line from 2005 to 2010 shows a much larger increase (a greater slope) in what looks like a major increase in the people ready and willing to work who have been left without jobs for more than 27 weeks. While some may argue that this is due to unemployment compensation, to have an effect starting in 2005 means that something must be entirely new about these payments that was not present in the 1970s, 1980s, or 1990s. Instead, we will argue that structural factors connected to offshoring, new technologies, and financialization have created this new and hazardous era of structural unemployment. In particular, the unusually slow recovery of employment after the quick recovery of stock prices is a structurally bad omen.

Fourth, a further form of structural unemployment has to do with race and ethnicity. In the US, African-American and Hispanic unemployment rates are consistently higher than white rates. In figure 1.4, we can see that African-American unemployment is more than 6 percent greater than Hispanic and about 10 percent greater than white unemployment rates. These differences get a bit smaller as we move into the 1990s, but in the "great recession" we go back to big structural differences from 2008 to 2011. Rates for black and white women are sometimes a bit lower, but they are much

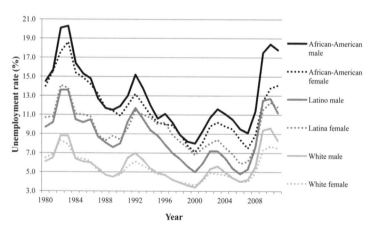

Figure 1.4 Unemployment rates, US, by race and gender, 1980–2011
Source: Bureau of Labor Statistics.

larger for Hispanic women. And one consequence is that African-Americans file for bankruptcy twice as much as whites, which creates a generational effect on wealth accumulation (Cohen and Lawless, 2012:181). This is a huge structural difference in unemployment that is not inherently due to free market behavior and is most often attributed to various forms of direct and indirect discrimination. Much of this structural unemployment has to do with the cultural matching that employers use as shorthand to get at skills and motivation (Rivera, 2012; Moss and Tilly, 2001; Turco, 2010). Employers in suburbs and small businesses, even when skill requirements are lower, are less likely to hire black men than in central cities and larger firms. This is driven by employer's poor perceptions of the motivation and performance of African-American and also Latino workers. African-American women are also negatively impacted by employee perceptions of skill; however, black men have a rougher road to employment (Moss and Tilly, 2001). In general, sociology gives employment discrimination and the structural unemployment it generates a great deal of attention.

Finally, another form of structural unemployment does not appear in the unemployment rate. To be unemployed, one must be able, willing, and ready to work. People who are not so and who do not have jobs are not included. Some of these workers may be spouses who stay home to take care of children. Others may be retired or disabled. In the face of unemployment some workers may decide to retire early. Others who may be younger may collect unemployment compensation for a year or two, but then if they cannot find work, they face major difficulties in getting food, shelter, and money. According to Bureau of Labor statistics, the overall participation rate of the US workforce has been steadily going down from 69.5 percent in April 2000 to 63.4 percent in May 2013. Further, from 2000 to 2012, the number of workers claiming disability has doubled from 1 per 100 to 2 per 100 (BLS/CPS, 2013). Comparing employment ratios to those in other countries, Germany has 7.7 percent and Sweden 8.7 percent more of its labor force at work than the US (see (b) in table 1.1).

A troubling study by National Public Radio of one Alabama county in 2013 showed that one in four people in the county were on disability, and that for laid-off workers with no schooling beyond high school, there were no comparable jobs that they could do (Joffe-Walt, 2013). Part of the problem was that many workers had medical conditions that prevented physical labor, but a desk job was not in the realm of possibility. The doctor who certified these people as disabled said he signed the statement of disability because there was just no way that these people would ever find a job in his county. As a result, much of the doubling of US disability rates masks the true rate of structural unemployment.[3]

A further problem is the stigma that often accompanies dispiriting unemployment (Goffman, 1963; Letkemann, 2002).[4] It is especially harmful when the unemployed internalize this stigma and confirm themselves as unemployable. In a comparative analysis, Ofer Sharone shows that US workers view the job search based on interpersonal chemistry and emotion work rather than on the competition between workers with specific skills. The American approach stresses the self-advertisement and the almost intimate chemistry of the interview. This plays into the American bias toward individuals to make the job interview "a bit like going to the prom" (Sharone, 2013:1442; Uchitelle, 2006; Schlozman and Verba, 1979). This Goffmanian presentation or marketing of the self is somewhat distinctive of the US, where job placement institutions are less prominent (Janoski, 1990). But the flipside of this, which Sharone implies, is that these presentations say "I am not a grumbler, grouser, or collective organizer of an oppositional culture" (whether based on race, gender, or union sympathies). In other words, "I am on the employer's side." And when not getting the job, American workers blame themselves for not having presented themselves effectively, while Israelis and most Europeans take a more collective view.

In the recent recession, the refusal by some employers to hire the unemployed, including advertising that the unemployed need not apply, is being considered by some legislators as a form of discrimination. The chances of this becoming law are probably small, but the idea of the stigma of being unemployed is an important concept. Governments have to be concerned not only with trying to create jobs and investor confidence, but also with the mental health, well-being, and confidence of the unemployed. Otherwise, governments and employers become complicit in creating disabled citizens who drop out of the labor market when they have significant skills and abilities to offer. This rationale of avoiding stigma is often an unstated basis of many programs to help the unemployed.

Unemployment, Inequality, and Labor Market Segmentation

The panorama of unemployment in AICs is more complex than one would expect. While there has been increasing financial and political pressure on the welfare state with various debt crises, the financial stability of the welfare state in most AICs is still relatively assured (Brady et al., 2007). Deindustrialization has increased over time with declining manufacturing, and globalization has definitely increased income inequality, with declining wages and rising profits for many corporations. Job stability has decreased for men, but there is some evidence that it has increased for women (Hollister, 2011; Farber, 2008) mainly due to the anti-discrimination policies of government, the diversity policies of corporations, and the increasing acceptance of female employment working its way through multiple generations of women of diverse ages (i.e., younger female cohorts who expect to work replacing retiring cohorts of women who have worked much less). The loss of manufacturing has increased balance of trade deficits as it has become increasingly difficult to export global services as much as manufactured goods.

This result is complex but two things are clear. First, declining manufacturing results first in unemployment and then in the unemployed taking lower-paid jobs in place of their previous middle-class jobs. It also decreases demand in AIC economies, since those with previously high incomes now have much less money to spend. The result is both higher inequality in the US and lower economic growth (Dwyer and Wright, 2011; Wright and Dwyer, 2003). The Gini index in the US after taxes are taken out and social security payments are made is much higher than other industrialized countries (see (c.)in table 1.1) (World Bank, 2013). Sweden at .259 and Germany at .295 are much lower than the US figure of .378. Income inequality in the US before government action has grown from moderate equality at .350 in the 1950s to the highest rate of inequality among AICs at .420 in the first decade of the new millennium (see table 1.2). This shows that the middle class has been hollowed out and much of the decline is due to their being unemployed and then sliding down in terms of labor market segments.[5]

Second, although offshoring may result in higher profits for AIC corporations, these profits go to highly paid managers and the owners of stocks and bonds (Goldstein, 2012). Corporations have no obligation to invest in AICs, so many of them send jobs overseas to cut wage-related costs. As a result, higher corporate profits exacerbate structural unemployment and inequality within the AICs despite creating more jobs in LDCs. This greatly contributes to balance of trade deficits and sovereign debt crises. From a global economic perspective, the world may be more efficient, but from the perspective of employees in AICs, there are fewer jobs,

Table 1.2:   Inequality, unemployment rates, and the declining middle class, US, 1950–2013

Period	Gini index of inequality before taxes and transfers	Range of unemployment rate (%)	Health of middle class
1950–9	.350	2.6–7.8	Growing to strong
1960–9	.340	3.9–7.0	Strong
1970–80	.366	5.9–9.0	Strong but slowing
1981–9	.379	5.0–11.0	Declining
1990–9	.399	5.6–6.8	Strong decline
2000–7	.420	4.0–4.6	Weak
2008–13	.419	9.2–10.1	Very weak

Source: US Census Bureau. http://www.census.gov/hhes/www/income/data/historical/measures.

lower income, greater inequality, and a greater possibility of crisis and decline (Friedman and Mandelbaum, 2011). This leads one to ask if the AICs will be headed toward a long-term surge in structural unemployment. In the next few paragraphs we look at where unemployment occurs in segmented labor markets.

We refer to structural unemployment as a "process" over time rather than a "state" at any one moment. This means that we regard structural unemployment as a shift from employment in a middle- or upper-class job into unemployment with a consequent readjustment of aspirations to move to a lower-paid segment of the labor market. Thus, structural unemployment at this point in time reflects a "hollowing out" of the middle class whereby inequality is increased and the average worker loses the capacity to maintain their previous standard of living. We use segmented labor market theory and dynamics to illustrate the unemployment and downward mobility process. While this model is a simplification of a complex economy, segmented labor markets make a large portion of these shifts much clearer.

One useful approach to map these movements in segmented labor markets is by use of a two-by-two classification of (1) labor market control by firms (corporations) or occupations (professions or craft unions), and (2) whether or not the labor market has internal labor markets with promotion possibilities or little chance of upward movement. There are five segments, according to Robert Althauser and Arne Kalleberg (1981):

1. *FILMs* or firm internal labor markets are represented by high-level management training programs with managers on the path toward being a CEO;
2. *OILMs* or occupational internal labor markets represent professionals like doctors and lawyers who have medical or bar associations that control much of their work;
3. *FLMs* or firm labor markets include many mid-level and moderately well-paid jobs such as white-collar or clerical jobs;
4. *OLMs* or occupational labor markets consist of the semi-professions like teaching and nursing but also the skilled trades with strong craft unions; and

5. *SLAMs* or secondary labor markets have the worst jobs with low pay, few benefits, and little job security.

In figure 1.5, we map the movements between segments that are due to unemployment. A few top managers might move to unemployment and then into middle-range jobs, perhaps as management consultants (FILM to FLM), and a few professionals may be out of work and then drift downward (OILM to OLM). But the biggest movement is from mid-range white-collar jobs into poorly paid jobs (FLM to SLAM), and semi-professional and craft work to these same secondary labor markets (OLM to SLAM). This downward trend drains the middle class since they are the most threatened segments of the job market. The straight arrows indicate

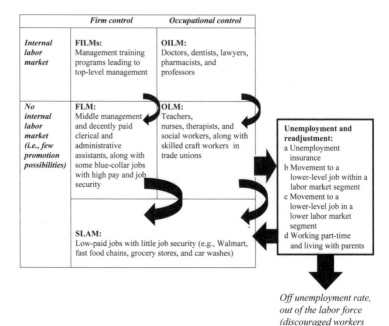

Off unemployment rate, out of the labor force (discouraged workers and those on disability)

Figure 1.5 Five types of segmented labor markets
Arrows show workers going from one labor market segment to unemployment and then to a lower labor market segment. Curved arrows assume the path to unemployment to keep the figure readable.

falling into unemployment and then moving to a lower level. The curved arrows do the same, but for simplicity we omit the path to unemployment. This current downward mobility contrasts with the upward mobility of the 1950s and 1960s. It is important to note that in the "process of downward movement," unemployment serves as a period of "aspirational readjustment" during which employees give up the wage levels of their previous jobs to accept lower pay among the only jobs that are available. This is the neo-liberal "cooling-the-mark-out" period that ends with employees from Ford or IBM taking jobs at Walmart or McDonalds (Goffman, 1952). The process of structural unemployment is slow and painful, and by the end of the unemployment period, these workers are drained not only of motivation but also of anger as they can think mainly of survival at their new and lower level of existence. But beyond downward aspirations, long-term unemployment increasingly leads to diminished confidence, deteriorating skills, mental depression, family conflict, and damaged marriages. Clearly, the unemployed should be looked at as perishable human beings who need re-employment in the short term to maintain their confidence and avoid stigma.

Four Causes of Structural Unemployment

The basis of our explanation can be seen in the four factors that cause structural unemployment: (1) the shift to services and skill mismatches; (2) downsizing, outsourcing, and off-shoring; (3) changing technology; and (4) structural finan-cialization. These changes have fundamentally changed the labor market, and the heart of this book lies in explaining them. On the left-hand side of figure 1.6 are some of the causes of the four major factors we will discuss in this book. Some of these causes point to the rise of a global economy, with the fall of communism, market deregulation with neo-liberalism, and the new world trade regimes populated by stronger economic institutions like the General Agreements on Tariffs and Trade (GATT), World Trade Organization (WTO), International Monetary Fund (IMF), and World

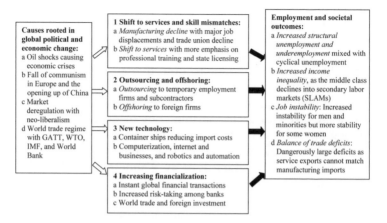

Figure 1.6   Four main causes of structural unemployment and inequality

Bank. These factors clearly influence financialization, which went global before other aspects of the economy. Greta Krippner in her explanation of financialization discounts the impact of globalization and corporate changes, and pinpoints the social, fiscal, and legitimation crises of the 1970s, which are connected to the oil price shocks of 1974 and 1980, and the double-digit inflation from 1972 to 1982 (Krippner, 2011:10–23). Some of this is based on the world systems theory of hundred-year fluctuations of Kondratieff cycles, and on the idea that the US has left the positive-sum material expansion phase of 1860–1960 (i.e., manufacturing emphasizing engineers in the A phase) and entered into a zero-sum financial expansion phase from 1969 to the present (i.e., financial services emphasizing investment banks and speculators in the B phase). This theory is largely laid out in systemic cycles of accumulation by Giovanni Arrighi (2007; Arrighi and Moore, 2001). However, explaining world systems, century-long cycles, the rise of Fordist technology, and the fall of communism are beyond the scope of this book, and we will stick to explaining how the four factors impact labor markets and structural unemployment.

Little research focuses on how these four factors have changed outcomes in employment, especially because existing research in the social sciences infrequently puts these issues together. First, most of the focus is on the shift from manufacturing to services and the subsequent mismatching of the skills of the unemployed with what the service sector now demands in terms of skills. Blue-collar skills from manufacturing fit poorly with a rising service economy. Although skill mismatches exist as an important part of structural unemployment, the role of such mismatches is often exaggerated as the sole cause of structural unemployment. Some of the expansion of services is really due to outsourced work from manufacturing employers with no real change in skills, and additional aspects of the mismatch are due to employers' reluctance to train workers and pay them a competitive wage when those skills are scarce. Consequently, we attribute the skills mismatch problem not only to workers but also to the lack of willingness to train by employers and the state.

Second, research on offshoring tends to be mainly in the field of economics, usually under the heading of whether and how globalization is efficient. There is very little social science research on why investment does not produce good jobs back in the AICs.[6] We discuss lean production and find that two major types of lean firms, represented by Nikeification and Waltonism, show a distinct lack of concern for jobs in the US and a very high proclivity for not only outsourcing but more importantly offshoring jobs to Asia, Latin America, and other areas of the world. These donut corporations that do not produce their own products create a problem for manufacturing in the US, especially since the third decade of trade deficits can be laid at the door of lower and lower levels of manufacturing exports.

Third, research on information technology is the rage, but its influence on jobs tends to be ignored or assumed. And the social impact of the web and robotics on labor markets is a severely understudied area in the social sciences. Most of the social science focus on the web is on social media and its impact on marketing or politics. We show that technology is negotiated rather than deterministically imposed, and that the containerization of ocean shipping as a technology specific to offshoring, and the computerization of all modern work as a transformative technology, both contribute to structural unemployment. Further, through a "Bravermanic leap,"[7] offshoring is beginning to affect the professions, such as the law and medicine.

And fourth, there is much research on the financial collapse of 2008–9, but little on how financial crises have come to be repeated and how they structurally impact upon labor markets. Financialization undermines the creation of stable and decently paid jobs in the US, and we show how it has promoted the short-term horizons of "shareholder value theory" that gnaws away at stable employment. We discuss how the globalization of financial markets, the increasing flow of profits to financial, insurance, and real estate (FIRE) firms, exponentially increasing CEO salaries, and vastly increased speculation have made employment less stable. This is followed by a discussion of how this came to be accepted by both the state and the public as inequality of incomes has emptied out the middle class.

Much, but not all, economic research tends to view the opening up of markets as a good thing because it increases world trade. We question the economic approach to world trade that uncritically touts "comparative advantage," but we also question critical studies that ask for protectionism. This book recognizes the positive aspects of trade, but argues that the four causes of structural unemployment must be understood and the interests of citizens, corporations, and governments must be balanced. At the present time, corporate interests through the market control much of government to the detriment of many citizens in AICs who are seeking work.

Policies to Reduce Structural Unemployment

The most-discussed solutions to unemployment are two diametrically opposed macro-approaches: to stimulate demand with Keynesian spending policies, or to stimulate investment with tax cuts (sometimes based on the Laffer curve, which says that cutting taxes creates jobs, growth, and eventually greater tax revenue). But both policy responses may simply increase offshoring. In other words, demand stimulation causes US workers to buy more Chinese-made goods sold at Walmart, and tax cuts allow corporations to invest more money in China to create more foreign jobs. As a result, both policies may even increase structural unemployment, although they may increase jobs in LDCs.[8]

In sum, the US needs policies based on an active state model that focuses on more long-term structural and institutional solutions. This approach would be more finely tuned than the typical short-term fiscal (e.g., shot-in-the-arm spending programs, or the Federal Reserve's quantitative easing) and tax policies (e.g., tax cuts). It can restructure policies more specifically toward job creation in labor markets by reconfiguring overall education and training, and regulating market and other economic institutions. Some of these policies could be permanent and some could be countercyclical, coming into effect when unemployment researches a certain rate. It may take 30 years to equilibrate US and Chinese wages, but it will leave one or more generations of workers writhing in downward mobility and lower horizons for a lifetime. A much more humane response to unemployment is necessary that will target people in the short run who are unemployed and suffering.

So we present four types of policies to combat structural unemployment: (1) job training with educational restructuring followed by job retraining, expanded vocational education, and more effective job placement; (2) job creation with a national infrastructural bank; (3) a more unified and entrepreneurially focused approach to research and development (R&D); and (4) more effective market stabilizing policies.

First, active labor market policies try to get the unemployed or those in insecure jobs into new jobs or job training for more highly skilled jobs. This requires a major restructuring of American education because of its inefficient approach to training workers who do not intend to go to college. The American high school doesn't work for nearly half the students who go there. The OECD shows that the US is one of the few countries in the world that does not offer adequate vocational training to students in secondary schools (2008). The German apprenticeship system integrates high-school-age workers into the labor force and gives them much more specific training. While the German system has disadvantages, the US education system needs a much more targeted approach, and we supply a workable solution.

Second, job creation policies are effective in promoting and temporarily creating jobs (Neumark, 2011). The biggest program, which follows President Obama's recommendations, is to create a national infrastructure bank that will be immediately ready to start projects that need to be done using employees who need jobs. The infrastructure bank would be ready in a countercyclical fashion to supply the money and engineering expertise to start new work as soon as possible. The financing of the bank would come from existing highway dollars, bonds, and tax revenues.

Third, unemployment needs to have a much more prominent place in the decisions of the WTO, the IMF, the World Bank, and the UN. These international organizations that promote trade need to be more concerned about the unemployment that comes about as a result of open trade! Also connected to trade are innovation and entrepreneurship. The amount of money the US has allocated to R&D has declined from 38 percent of world totals in 1999 to 31 percent in 2009 (NAS/NSF, 2013). While the US still leads Asia (24 percent) and the EU (23 percent), this relative decline needs to be reversed.

Fourth, market volatility increases the possibility of financial collapses, which create uncertainty or pessimism, and this causes employers to avoid new hiring. This instability as a cause of structural unemployment can be addressed by three measures related to taxes and one restricting risky investment. Avoiding excessive speculation, arbitrage, and churning increases market stability, and this can be done with a global investment tax (e.g., Tobin tax) and a value at risk tax (VaR). Third, the closing of loopholes on corporate taxes would increase tax revenues to fund other programs for job training and job creation programs. Finally, exposing commercial bank operations on everyday savings and checking accounts can be prevented by the Volcker Rule proposed in the Dodd-Frank Act (discussed below). This would reduce bank exposure by keeping our savings and checking accounts out of risky hedge and equity fund investments. All of these measures would increase financial stability.

What Comes Next?

The next chapter will explain the decline in manufacturing jobs and increase in service jobs that require different skill sets that have caused a structural mismatch in the labor market. Chapter 3 will examine the impact of offshoring and outsourcing and the changes that have come about in corporate organization through lean production. Due to foreign investment, an inexorable flow of jobs from AICs with high wages and benefits has occurred to LDCs with low wages and benefits. Chapter 4 looks at the changes in technology that have occurred in the past half-century and how these have impacted upon jobs. New technologies – container ships, computers, the web, and robotics – have destroyed many jobs and created a few new positions. The result is a balance of jobs and working conditions that is unfavorable to workers in AICs. Chapter 5 looks at structural financialization with its instantaneous communication and investment, which tend to intensify cyclical downturns. Thus, finance becomes a structural factor in itself in creating unemployment. Chapter 6 shifts gears from the problems to the possible solutions to structural unemployment. A range of government solutions includes incentivizing internal investment, and active labor market policies that target job training, job placement, and creating jobs. Finally, in the conclusion we will examine rebalancing the power of corporations and the nation-state, and coming up with a new social contract between management and labor.

2

Shifting from Manufacturing to Services and Skill Mismatches

As far back as *The Coming of Post-Industrial Society* in 1973, Daniel Bell predicted that employment in AICs would continuously shift from industrial factories to service industries. With blue-collar workers experiencing a precipitous decline, the consequences shrink the middle class and increase structural mismatches and unemployment. Since the early 1970s, it has been clear that AIC economies have shifted from manufacturing to service jobs. Steel, auto, and other manufacturing workers have lost jobs in the rust-belt states and it is difficult for them to fit into the new service economy. Wages have lagged and inequality has increased greatly, going from a Gini coefficient among the lower figures in the West to the highest among AICs in the new millennium. While a certain amount of shifting from manufacturing to services was necessary over those years, we will show that this change exceeded the levels that are healthy for an advanced economy. Furthermore, the explanation of unemployment that flows from this scenario – the skill sets of manufacturing workers do not match the needs of the service sector – is rather exaggerated, sometimes creating more problems rather than solving them. The skill mismatch argument is one of four important causes of structural unemployment, but it is certainly not the only cause. We will present a balanced picture of its effects in this chapter, emphasizing the roles of individual employees, employers, the state, and educational institutions.

The Shift from Manufacturing to Services

The shift from manufacturing to services employment can be clearly seen in figure 2.1. There is a large increase in the number of service jobs, and a steady decrease in manufacturing jobs after the first oil crisis and since 1978. This decline strongly contributes to skill mismatches. For many years, manufacturing in the US provided middle-class jobs for individuals with high school or even lower educational attainment. With the loss of manufacturing jobs, these so-called "semi-skilled" workers do not have comparable options. While consumers in the US may be pleased that the shift of manufacturing jobs to lower-wage countries results in lower-priced manufactured goods, they may find it difficult to take advantage of these low-cost goods if they do not have a job that pays them a sufficient wage to purchase them. A generation ago, people could count on working in manufacturing and earning enough to live the "American dream," but

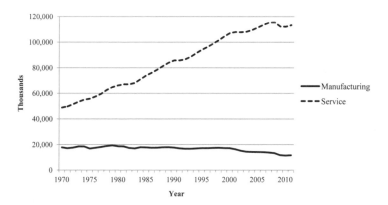

Figure 2.1 Number of manufacturing and service jobs, US, 1970–2012
Source: Bureau of Labor Statistics.
Numbers are not seasonally adjusted.

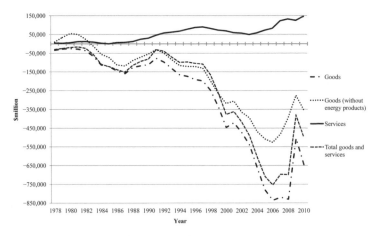

Figure 2.2 Trade balance of payments and exports with energy products (petroleum and natural gas) removed, US, 1978–2010
Source: Bureau of Economic Analysis.

today they are faced with grim job prospects. Unfortunately, most new service jobs are mainly in lower segments of structured labor markets with low pay and few if any benefits. It is clear that the standard of living of a unionized auto worker was and still is dramatically greater than that of a Walmart greeter.

Manufacturing, along with the middle class, grew after World War II and until its peak in 1978 in the US, but the decline beginning in 1978 continues to this day, where only one in ten Americans work in manufacturing (Moretti, 2012). There are serious consequences of this decline. Figure 2.2 shows America's negative balance of trade for goods beginning in the mid-1970s and continually increasing. Although the balance of trade for services is positive, it is not nearly enough to offset the large and negative trade deficit for manufactured and other goods. This balance is negative because the US is buying substantially more goods from overseas than it is selling to other countries (the lines in the graph are based on *net* exports). Even when we eliminate the enormous amounts of money representing oil imports from the total balance of trade figures (the dotted line in figure 2.2), the trade deficits for goods production still do not differ very much from the total figures (BEA, 2012). Although the US is exporting more services than it is bringing in, the service exports do not cover the imports of goods. This is understandable when one realizes that it is much easier to export a manufactured good that is separable from those who make it than to export a service that most often requires the physical presence of the service worker. Some services can be exported, like financial services that can be done anywhere, but there are many that require a doctor's scalpel or kindergarten teacher's guiding hand that make the exporting and transporting of services much more difficult than one might imagine.

Bell predicted some of this by saying about offshoring, "The reduction in costs of transport, and the differential in wages, has made it increasingly possible for American multinational corporations to manufacture significant proportions of components abroad" (1973:158). Bell suspected the US would see a substantial decrease in the proportion of exported goods in the balance of trade, asserting that the differential in wages was a motivating factor for many jobs to be moved. Consequently, there was a major shift in the production of physical goods away from the wealthier countries of the world with high labor costs to the poorer countries with much lower labor costs (Moretti, 2012). As of 2007, services accounted for more than 75 percent of US gross domestic product (GDP) and created over 19 million jobs during the 1990s (Daniels, 2007). But not enough of these services were exported to make up for the decline in manufacturing. This reveals the structural shift in the US labor market, and the basic accounting problem for the AICs that come with it.

But trade deficits are a problem for all Americans because deficits (1) devalue the currency, making it harder to buy imports, thus eventually leading to inflation (foreign goods cost more); (2) are almost a direct measure of structural unemployment; (3) cause nations to become major borrowers, which increases governmental and private debt even further; and (4) cause a decline in political power and influence (DeLong, 2010b:4–6). In other words, debtor nations soon become beholden to other countries.

Overestimates of the Shift in Services

While we largely agree with the implications of the shift from manufacturing to services employment, there are three points that need to be made so that one does not overestimate this shift. First, just as the shift from agricultural to manufacturing employment in the last century did not mean that people no longer eat food, one should keep in mind that manufacturing and construction are still enormous components of the revenues that corporations generate. Thus, despite the shift to services, consumers continue to pay out large percentages of their annual income for automobiles, houses, iPads and computers, and multitudinous other items from pots and pans to lawnmowers. One should not confuse the benefits of high revenues and profits that large corporations make by transferring many of their workers to service firms with the decline of the manufacturing labor force. After all, these workers are doing the same work despite their reclassification.

Second, the US is one of the most extreme examples of the shift from manufacturing to services. Germany, Sweden, and Japan exhibit a much higher proportion of manufacturing and goods production than the US. Although most Western countries have declined in manufacturing employment, the US did so by 28 percent and Germany by 10 percent from 1990 to 2011. Yet the latter's cost of direct wages is much higher, at $37.14 an hour in Germany compared to $23.70 an hour in the US (Levinson, 2013:10–13). This strength in employing more workers in manufacturing has kept German balance of trade figures in the black for many years since domestic manufacturing generates more exports.[1] Explaining this is difficult within the typical American discourse on trade and the economy.

Third, outsourcing in terms of subcontracting work to specialized firms exaggerates the amount of the shift from manufacturing to services. Prior to outsourcing, security guards, cafeteria employees, copying, and other tasks at General Motors were considered to be in the manufacturing sector. In the 1970s and 1980s, the automobile companies began to outsource many aspects of their work. At one point,

GM also outsourced secretarial pool and other services, as long as the material was not confidential. After these "manufacturing jobs" were outsourced to subcontractors in the US, they became services. More recently, firms such as Toyota have outsourced much of their human resources departments to companies such as Manpower and Kelly Services (Vidal and Tigges, 2007). This moves another set of staff services from manufacturing into services.

Channeling Profits Away from Labor

While corporations view outsourcing as a way of increasing efficiency and reducing costs, one can view this from a more sociological perspective. When the firms separate these services from the corporation, they also sever the profit relationship. If a high-performing corporation makes record profits in a year, it has no responsibility to share these profits, made during good times, with the subcontractor firms that they rely upon. Instead, original equipment manufacturers (OEMs) most often tend to squeeze their subcontractors to create even more profits. One recent example involves Jaime Dimon, the CEO of J. P. Morgan-Chase, upon his visit to Congress to testify about rogue trading (Jamieson, 2012). He was confronted by Adriana Vasquez, a 37-year-old single mother of three children, who said "Despite making billions last year, why do you deny the people cleaning your buildings a living wage?" (see box 2.1). CEO Dimon brushed her off with "Call my office" where it was revealed that although Morgan-Chase earned $19 billion in 2011, Ms. Vasquez worked for a subcontractor hired to clean Morgan-Chase's buildings, was paid $8.35 an hour for working 5 hours a day, and Morgan-Chase claimed that they had absolutely nothing to do with her wages. Similarly, when Toyota executives are asked about the pay or status of their temporary employees, some of whom work for two or more years actually manufacturing automobiles on an assembly line, they say that these workers do not work for Toyota. They work for a temporary staffing agency, which is a service firm, not a manufacturing firm. Any corporation can build a wall between themselves

Box 2.1:   Employees experiencing mismatch or transition from manufacturing

Frank Robinson, a 55-year-old man working in Metro Detroit for one of the American automotive manufacturers, found himself out of a job when the plant he worked at closed. His chances of other manufacturing work are very slim, as manufacturing has declined in the US, and his advanced age discourages him from investing in more education. After being on unemployment until it ran out after two years, Frank took a job selling hardware at Lowe's with a 40 percent wage cut from his previous job.

Jean Rozinski is 36 and was laid off from Midwestern Manufacturing Inc. where she had done assembly in engine parts for pumps that were used to eliminate water in oil rigs overseas. As she perused the classified ads and online job search sites, she found opportunities for certified medical personnel, certified public accountants, and other service jobs which require a different skill set than what she has. And even if she were to take the available service jobs that she does qualify for, she would suffer a massive pay cut and likely go from a comfortable middle-class income to a poverty-level existence. Undeterred, she started a community college course as a licensed practical nurse. Jean finds the courses interesting but her background in chemistry and biology is weak. She worries about the loans she has taken out to finance her tuition and living expenses, which now are more than $25,000.

Bob Jerecki worked for a long time as a slag remover in an open hearth oven at McClouth Steel in Trenton, Michigan. As production shifted to the more efficient basic oxygen process, he got a job in quality control in testing the carbon content of steel. However, competition from overseas kept pushing the price of steel down. McClouth kept cutting jobs as it was late in modernizing its equipment. By 1995, McClouth Steel laid off most of its workers and just kept a skeleton crew. Bob stayed on hoping that the company would stay solvent, but it declared bankruptcy in 1998. Several attempts were made to restart the plant and as of 2011 the company owed nearly $5 million in back taxes. Since then Bob has worked as a security guard at half his former pay while trying to get a job at the Flat Rock Ford plant. At the age of 58, he doesn't feel that it is worth it to go back to school. Now many state governments are buying steel from China for their bridge projects including $34 million for steel for the Verrazano-Narrows Bridge in New York (Navarro, 2013).

Adriana Vasquez came to the US when she was 23, and is now a 37-year-old single mother of three children. She has worked as a cleaning lady, and currently works as a janitor cleaning the offices of J. P. Morgan-Chase in Houston, Texas. She is currently paid an hourly wage of $8.35 and earns an average of $8,684 annually. Morgan-Chase has outsourced the work in their corporate offices to her firm. The janitors are seeking a raise but the cleaning contractors have countered with an offer of 50 cents to be phased in over the next 5 years (10 cents an hour in each year). Adriana cleans 24 bathrooms on 11 floors from 5:30 p.m. to 11:30 p.m., 5 days a week. She describes her workday as stocking her cart with chemicals and supplies, finding the empty floors where the tenants aren't in the way, cleaning the bathrooms, and then moving onto the floors where people have worked late. The executive floor receives special attention with scrubbing the grime in the toilets, dusting "every inch" of that bathroom, and shining the fixtures (Jamieson, 2012).

Tim Zaneske is 44 and was laid off from his information technology job in 2009. He is married and a father of two, but he had to declare bankruptcy after running out of money from his 401k for his house payments. After only getting two interviews over two years, he finally got a part-time contract job in information technology. Tim is happy to be in a job that is related to his training, but he would like it to be full-time. In Michigan, where he lives, 36 percent of the unemployed have been searching for a year or longer (Yung, 2011).

and their subcontractors, and have no legal obligation or even human concern about how much these people earn while working in their corporate offices or factories. The ruse, legal as it is, amounts to the fact that Morgan-Chase and Toyota have tremendous bargaining power over these subcontractors. But our point is that these used to be considered finance or manufacturing positions rather than service jobs.

In sum, revenues from manufacturing are still enormous, but outsourcing disguises much of what used to be considered manufacturing jobs, with the side effect that these subcontracted companies can pay incredibly low wages to employees. In effect, these workers still actually work in the original equipment manufacturing corporations, although executives, with support from the law, deny it. Thus, outsourcing within a country, which effectively weakens wages, is the next step toward offshoring outside the country, which will be much of the topic of the following chapter. And many countries, such as Germany, Sweden, and Japan, show that higher-wage manufacturing employment is still possible.

Recent Shifts and Mismatches

Economists frequently claim that good jobs have not disappeared, but their characteristics and locations have changed (Holzer, et al., 2011; Holzer and Hlavac, 2013). The shift of manufacturing workers to services creates mismatches over the life course and even in the short run. Service jobs require different skill sets than those needed in manufacturing, and these jobs generally pay less and have fewer benefits. There are several labor market consequences of the skills mismatch.

When most economists discuss unemployment and exports, they often simultaneously refer to structural unemployment and skill mismatches. Skill mismatches occur when unemployed individuals looking for work lack the skills necessary to fill available jobs, or when the skill levels of the unemployed are supposedly too "low" for the jobs that are available. One major cause of skill mismatches has been the shift from a manufacturing economy to a service economy, but other causes may appear through educational systems that prepare students for the wrong jobs or do not supply the skills that are really needed in the labor market.

As an example, in what is now referred to as the "rust belt," many manufacturing employees have manufacturing skills that do not fit into service industry requirements. The automotive industry in Michigan has been hit particularly hard. Automotive assembly and manufacturing workers who lost their manufacturing jobs found themselves unable to enter a labor market for jobs with comparable wages. Further, many of their skills were not valued in the service sector (e.g., welding skills do not translate into nursing skills). The impact on the individual can be devastating. If they are able to find new work, former auto workers frequently end up working in low-wage service-sector employment for a fraction of the wage they once earned and with benefits that are not comparable to those of their previous jobs (if any benefits are offered). A high-school-educated American manufacturing worker who loses his job will rarely be able to find a job that utilizes his unique skill set, particularly in the service sector. This is a symptom of the shift to post-industrial society: service industries growing at the expense of blue-collar industries. This shift to service jobs often results in structural unemployment due to the skill mismatches it creates. As with Frank Robinson and Jean Rozinski (see box 2.1), who are displaced manufacturing workers who move into the service industry, this disjuncture of skills helps to increase socioeconomic inequality, as researchers have found that typically the ability of less-skilled workers to get jobs in the highest-paying service firms declined along with the prevalence of good manufacturing jobs from 1992 to 2003 (Holzer et al., 2011).

Some may argue that this is not structural unemployment, and that this is less an indication of skill mismatches than of the preference of unemployed job seekers. While some research has shown a substantial minority of unemployed people rule out entry-level service work (Lindsay and McQuaid, 2004), the wage difference between a "semi-skilled" manufacturing job and a "low-skilled" service job means that these unemployed workers would be accepting positions as the working poor. This becomes a structural issue. If low-skill service work compensates workers at a comparable rate to manufacturing work, this could potentially reduce structural unemployment. Still, blaming structural unemployment on the individual preferences of unemployed workers neglects the impact of broader changes in the economic structure in both the global economy and AICs in particular. The skill demands of employers have increased and changed in a number of ways due to the technical demands of computers, the emotion work of social interaction, and the overall shift from manufacturing to services.

Some have even argued that the demand for skills, specifically the cognitive tasks often associated with highly educated employees, has been on the decline since the year 2000 (Beaudry et al., 2013). They note that while the demand for cognitive skill had been on the rise prior to that year, it then reversed and forced high-skilled workers to a lower rung of the occupational ladder. In doing so, this created a domino effect where low-skilled workers were pushed even further down or possibly out of the labor market altogether (Beaudry et al., 2013). This is undoubtedly problematic and if this has gone on since 2000 and continues today, it appears this may be a negative structural change.

Still, others question whether the current unemployment issues are structural or cyclical, but the motivations behind these beliefs are somewhat political. On one side, Keynesian economists argue that unemployment is cyclical and that the government has the capabilities of stimulating job growth in order to lower unemployment. Economists like Paul Krugman maintain that those who argue that since the "great recession" the surge in unemployment is entirely structural are simply avoiding the quest for solutions. On the other hand, conservatives favor austerity policies and fiscal restraint because they see unemployment policy as wasting money, increasing debt, and reducing the real job generator – private investment.

The arguments of structural vs. cyclical unemployment go back and forth with valid points on each side, but they are expressed in dichotomous terms, ignoring the shades of gray in this debate. While it is true that some of the increase in unemployment since the "great recession" is not something one can totally attribute to structural elements, it is also true that a significant portion of this increase in unemployment is not totally cyclical. Additionally, while high unemployment over an extended period of time is often a good indicator of mismatch and structural unemployment, it is not the exclusive indicator. With economists possessing a strong understanding of policies that remedy cyclical unemployment, we focus our attention on the structural elements. Structural unemployment does exist, and some people are without work because they possess skill sets that do not match available jobs. As noted by Holzer and his co-authors: "The shift of better-paying jobs from manufacturing to other sectors thus implies a higher set of skill needs to obtain better-paying jobs, even for those without college diplomas" (2011:42).

Recorded unemployment in the US is high, but it should be at least 4–5 percent higher at 14.5 percent because many individuals have given up on their job searches. To some degree a longer duration of unemployment causes unemployment rates to be higher, but in other ways it can cause them to be lower. Long-term unemployment can cause people to drop out of the labor force after benefits are exhausted (Cappelli, 2012a).

Also problematic is the significant and substantial racial disparity in rates and probabilities of re-employment for those displaced workers, due in part to higher unemployment rates of minority workers among both men and women (Moore, 2010). A significant part of the problem is that employers often seek a "cultural match" (Rivera, 2012), which puts minority workers at a disadvantage. Since evidence is mounting that employers look for candidates who are culturally similar to themselves, which is not a meritocratic evaluation, white workers are at an advantage in the hiring process because they most often look and act like their most often white employers. While some argue that affirmative action constitutes reverse discrimination and gives minorities an unfair advantage, the racial disparities in unemployment rates tell a completely different story (Feagin and Sikes, 1995).

From the employers' perspective, searching for employees is now easier and cheaper than it once was due to LinkedIn, Facebook, and the internet. As a result, employers are taking their time or waiting for qualified candidates, contributing to the overall high levels of prolonged unemployment. In fact, employers may wait as long as possible to take advantage of newer technologies or offshoring opportunities so that expensive hires need not be made (Cappelli, 2012a, 2012b). This apparent luxury of employers to take their time in filling positions (as evidenced by the Beveridge curve) clearly comes at the expense of the unemployed worker struggling to pay food or electric bills.

Computers and technology have for some time been, and continue to be, transforming the labor market. The impact of technology on the labor market is explored in further detail in chapter 4 of this book, but the impact of computers and technology on employer skill demands warrants discussion here. Bell predicted that technological change would increase the demand for skilled workers and change the skills required of workers. Skills mismatches related to technology can manifest themselves in different ways. Let us consider an individual in her fifties with no formal education beyond high school who has lost her job and is looking for new work. High schools now have changed significantly, and computers and internet technology are incorporated into high-school classrooms and coursework in many AICs. When the worker we consider attended high school, computers did not exist, and in this worker's previous job there was minimal to no computer usage. As a result, this individual lacks the basic computer skills that are required of most jobs. In addition, being unfamiliar with internet resources for job searches may play a role, as employers shift from posting job openings in classified newspaper ads to posting online. For instance, Bob Jerecki in box 2.1 has little familiarity with the web other than a Facebook page and e-mail that he picked up recently. The skill mismatch created here is caused by changing job requirements due to technology and its incorporation into jobs, as well as the static skill set of the employee which has not evolved over time. This can even apply to experienced scientists who do not have the most current job skills that newly minted PhDs might have. This is not just a labor market issue, but also a matrix of technological and social problems that may include ageism.

People who are settled in their jobs can face skill mismatches stemming from technology as well. Over time, the incorporation of new technology into jobs changes their character and nature. Workers may find new technology invading their work life and be forced to adapt and learn the new software. For some workers who are not as comfortable with computers, this can be particularly troublesome and stressful. Some may even be resistant to the incorporation of technology. Refusing or struggling to acquire the new skills that have become necessary for the job will result in a mismatch and could be a cause for the employer to fire an older worker and look for a younger person. The structural changes caused by technological innovation have real, tangible consequences on individuals in their jobs. These examples illustrate the interactions of the causes of structural unemployment discussed in this book.

Employee involvement programs can also play a role in skill mismatches. These programs include self-directed teams, job rotation, quality circles, enhanced job training, and increased compensation for newly acquired skills that are directly related to job tasks (e.g., being able to do all the jobs rather than just one job in a section of the assembly line). Companies using employee involvement programs often grant employees more decision-making capacity and more input into the operations of the organization. The result of this is a need for a different skill set. Manufacturing employees working for companies that utilize employee involvement programs may be asked to perform quality control or process improvement tasks, which require other skills than simply the physical act of assembly (Handel and Gittleman, 2004). Lean production empowers employees through involvement, and the skills of employees in lean production environments may often differ substantially from the skills of an employee in a Fordist assembly line. While quality control, networking, and team work in employee involvement programs can result in higher job satisfaction, they often modify skill requirements and make job descriptions more daunting (Handel and Gittleman, 2004). However, employee involvement programs can serve to alleviate skill mismatches through enhanced job training that involves necessary skill acquisition. In this sense, the relationship between employee involvement programs and skill mismatch is not completely one-sided.

Thus, the shift from manufacturing to services according to Bell's prediction of deindustrialization is coming to fruition. This shift has several major negative impacts on the labor force: skill mismatches and resulting structural unemployment, increased wage inequality as the higher-paying manufacturing jobs being offshored are replaced with lower-paying service jobs, and large balance of trade deficits.

Education and Skill Mismatches

Structural unemployment due to skill mismatches and wage inequality can be illustrated with the example of Frank Robinson, a Michigan automotive manufacturing worker, who lost his job but is now a sales associate in a hardware store (see box 2.1). This displaced worker found himself with a skill set that service-sector employers did not need, and an educational background that was far below what was required for a service-sector job that would pay auto-sector wages. Education is the most available and frequently used measure of workers' skills, and many manufacturing workers did not pursue education beyond high school (Handel, 2003). This is a potentially huge problem in the US as the large cohort of baby boomers working in manufacturing is likely to be affected by this. Some have suggested that the skill mismatches related to education reflect a decline in the skills of the workforce; however, there is little empirical basis for an actual decline. There is an emphasis in formal education on developing cognitive skills, but for employers, studies have suggested a greater weight is placed on non-cognitive factors, including work effort and cooperative attitudes (Handel, 2003). In fact, the mismatches between manufacturing and service jobs often relate to interpersonal skills. In service industries, interpersonal skills often take priority. Although working with other employees on an assembly line requires some interpersonal skills, customer service necessitates a very different skill set from what is required of assembly line auto workers, for example. Traditional manufacturing jobs in a Fordist assembly system do not necessarily help to promote and strengthen these skills.

Education, though, does play a role in the area of skill mismatches and structural unemployment. College can be referred to as an intermediary (Sarbaugh-Thompson et al., 1999). Intermediaries are organizations that help to mediate between hiring firms in the labor market and their prospective employees, and include educational, training, and employment institutions or agencies. They are "organizations – public, private, nonprofit, or membership-based – that help broker the employment relationship through some combination of job matching, training, and career support services (Benner et al., 2007:10). Skills necessary for jobs are often taught in on-the-job training, but the competencies that may be developed into these skills are often cultivated by intermediaries. Now more than ever, intermediaries utilize online channels for providing services. Job boards (e.g., monster. com or careerbuilder.com) or professional networking sites (e.g., LinkedIn.com or academia.edu) provide opportunities for workers to search for jobs that match their skills and for employers to seek out employees that fit in their organizations. In addition, job training is available online where people can earn university degrees from home or certifications that signal marketable skills to employers. Although many economic studies generally seem to view higher-level cognitive skills as being in short supply, employers tend to complain more about work attitudes and basic skills of non-college-educated employees and see education as a sign of a more reliable, hardworking, responsible, and self-disciplined worker (Handel, 2003). Still, when the education system does not recognize the skills needed in the job market (whether in live classrooms or online education), this structural deficiency results in skills mismatches in the labor market and increased structural unemployment.

New worker skills and education are increasingly becoming prerequisites for good jobs, and many employees currently only have some of them (Holzer et al., 2011). Employees need more computer, mathematical, management, and social interaction skills than ever before. They also need specific training in organizational techniques, government relations, and technical matters that differ from medicine to financial counseling. Well-paid jobs in healthcare, technical sales (e.g., MRI scanners), and advanced retail (e.g., overseas buyers) require more specific technical training, statistical analysis, and language skills than did jobs in the past. Improving general academic skills is just the beginning that leads to further training that will produce a labor force more attractive to most employers. Community colleges and technical education centers are the intermediaries that more directly address these needs and issues for the workforce (Holzer et al., 2011).

Labor Market Intermediaries and Job Placement

Labor market intermediaries (LMIs) are of specific importance for low-income individuals who may have weaker
or less effective social networks, as these intermediaries
can help connect individuals with opportunities they would
otherwise not be exposed to (Benner et al., 2007). Making
these connections is fundamental to overcoming some of
the unemployment that may be misconstrued as skill mismatch but in actuality is individuals and jobs not finding
one another. The matching process is indeed complex, and
factors other than skills play a role, including social networks
and connections which may lead some demographic groups
toward certain employment sectors and lead some employers
away from certain demographic groups (Andersson et al.,
2005). The access that minorities with few skills have to
organizations that pay higher wages is severely limited,
and their blocked access helps to perpetuate socioeconomic
inequality along racial and ethnic lines. Evidence of this is
the disproportionate use of lower-paying temp agencies by
minorities.

Temporary agency workers tend to be younger, more
often foreign-born, more likely racial or ethnic minorities,
usually from a lower-income family, and with lower educational levels (Benner et al., 2007). Thus, much outsourcing
relies on low-income, low-education, and racial or ethnic
minority workers. The unemployed use these intermediaries,
while more advantaged workers typically look to higher-level
intermediaries to help improve their careers. They use community colleges or vocational schools, or professional associations (Benner et al., 2007). Table 2.1 provides a typology
of LMIs that may be useful in understanding the variety that
exist and their organizational types. Educational institutions
(community colleges, for example) are a common form of
LMI. While the US had the highest high-school graduation
rates in the beginning of the twentieth century when the
economy thrived, many other countries in the world have
caught up and even surpassed the US, causing the American

Table 2.1:   An organizational typology of labor market intermediaries

Organization type	Examples
For-profit sector	Temporary employment agencies and headhunters (e.g., for SLAMs: Manpower Inc. and Kelly Services; for OLMs and OILMs: Robert Haft Services, Nurses Registry, Kronos Consulting, and Accountemps)
	For-profit training providers and vocational schools (e.g., ITT International and Sullivan University)
Nonprofit or community	Nonprofit employment training and placement services for disadvantaged workers (e.g., Empowerment Centers, Job Corps, Goodwill Industries, etc.)
Membership	Union-based initiatives and professional associations (e.g., Longshore Workers Hiring Hall; Millwright Union Hiring Hall; Pipefitter Hiring Hall; professional association employment services)
Education	Community college and university placement offices
Public sector	US Employment Service, one-stop career centers, private industry councils, and Temporary Assistance for Needy Families welfare-to-work agencies

Source: Benner et al. (2007). © 2007 Russell Sage Foundation, 112 East 64th Street, New York, NY 10065. Reprinted with Permission.

economy to slow down (Golden and Katz, 2008). Increasing high-school graduation rates may not be the simple solution it appears to be – the US education system is far from perfect, and differences in educational systems from country to country often result in workforces with very different skill sets between countries.

In comparing the education systems in the US and Germany, valuable insights can be gained related to structural unemployment. First, look at the US education system. There was little change to the structure of the education system in the US after World War II and vocational programs have not been effective among US high schools (OECD, 2008; Janoski, 1990). The US, in fact, has never had a well-developed vocational education program when compared to other countries (Cappelli, 2012a). Vocational training in the US occurs after high school, when most job-specific skills and trade knowledge are acquired by students. Apprenticeship training in the late 1930s served as an attempt for labor and management to work together on vocational training, and labor unions and management primarily funded this training (Janoski, 1990). Structural limits to these apprenticeship training programs in the US arose, however, as management was sometimes reluctant to plan the programs out and labor had an interest in limiting the supply of craftspeople (and thus keeping greater control over their wages) (Janoski, 1990). After high school in the US, students may choose to join the military to learn skills during their service, or perhaps go to college and gain white-collar professional skills (and some blue-collar skills as well). These ventures most often have federal and state funding.

A review of the education system in the US for less academically oriented individuals who do not go to college shows that these students lack meaningful options to gain marketable skills. In comparing US job training with that in three other countries, Kathleen Thelen goes so far to say that the incentives facing young and ambitious workers have "led them to avoid vocational training . . . like the plague in favor of academically oriented education" (2004:284). As a result, "workers could not be sure that any investment they made in company skills would be rewarded through systematic advancement" because "career ladders often had low and concrete ceilings" (2004:214). Structural unemployment caused by skill mismatches may be an indicator that other intermediaries for training employees are failing to train in the skills needed in the economy. If this is the case, a structural disconnect between intermediaries (like educational institutions) and employers is one source of skill mismatches that does not originate from workers.

Not all countries have the same educational structure, and in general, school systems can be classified into horizontal systems like that of the US, and vertical systems like those of much of continental Europe. While in the US, job-training programs focus on socialization in unskilled jobs, German job-training programs maintain a focus on high-skilled jobs (Hoffman, 2011; Halpern, 2006; Thelen, 2004; Hamilton, 1999; Janoski, 1990). In education, most striking is the difference between the horizontal system in the US, which keeps students together until the age of 17, and the vertical German system, which separates students at an earlier age. After four years in elementary school, students in the German system go on to either a lower vocational (apprentice) school, a pre-business school, or a pre-engineering school, or go on the academic or professional school route (which excludes business or engineering) (Janoski, 1990; Smil, 2013). This means that when students are aged 10–12 many are taking courses more specialized in their career fields. Where in the US a high-school graduate typically has no major marketable skills from their education, in Germany students who are the same age and chose a vocational track are certified skilled craftspeople and artisans. Intermediaries in the German education system help to prepare students for a variety of jobs based on the needs of the economy and the potential and orientation of the students. More academically oriented students may be encouraged to go on to become scientists, lawyers, or researchers, whereas those who are less academically oriented have other meaningful options.

There are, however, drawbacks to the German system. As it stands in the US, students who have barely reached their teens are expected to decide their future. Whether they go to school or not, finding a stable career (not just a job) is a laudable goal for many young men and women. Still, for many American 18-year-olds, it is difficult to decide on a career (Halpern, 2006), and this tends to be prolonged in the US system. If these individuals decide to go to college, the expectation is not lifted; college students often have trouble selecting a major that will position them for a career outside of the academy. In the German system, these problems are exacerbated by the fact that career choices need to be made at a very young age. Still, in spite of its drawbacks, it appears that the intermediaries in the German system are better positioned to combat structural unemployment than intermediaries in the US, which appear to be stymied by the gaps in the structure of the American education system. In chapter 6, we will propose solutions for this seeming dilemma of "choosing too early" or "choosing too late."

Firms and Skill Mismatches

While some of the responsibility for skill mismatches rests with employees' willingness to train and with what labor market intermediaries provide, employers also play a largely unrecognized role in creating skill mismatches. Employers create the perception and reality of skill mismatches in three ways: (1) the private sector's stake in the reserve army of the unemployed chills out some firm training; (2) firms may have unusually high expectations but do not provide the social capital to create new training for a skilled workforce; and (3) firms may refuse to offer higher wages for higher skills, and prefer offshoring when there is no skill mismatch at all.

First, concerning the reserve army, with a large number of unemployed individuals, employers have the capacity to be more selective and keep wages low. In fact, with the advent of online job applications, the typical applicant pool is so large that restrictive criteria (that barely anyone meets) are often used to narrow down the applicant pool. Human resources software is often used to filter out applicants, and the artificial intelligence built into the software's algorithms is often far from perfect (Cappelli, 2012a). Karl Marx (1977) referred to the unemployed as the "reserve army of labor," and believed the presence of this army was advantageous to the capitalist. While this has always been the case in the US with undocumented immigrants working in agricultural fields, it is somewhat new to the general white-collar labor market, especially markets for college graduates. Surplus labor, even for highly skilled workers, keeps wages in check because managers may simply threaten to hire others with similar skills in the US or abroad.

Second, a current trend is for employers to refuse to train new workers and expect candidates to meet the job requirements of a long-experienced employee doing advanced job tasks. As a result, there is a tendency for firms to only select overqualified candidates, if they are available, by simply prioritizing work experience and educational attainment over the firm training. Those with a good general education but no firm-specific or highly specialized skills do not get the job. This saves money by avoiding the cost of on-the-job training for new employees (Cappelli, 2012a). So college graduates who find it difficult to find jobs are not to blame, as they are frequently pursuing degrees in fields that are in high demand. Cappelli gives the example of Owen, who followed up his liberal arts degree with a two-year health vocational diploma, only to find that employers want two such diplomas with one of them being in an entirely different area. In the labor market, younger workers are often being bypassed in favor of experienced employees who require less training and therefore cost their employers less money (Cappelli, 2012a; Quijano, 2012). In general, employer training is now in short supply. A 2011 survey by global management consulting firm Accenture revealed that only 21 percent of employees had received *any* employer-provided formal training in the previous five years. Conversely, this means that 79 percent had received no training in half a decade. So while employers complain, as 52 percent did in a manpower survey in which they blamed talent shortages for their hiring difficulties, the skills gap and skill mismatches they encounter are in large part the result of their own weak efforts to train employees. This may also be coupled with employers stiffening job requirements and discriminating against unemployed applicants in order to narrow down the pool of applicants (Cappelli, 2012a; Wolter et al., 2003).

The third trend is for employers to refuse to pay higher wages when there is a shortage of workers. Economists see this as contravening the basic economic law of supply and demand. If you need workers for a special skill and they are in short supply, then you should pay more money for them.

This will attract more workers to this area and eventually the wage pressures will subside. A Boston Consulting Group (BCG) survey shows that the skills gap is more limited than as portrayed in the media. In locating wage growth areas where there is a purported skills shortage, BCG found that many manufacturing employers are "trying to hire high-skilled workers at rock-bottom rates" (BCG, 2012a). As BCG states, this "is not a skills gap," it is a "wage gap" created by employers. In Adam Davidson's examination of a manufacturer in Milwaukee he found that trained workers with a technical associates degree in a relevant field start out at $10 an hour, which rises to $15 and then to $18 after years of good performance. The BCG surveyors Harold Sirkin and Michael Zinser refer to this as a "fake skills gap" (Davidson, 2012). A shift supervisor working at McDonalds makes $14 an hour, which is the same pay that a highly trained manufacturing employee makes in computer-aided design/computer-aided manufacturing (CAD/CAM). Joseph Goldenberg teaches computer-aided machine tool processes at Queensborough Community College and he finds that students do not want to work in these types of manufacturing jobs because the pay is too low (Davidson, 2012; BCG, 2012a, 2012b; Guenther, 2012). The cause of this fake skills gap is wage competition with China and not the local labor market. As long as sending these jobs to China is a possibility or manufacturers in the US see that they may compete with manufactured goods from China, they will not respond to local labor market conditions and instead refuse to pay the wage premiums that shortages of skilled workers in the US would demand. Davidson shows specifically how one manufacturing company negotiates the decision about this offshore versus inshore tradeoff.

The Magnitude of Skill Mismatches

How big a problem are skill mismatches? Recent research has looked into the role skill mismatches played in the increased unemployment resulting from the serious recession in 2008, finding that mismatch accounted for between 0.6 percent and

1.7 percent of the observed *increase* in the unemployment rate from 5 percent at the beginning of the recession to approximately 10 percent in October of 2009 at its peak (Şahin et al., 2011). This proportion attributable to mismatch is substantial (i.e., 12 percent to 34 percent of the increase in the unemployment rate) (Chen et al., 2011; Şahin et al., 2011). Thus, while some skill mismatches are more apparent than real, other mismatches are meaningful.

The unemployment that appeared after the 2008 recession is different since its duration is at historic levels, which suggests that a portion of the unemployment stemming from 2008 is structural, not cyclical, as it has outlasted the business cycle (Chen et al., 2011). Using a skill mismatch index, researchers with the IMF found that in the US during the "great recession," skill mismatches increased overall and particularly in states where manufacturing accounted for a large share of GDP (Estevão and Tsounta, 2011). This general trend is reflected in the story we noted earlier about the displaced manufacturing workers in the Midwest. Skill mismatches are structural phenomena that have a real impact on people's lives, and they have been accentuated by the "great recession" of 2008. With cyclical unemployment, individuals may find themselves out of work for a short time during an economic downturn, but the structural implications of the "great recession" result in longer unemployment duration and a structural change in the economy. Long-term unemployment and skill mismatches have drastic impacts on individuals and families who find themselves with a skill set that their economy no longer values. Unfortunately, skill mismatches continued to rise in most states in the US even after the official end of this "great recession," in part explaining why unemployment rates have not recovered to pre-recession levels (Estevão and Tsounta, 2011). These stubbornly high unemployment numbers provide yet another indication of a structural economic change. Structural unemployment is a problem in many AICs, and both real and fake skill mismatches contribute to the problem.

The recent recession shows that the power of the individual to combat skill mismatches can be limited by the housing market. Jobless individuals can at times be trapped in economically depressed areas due to poor housing market conditions. So on top of skill mismatches, being unable to sell your house contributes to being unable to move without suffering a large financial loss. See the example of Tim Zaneske in box 2.1, who lost his job and then lost his house before a low-level job in computers became available (Estevão and Tsounta, 2011). Some refer to this situation as a spatial mismatch. Detroit is a city with high unemployment, a poor housing market, and an auto industry that has seen a large decline in manufacturing jobs. It provides a cautionary tale of how skill and spatial mismatch can impact an industrial city. Las Vegas has had a similar decline in its housing market but with a service industry economy. Both Detroit's and Nevada's populations have been shrinking at an astonishing rate since 2008, and Detroit's is now as low as it was a hundred years ago. Part of this is due to the fact that as manufacturing jobs are lost, service jobs disappear as well because there is a lower demand for service work in the region (Moretti, 2012). So mismatch hardly applies to situations where there are no manufacturing or service jobs, and one cannot sell one's house. As a result, these people are trapped.

Conclusion

There are ways to address the problem of skill mismatches, but in order to do so, the participants must recognize the positive roles that employees, employers, the state, and educational institutions play in the process. First of all, *employees* can no longer take a narrow view of education and training. The days of asking questions like "Why do I have to learn statistics to be an auto mechanic?" have given way to a recognition that the flexibility of new labor markets demands that employees have wide-ranging skills and the ability to change into jobs that are foreign to their present skill sets. The days of math or language blocks are over as the auto mechanic has to interpret computer output on engine performance for a range of American, German, or Japanese cars.

Second, *employers* can no longer take a narrow view of employee training and pay the lowest wages possible when their profits are actually rather high and they are hoarding cash. The structures of employee training are in large part also due to employer behavior, especially employer decisions to avoid giving intensive training and just hire the "perfect" but low-paid employee. Further, many employers are dumping their responsibilities to employees by outsourcing (e.g., Adriana Vasquez in box 2.1), which is simply not ethical. So the skill mismatch may be a reality, but it has been misused in covering up a large portion of the problem and who is responsible for it. It is both an employee and an employer problem, and it will require an employee and an employer solution!

And third, *the state* can no longer passively allow a stagnant and outdated curriculum in the general education or vocational part of high school to produce workers with skill sets that have minimal economic benefit. Certainly educated individuals are more informed citizens and active members of their communities, but for practical purposes, *educational institutions* have some responsibility to generate the workforce needed by the community (US-JEC, 2011). Educational institutions and firms should be in open dialogue with employees and employers to assess economic needs. Educators must help provide workers who will be in demand in the labor market and who will be well trained to do their jobs upon completion of their education. These strong lines of communication with employers will ensure that the skills and training schools provide are needed. This should also involve their "coproduction" of training within firms. The investment of individuals in education is one which they expect to reap the rewards of through employment; but for this to happen, the skills for those not bound for college need to be marketable and match the economic climate as much as possible.

All too often when the unemployed are blamed for their situation, the role of the employer and the role of the intermediary are both ignored. The individual cases in box 2.1 clearly illustrate that the individual is not solely to blame. If an unemployed worker goes back to school but is educated in a watered down program or an unnecessary skill, the intermediary is partially to blame for offering training in obsolete skills. For practical purposes, workers are now expected to adjust and adapt to the changing demands of the labor market. On an individual level, today's workers face new demands due to structural changes in the economy. What has been described as the "new career contract" is the move from the organizational to the protean career, where productive workers must possess the meta-skills of identity growth and adaptability. This creates a "decoupling" of "the concept of career from a connection to any one organization" (Hall and Mirvis, 1995:19). In the old organizational career, people often worked for the same employer and were promoted within that entity for the duration. However, in the protean career, the concept of "career" is decoupled from the organization, and the contract becomes one with the self and one's own work. The protean career concept requires continuous learning and adaptability, which are key ideas from lean production (Hall and Mirvis, 1995). Although it has some positive aspects, the new career contract is an individual-level way of addressing the problem of structural unemployment in the changing labor market. But it does not mean that employers should abandon training. As we have shown, skill mismatches are not simply an individual problem; corporations and governments also have work to do in order to alleviate the structural unemployment that results from skill mismatches.

Skill mismatches do exist, though they are often exaggerated; however, using the term synonymously with structural unemployment is a mistake. Skill mismatches account for a small portion of unemployment because there are many other structural factors, such as offshoring, technology, and financialization. The next chapters address these explanations of unemployment.

3

Transnational Corporations Enthralled with Outsourcing and Offshoring

There has been an inexorable flow of jobs from AICs with high wages and benefits to LDCs with low wages and benefits (2a and 2b in figure 1.6). The famed manager Jack Welch from General Electric proselytized for offshoring and promulgated the idea of "factories on barges" so they could move to wherever labor is cheaper and taxes lower (Surana, 2011; Palley, 2007). In the AICs, multinational corporations and shareholders benefit from offshoring because the corporations make increased profits as they move production and a certain amount of services to low-wage countries. However, workers in these developed countries have little share in the profits as wages within their country stagnate, and workers tend to be laid off. Workers then have to look for lower-paying jobs and suffer much higher unemployment rates, and new workers especially have difficulty finding jobs. The end result is a bifurcation of benefits: managers, investors, and professionals gain, while blue- and white-collar workers and new graduates lose (Goldstein, 2012). Alderson (1997, 1999, 2004) shows that outward foreign direct investment (FDI) from the US causes major declines in the American manufacturing sector. While FDI has a complex relationship with unemployment as a whole, it does cause downward movement in segmented labor markets. Conversely, FDI into China (see figure 3.1) causes major increases in jobs that pay much higher wages than work in village agriculture, though

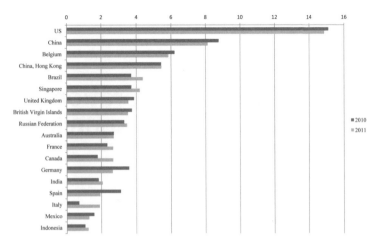

Figure 3.1   Inward foreign direct investment as percentage of world total, 2010–11
Source: United Nations Conference on Trade and Development (UNCTAD STAT), unctadstat.unctad.org.

at the cost of many citizenship rights (Janoski, 2013).[1] FDI leads to greater wage inequality and the loss of manufacturing jobs and exports, which then lead to balance of trade deficits for the US. This is because manufacturing imports to the US since the early 1970s have overwhelmed the low levels of service exports as manufacturing exports have declined (as shown in figure 2.2). In the new world of globalization, offshoring and outsourcing have become dominant themes. Meanwhile, the balance of trade in most AICs has been driven strongly negative, which ultimately connects up to various forms of government and private debt that inevitably lead to financial crises and political conflicts over government deficits.

The Rise of Lean Production

Along with globalization, a strong trend has emerged in terms of lean production which major producers and corporations may neglect at their peril. The implementation of lean production varies considerably in firms, but various portions of its core principles are observed by most. In the world of corporations, three major types of lean production have emerged. Two of these new types of organizations – the ones we describe as Nikeification or lean production two and Waltonism or lean production three – have some distinctly negative forms. Manufacturing becomes a donut hole as the missing middle represents production that takes place abroad. This has major implications for unemployment and income inequality in both the AICs and LDCs. This chapter will first review a number of companies that provide examples of these three types of organizations, and then look at their implications for employment in society as a whole. The three types will be represented by (1) Toyota; (2) Nike, Apple, and General Electric; and (3) Walmart.

Lean production is a somewhat misleading name for the change in the division of labor from Fordism and Taylorism. It implies a cutting process that is not particularly descriptive of many of the aspects of team work and social capital used by some firms. The Japanese themselves did not use the term until it became popular in the US. "Toyotism" as described by Christian Berggren (1992) is a more accurate and less ideologically biased term. However, since "lean production" as a term descriptive of the division of labor was first used by John Krafcik (1988) and popularized by James Womack, Daniel Jones, and Daniel Roos (1990), we will use it in this book but caution the reader that its meaning goes beyond the narrow connotation of "lean." As such, lean production has four basic principles (Liker, 2004; Toyota, 2004):

1 *The philosophy of hiring employees for the long term* provides training for core employees, who stay to create a learning organization with reflection. They are oriented toward gaining market share using retained profits, and avoiding short-term distractions such as paying stockholders with high dividends and increasing the price of stock.

2 *A supply-chain network based on just-in-time inventory processes* creates a tightly connected production process

that emphasizes standardized work and continuous process flow. This requires establishing a network of trusted suppliers who then work with the OEMs on design, supply, and production.

3 A *problem-solving culture* focuses on quality using visual and statistical control (often summarizing the entire recommendation on one A3 diagram), management by walking around, leveling out the workload, and creating a culture of stopping to fix problems.

4 *Strong, small teams* (with 5–8 members) are led by a coach and facilitator. They grow leaders "up and in," and make decisions slowly with consensus.[2]

One should be careful about a too rigid adherence to these principles, since Emi Osono, Norihiko Shizumi, and Hirotaka Takeuchi show that Toyota often violate some of their seemingly core principles – they move gradually but also take big leaps, are frugal but also spend huge sums, operate efficiently but also redundantly, cultivate an environment of stability but also paranoia, respect hierarchy but also allow dissent, are simple but also complex (2008:9). However, the culture of promoting and nurturing employees and suppliers is quite strong and not often ignored.

Offshoring is a more specific term than outsourcing. It means transferring the actual production of the final product to an overseas or foreign location. Most often the offshoring is subcontracted but companies may sometimes own plants overseas. Outsourcing means a form of subcontracting that occurs within one country, and it is often connected to the employment of temporary workers within the home base of a corporation or company. The parent company will even outsource the payment and hiring of these jobs to a separate firm. Hence, they are officially employees of the subcontracted firm while doing work directly for the parent firm. However, companies can also directly hire temporary employees without an intermediary. Lean production has a strong connection to temporary employees, which somewhat contradicts principles 1, 3, and 4 above, but few works on lean production even mention this (see Lepadatu and Janoski, 2011). Temporary employees are more like the dirty little secret of lean.

Offshoring and outsourcing are often connected to new forms of organizational alliances and cooperation. This is sometimes referred to as alliance capitalism (Rugman and Boyd, 2003), the networked theory of the firm (de Lange, 2011), or the modular organizational form (Schilling and Steensma, 2001; Sturgeon, 2002). The term "modular organizations" refers to loosely coupled networks of organizations that negotiate supply, production, marketing, distribution, and even R&D activities with other firms. While some see this as a new development, firms have been networked in this way for a long time and the factories of the 1800s were often subcontracted groups headed by foremen (Nelson, 1996). Fordism and Taylorism brought production within the organization, but lean production has pushed some of it out as if by centrifugal force to achieve lower costs. Two major concerns about these somewhat open networks involve (1) gaining expertise for critical production or development problems without paying too much for it, and (2) keeping company secrets secure despite an open network. With these loosely coupled arrangements, critical information has to be carefully managed. Thus, joint ventures have to balance loyalty and trust in their supplier relationships. The boundaries still exist but are sometimes porous and sometimes not. The modular firm is important because offshoring is directly related to new forms of lean production. Our argument is that lean production is most effectively and completely portrayed by Toyota (hence, Toyotism) and less so by Nikeification and Waltonism.

Changes in Organizational form due to Lean Production and Offshoring

In the late twentieth century, Taylorism and Fordism gave way to Toyotism, Nikeification, and Waltonism, which we will refer to as lean production one, two, and three. The first lean production regime, Toyotism, refers to the most complete application of the definition of lean production (i.e., principles 1, 2, 3, and 4 above) without much in the way of offshoring, and the next two regimes move to more emphasis on supply chains with offshoring (i.e., a modification of principle 2) and much less application of the team and longevity aspects of lean production (i.e., principles 1, 3, and 4). These last two forms may even embrace "shareholder value theory," which is an anathema to Toyotism. Below, we discuss these new forms of production in more detail.

Lean production one

Lean production one (LP-1) or *Toyotism* implements the four aspects of lean production in the definition influenced by Jeffrey Liker (2004). These organizations have a long-term philosophy toward learning through employees they employ for the long haul. They are oriented toward gaining market share with retained profits and as a result are not the darlings of Wall Street. They establish a strong supply-chain network based on loyalty and trust, and within the OEM or parent firm itself they use a team-based problem-solving approach with team leaders, promotion from within, and strong analytic techniques. Generally, LP-1 is wary of alliances outside of its supply-chain network, but on occasion it will engage in alliances or networks with some firms (e.g., Toyota generally avoids alliances but did cooperate with GM for a decade or so in New United Motors Manufacturing Inc., and has had some R&D cooperation with Ford on battery, hybrid, and other technologies). Like all other companies, it has made joint ventures in China. But in large part, the thought of subcontracting its final production processes to another company is an anathema to Toyota. This is mainly because extensive subcontracting violates Toyotism's "up and in" and "strong team" approach. Further, this policy would involve revealing many company secrets. In other words, in LP-1, organizational boundaries are strong but the long-term and privileged supplier network is more or less considered to be within these boundaries.

Lean production two

Lean production two (LP-2) or *Nikeification* implements strong supply-chain programs, and often has strong teams in

R&D, product development, and marketing. But these organizations use extensive outsourcing and offshoring in taking advantage of expertise that they do not consider to be in-house or within their core competencies. However, most offshoring is not for new technologies or processes, but simply to take advantage of low labor costs, so one should not make too much of the widespread pursuit of "external expertise." Since these companies are often in fierce competition with their rivals, they may change suppliers or joint venture partners at critical points when developing new products so that firms do not gain too much knowledge of their internal operations. The self-managed teams they use (an idea from socio-technical theory) in their AIC corporate offices in the US show some evidence of more independence and creativity than lean production teams (Weisbord, 2004); however, these organizations are not particularly concerned whether or not their offshore plants actually engage in team work and "up and in" procedures. As Kate Raworth and Thalia Kidder state, offshore lean production will "work harder rather than smarter" in terms of speed-up, overtime, harassment, and abuse, rather than keeping employees for the long term, training them "up and in," and using teams to solve problems in China (2009:173–4). Further, the labor conditions for these 18- to 30-year-old workers (usually women) are quite exploitative (Lee, 2007; Silver, 2003). Nonetheless, they are heavily involved with supply-chain management and just-in-time inventory. Closure is weaker in these offshore plants with various aspects of pilfering products common, sometimes for competitive startup purposes. Also, China has specific technology sharing agreements attached to the joint ventures. However, the R&D of LP-2 firms changes products so fast and often as to make these knock-off products ineffective in stealing any of their "important" shares of the market. In general, these firms are much more concerned about short term profits than the LP–1 firms.

Lean production three

Organizations that use lean production three (LP-3) or Matt Vidal's *Waltonism* do not produce anything that they sell (some have subcontractors that produce second brands under their label, but these are not company-owned). They have little or no interest in strong teams or promoting "up and in." Instead, they employ strong-armed bargaining techniques with suppliers of goods that they then resell to consumers. Their aim is to generate the lowest price possible, but they do not have any particular recommendations about how the subcontractors should produce these products. This pursuit of the lowest prices has pushed these companies to outsourcing and then offshoring to low-wage countries. Some producers using this model have generated a great deal of community opposition and some worker protest (e.g., Walmart). But they have been highly successful and Walmart is the largest American corporation measured by employment.

While one might question whether this is a lean production model at all, these organizations do have what might be termed the strongest just-in-time inventory process in the world, with Walmart having its own satellite system to track production and deliveries (Vidal, 2010). Their bargaining process with suppliers is sometimes viewed as brutal, but they do produce lower prices for consumers. LP-3 organizations are merchandising firms, not manufacturers, and hence they produce no physical products. One could say that they produce services. The result is "lean" in the much more narrow sense of the word. It would represent bargaining pressure on suppliers that probably squeezes out waste, it definitely reduces their profits, and it does not create a trusted network of suppliers who are brought into the inside workings of the firm (Hamilton, 2006). However, the squeezing of supplier profits could be said of many of the lean production models.

Offshoring

These three lean process models are based on Toyotism, but offshoring is in part due to two other major changes in technology that affect the production process. The first technological change is the introduction of computers, which has a multifaceted impact on manufacturing. Computerization has aided in the instantaneous tracking of parts when they are inserted into a product during assembly and when the actual product is bought (i.e., aiding the pull process). Suppliers and the parent company can know very quickly how many parts need to be produced in a short amount of time. Computers also have led to the offshoring of information technology work, and even services work that can be communicated by the internet. The second technological change has to do with a seemingly low-tech but major change in the transportation of goods across oceans. The container ship has gone from a rebuilt oil tanker transporting 58 containers across the ocean in 1951 to the *Emma Maersk* moving over 15,000 twenty-foot equivalent units (TEUs, the standard unit for a ship's cargo-carrying capacity) in 2010. Container ships did away with the extremely time-consuming process of loading individual packages and boxes into the holds of commercial ships. However, lean is pushed further with these vessels because they often have very small crews (e.g., 10–20 crew members). The use of container ships vastly reduced the number of longshoremen and the size of their unions, since they have been more or less reduced to crane operators to remove the containers (see chapter 4).

How did we get from Toyotism to unemployment?

Four movements cause the shift toward structural unemployment. First, the original model of Toyotism may be considered a "jobs machine" despite some outsourcing and use of temporary employment as a buffer to protect its permanent employees from unemployment. The first shift was to use the word "lean," a term that Toyota did not use, and this emphasized cutting inventory but also employees. The second shift to Nikeification dropped the buffering of production employees as these jobs were offshored, but maintained the buffering of creative design and technology staff. Third, the pricing negotiation mechanisms in Waltonism brought us closer to Marx's view of the declining rate of profit and the immiseration of subcontractors and their workers. Fourth, the donut hole gets bigger when design and high technology shift offshore. Former Intel CEO Andy Grove (2010) makes the argument that production expertise in actually making the product begets design and technological knowledge. This process has been further intensified by China's policy of technology transfer. These factors are aided by conservative tendencies in the US that brought "lean" into the world of neo-liberal budget cutting, which brings politics closer to private shareholder value strategies (to be discussed in chapter 6).

Toyotism's emphasis on creating jobs by increasing market share and protecting jobs by buffering its permanent workers has disappeared. The logical conclusion of this progression is Vizio, the largest US TV producer, with 188 design and finance employees in California and 226 call center employees in South Dakota (Patel, 2012). Although Vizio sells over a billion dollars' worth of TVs, it doesn't have any employees who actually make them. In other words, the Americanization of lean production has produced a near anathema to the original concept of Toyotism, and in the process has greatly increased structural unemployment.

Examples of Various Lean Firms

There are five specific organizations that illustrate some important processes involved with lean production and outsourcing. First, Toyota represents the job-creating organization that pursues market share and does much less offloading of employees. Second, Nike, Apple, and GE represent successful companies that have become full donut corporations in that production is no longer contained within their organizational boundaries. Nike started as a donut corporation with little intent to produce in the US, while Apple came to overseas production after some internal US production. GE is particularly important because it encourages offshoring to other long-standing manufacturing firms. Third, Walmart, now the largest employer in the world, has become so as a merchandiser by buying goods that have been outsourced from many different types of manufacturing corporations. These last two models of lean production do not cover all corporations, but they exemplify some of the most successful corporations in the modern era that offshore jobs.

Toyota as the Premier Lean Production Corporation Expanding Jobs

Toyotism, or lean production with the four principles mentioned earlier in this chapter, was developed by Taiichi Ohno of Toyota and Professor Mauro Ishikawa under the quality control guidance of W. Edwards Deming. They used the term "Toyota production system" (TPS).[3] Toyota is the exemplar of LP-1, which implements all four aspects of lean production outlined above. Lean production has already been discussed in this chapter, so the focus in this section is on two lesser-known principles that make Toyota a distinct exemplar of LP-1: (1) the heavy focus on team work, using the "up and in" focus on employment security and promotions; and (2) the avoidance of short-term foci on the stock market and profits.

First, Toyota is noted for its heavy emphasis on developing employees for the long term through team work and promotion from within. This often results in the sometimes contradictory focus of keeping more employees in the US and Japan than they seemingly need. While Toyota makes full use of temporary employees in both countries, it still often carries more employees than it needs. This contradicts the more American or capitalist focus on only having as many employees as necessary to minimize labor costs. Further, because of this, Toyota is not a donut corporation: there is no "hollow production core," as production is done within the company, with subcontractors being tightly connected to the firm through contracts and the overlapping exchange of personnel. However, the company and its suppliers have tight boundaries that keep information within the organizational network.

Second, the company strategy is long-term and focused on automobiles (unlike Honda, which sees itself as an engine company doing automobiles, lawn-mowers, jet engines, and other products). Although corporations need profits to survive, Toyota's main goal is to expand its market share. So focusing on profits and dividends is not part of the Toyota management culture, and this contradicts shareholder value theory. Toyota's principles are the polar opposite of many American management principles, which are exemplified below by General Electric. In effect, Toyota employs all four principles of lean production while Nike and Apple focus on two, and GE and Walmart focus only on one. Again, the contradictions of *Extreme Toyota* (Osono et al., 2008) apply, with the company seemingly pursuing profits in one period only to spend them for increasing market share and taking large risks on new products (e.g., Lexus, and Prius with its hybrid technology) in another. Much has been written on lean production at Toyota, but one must keep it clear that all four principles apply, and principles 1 and 4 are not "lean" in the sense of cutting employees and focusing on short-term financial goals.

Nike as a Donut Corporation from the Beginning

Nike has become a world-renowned athletic equipment and apparel company with a stated mission: "To Bring Inspiration and Innovation to Every Athlete* in the World," further broadening their market by explaining in a footnote "*If you have a body, you are an athlete" (Nike, 2011). Nike emerged out of the initial low-cost production advantage of Japanese production of shoes in the early 1960s. While a weak attempt was made by Nike to produce in the US, this was soon given up to produce in the then lower-wage area of Japan. Nike was founded by Bill Bowerman, who coached the University of Oregon track team, and one of his former runners named Philip Knight (Nike, 2011). They originally contracted to sell Onitsuka shoes but quickly started making their own shoes in Japan. In 1974, the US government imposed large tariffs on Japanese footwear and the yen continued to rise against the dollar, so Nike moved production to Korea, Taiwan, and Maine (for only two years). Knight subcontracted numerous factories to keep up with the rapid change in technology with each factory producing different products. At the time, the production wage difference between the US and Asia was $8-$11 an hour versus a mere $1. As a result, the New Hampshire and Maine assembly plants were soon closed (see Bill Kingston in box 3.1).

Nike's comparative advantage was two-fold: (1) create cutting-edge technology with the marketing of the shoes around famous athletes, and (2) produce the shoes at a very low cost in Asia. According to the Fortune 100 (Fortune, 2012), Nike employs more people within the US than outside. Nike's headquarters in Beaverton have nearly 8,000 workers, most of whom are quite well paid (average salaries of about $100,000), but the overwhelming majority of Nike's employees in the US are part-time. In East Asia, production factories have many more workers and a number of controversial issues – physical and verbal abuse, working conditions, and hourly wages (Todd et al., 2008). These subcontractors who make the shoes are not included in the official Nike employment statistics, but the company now has a staff of ninety employees to monitor them.

By the late 1980s, Nike created a specific product for each sport and outfit for each team with their individualized production. Marketing and advertising along with R&D comprised the largest portion of their US employment. Using star athletes like Michael Jordan, Tiger Woods, and LeBron James, Nike's spend on advertising went from $383 million in 1993 to over $3 billion in 2012, which includes sponsorship contracts, especially on hard-edge "just do it" television spots and extensive promotions. Nike also moved from independent marketing agents in the field to corporate sales within the company. Nike provided the employees with higher salaries and health benefits, but cut their commissions drastically. Each territory is equipped with at least two footwear and two apparel representatives (Geisinger, 2012).

Nike's worth is largely due to their ability to offshore production. They create a product that is manufactured by low-wage labor in overseas plants that are not officially part of Nike. In doing so, Nike subcontracts with three different types of factories (Donaghu and Barff, 1990). First, quality partners were set up in Japan, but are now in Taiwan and

Box 3.1:   Employees experiencing unemployment due to offshoring and outsourcing

Bill Kingston worked on waffle sole assembly in the Blue Ribbon Sports plant in Exeter, New Hampshire. He started in 1974 a couple of years after high school and the company had 250 workers by the end of the year. A stitching plant and a distribution center were added, so times were good. But in 1979 new plants were set up in Taiwan and Korea, and the American plants had outlived their usefulness. In 1980, the company changed its name to Nike. Bill lost his job that same year at the Exeter plant and went on unemployment for four months as the economy hit a big recession. He then got a job at the Phillips Exeter Academy where pay was lower and working around rich kids was, he said, "weird." He looked into becoming an apprentice electrician, which would have led to higher pay, but he didn't have the connections to do so. He moved to Nashua and got a job in maintenance at a hospital complex. He has better benefits and has stayed at the hospital. He is now 56 and just hopes to keep his job till he retires.

Michael Rossi started working at Apple in 1984 in Fremont, California, keeping track of parts for hard drives. Apple offered him the chance to get in on the ground floor at the new plant in Fountain, Colorado, 30 miles south of Denver. He and his wife Fresca moved across country, and they bought a house after he landed a supervisory job in shipping. But in 1996, Apple sold the plant to SCI Systems with the agreement that they would make Macs for the next three years. The employees were never sure what would happen after that, but in 1999, Apple severed their agreement with SCI systems, and Mike was out of a job. He tried to hire on at another Apple manufacturing plant, but found out that they shifted all their production to Singapore and China. He tried real estate in 2001 but didn't do well, and two years later Mike and Fresca lost their house. In 2003 they moved back in with her parents in California, and in 2004 found out that Apple had closed their Elk Grove plant. He remained out of full-time work for two years until he found a job in inventory. At 55, he found a more secure job in another electronics supply firm.

Trish McFadden is a 33-year-old woman who grew up in an inner-city neighborhood with her mother, who had two jobs in a nursing home and a restaurant. It seemed that she was always at work. After graduating from high school, Trish took a minimum-wage job transporting patients in a local hospital. The hospital provided educational benefits to become a nurse, and she had signed up. But she was injured lifting a patient and unable to do her job. Trish was transferred to an office job scanning medical records to digitize them, but then the job was subcontracted through another company. After she had worked briefly with the subcontractor, all paper medical record files had been converted to electronic form – Trish and the other workers were laid off. She was unemployed with no marketable skill set gained in high school and no access to affordable training. With wages that barely covered food, clothing, and lodging, Trish was unable to further her training and was essentially trapped.

Diedre Simmons is 30. She worked doing software development for Siemens, a German electronics firm. In 2005, Siemens announced that it would move 15,000 of its software programming jobs to India, China, and Eastern Europe. But Diedre was asked to stay on for a few more months to train her insourced replacement from India before she was laid off in her Florida office. Meanwhile, the Siemens Information Systems Development Center in Bangalore has added 3,000 jobs. Soured by the experience, Diedre is now looking to get out of information technology and into nursing. In 2012, she read that Siemens was getting a lot of publicity for creating advanced training programs for American workers. She said that made her mad.

Donald Jackson is 65. He worked doing software development for IBM for twenty years until 1993, when he was laid off from the mainframe manufacturing plant. In the early 1990s, IBM was undergoing a radical shift in their operations. Don was on unemployment for three months and then decided to move from New York to North Carolina for a job as a computer operator at a state university. It was a considerable pay cut (30 percent) but the benefits were somewhat comparable. Then two years ago, he retired from that job. Don is still bitter about how he was treated at IBM, but admits that the IBM of the 1960s and 1970s was heaven.

South Korea. They make the top-quality shoes in smaller batches (25,000 pairs per day), and are more likely to collaborate in innovations with Nike. Second, volume partners are large factories producing large amounts of standardized, lower-priced footwear (80,000 pairs). Production may serve companies other than Nike. Volume partners tend to own their own leather tanneries and rubber factories, but they are not particularly innovative. Third, new partners are often joint ventures and are located mostly in Thailand, Indonesia, and China because of their low labor costs. Each of these partners has an ability to meet the particular market needs of Nike. Having numerous partners allows for flexibility within the market, especially with innovations in technology and design. While wages in these Nike factories are extremely low, they increased by 18 percent in the 10-year period from 2001 to 2011 (Holmes, 2007; Walters, 2007; Townsend, 2011). Additionally, Nike claims to have changed its business strategy in 2007 with a renewed emphasis on sustainability and corporate responsibility (Nike, 2007).

To keep innovation going, R&D is a key to competitive advantage. Knight's *Futures Plan* requires that new designs have to be finished a year in advance to let retailers review new product lines before committing to the 6-month lead time orders (Holmes, 2004, 2007; Geisinger, 2012). R&D also invents new technologies to maintain their high-price premium lines (air cushions and spring pumps, Dri-FIT, and AirFree). Part of this technological shift to new materials is to avoid US taxes because their current products were often taxed on the percentage of leather in each pair of shoes, so replacing leather would avoid US government tariffs. Beyond its ability to reduce taxes, R&D has complemented Nike's marketing backbone with some very innovative and attractive products. The end result is that Nike is almost in the public relations business, with the Oregon football team being in the lead of the current revolution changing football uniforms.

Apple as a Donut Corporation

Apple is the iconic entrepreneurial startup out of a garage, with Steve Jobs eventually becoming the main CEO. After incorporating in 1976 in Cupertino, California, Apple went on to create computers, and then such innovative products as the iPod, iPhone, and iPad. It is now tremendously profitable and a worldwide symbol. Generally, Apple has developed an intense customer base to which it sells higher-priced products that have superior usability and some effective technical features. The design and innovations of Apple are often connected to Jobs' genius, but Gladwell (2011) points out that much of his innovation was with seemingly endless tweaking of existing innovations until they met his high standards of "perfection."

By 1996, a large amount of production work (assembling circuit boards, board testing, and final product assembly) were outsourced to suppliers and all iPod manufacturing was offshored to Taiwanese companies with factories in mainland China. Manufacturing still went on in Elk Grove, California, and Fountain, Colorado, but 250 were laid off at Elk Grove and actual production in the US ceased in about 2004 (see Michael Rossi at Apple and Diedre Simmons at Siemens in box 3.1) (Prince and Plank, 2012). Apple started quietly offshoring its production of computers with Inventec Appliances in Taiwan but nearly all manufacturing is now handled by Foxconn Industries, a division of Hon Hai Precision (Levy, 2006; Satariano and Burrows, 2011). The labor involved with an iPod requires about 10 minutes for assembly, usually done by 18- to 28-year-old women who are paid about $100 for a 60-hour working week (Portelligent, 2003, 2005a, 2005b; Kurtgenbach, 2006; Dedrick et al., 2011:14).

Terry Gou, a Taiwanese citizen, began Foxconn in 1974, and it became a primary manufacturer of Apple products around 1997. By 1998, Foxconn was producing the iPhone. In 2002, its production of Apple products increased tremendously as it grew to about 900,000 employees and later to over a million. Gou's firm was criticized for its harsh management and because 14 employees jumped to their deaths in 2010–11 from the top of his factory in Shenzen. Since then he has reacted with more openness and employee programs (Satariano and Burrows, 2011). Apple is generally insulated from bad press concerning Foxconn due to its overwhelming product popularity. It nonetheless launched an investigation, and quickly quieted the few negative stories with somewhat vague promises to improve the working conditions for its Foxconn workers in China and its other suppliers.[4] Nonetheless, nearly all of Apple's manufactured production came and still comes from China, and the CEO from 2011, Tim Cook, has made heavy equipment investments there (Lashinsky, 2012).

Apple maintains control over its supply- or value-chain networks in three ways. First, it is highly secretive in its technology design, especially in avoiding too much input from suppliers (compare the case of Microsoft, which sapped HP and IBM). In the personal computer market, it avoided lock-in to the Windows operating system (Shapiro and Varian, 1999). For the iPod it kept proprietary control over this user interface, and did the same through its iTunes store. Its extreme secrecy includes refusing to open up its digital rights management system to others, so that it can develop a "great deal of tacit knowledge in the areas of industrial design and user interfaces that others have tried and failed to imitate" (Dedrick et al., 2010:16).

Second, to control subcontractors, Apple has also been known to place electronic monitors in boxes of parts that allow them to track the parts moving through Chinese ports to Foxconn factories (Satariano and Burrows, 2011). Apple's approach to its suppliers keeps them from gaining any significant market power by keeping them dependent and by frequently enough switching key suppliers when they move to new models (e.g., their switch from PortalPlayer to Samsung on recent iPod models for their microchips) (Jacobides et al., 2006; Dedrick et al., 2010, 2011; Linden et al., 2011).

Third, Apple requires such large orders that it frequently crowds out competitors from using the same suppliers. Adam Satariano and Peter Burrows (2011) describe a relationship whereby Apple offers high volumes and upfront cash payments with strong downward pressure on costs (and hence supplier profits). These authors also indicate how Apple corners a market on lasers and high-power drills at key points leading up to their product launches when production needs to be high. Although not as charismatic as Steve Jobs, Tim Cook has been the master of leveraging Apple's supply-chain management into a major point of competitive advantage that contributes a substantial portion of their 40 percent profit levels. Thus, Apple simultaneously remains the darling of high tech in the US while downplaying its massive offshore production processes.

GE as the Proselytizer

General Electric (GE), a conglomerate producing a range of products from light bulbs to jet engines, is important as an older and traditionally managed firm that made a concerted move under former CEO Jack Welch to outsource and off-shore as much of its production as possible. While Nike and Apple had to do little to start offshoring, GE had to downsize and close many plants in the US. Further, while Nike and Apple tend to hide their offshoring, GE under Jack Welch broadcasts the idea.

GE began in the late 1890s as an electrical motor manu-facturer, but became a manufacturing giant of home appli-ances, consumer electronics, wind turbines, aviation engines, electric motors, lighting, locomotives, software, and certain kinds of weapons. It also produces basic products in terms of water, electricity (fueled by nuclear, wind, and gas), wind turbines, gas, and oil. Under Welch it moved into financial, entertainment, and health services. Since the 1980s, about half its revenues have come from financial services, with manufacturing providing the rest. The company has had many mergers and acquisitions, but our focus is on its offshoring.

In 1981 Jack Welch became the youngest CEO at GE, and he cleaned house with an emphasis on shareholder value. He was intent on reviving the company and wanted its many divisions to be first or second in the industry or to leave their market entirely. He became known as "neutron Jack" for downsizing employees; he had cut over 100,000 employees or about 25 percent of the company by 1985 (some by selling businesses and others by straight cuts).

Welch took three steps to make GE more profitable: (1) he changed the focus of overall operations to financial services, which he viewed as being more profitable, and in the process he cut unprofitable divisions and companies; (2) he adopted Six Sigma quality programs in manufacturing in 1995;[5] and then in the 1990s (3) he offshored and outsourced manufacturing whenever he could. The year before he became CEO, GE had revenues of $27 billion and a market value of $14 billion, and the year before he left GE had increased its revenues by a factor of five to $130 billion and market value by nearly thirty times to $410 billion. *Fortune* magazine named him the "Manager of the Century" (Fortune, 1999). At the end of his tenure at GE, Welch was widely regarded as a management genius (Slater, 1999; Lane, 2007).[6]

Although Six Sigma somewhat improved quality, the entry into financial services took resources away from manufacturing, especially as Welch cut basic research. His third step followed his "70–70–70" rule, which was to outsource 70 percent of production to other firms, offshore 70 percent of this outsourcing to low-wage countries, and send 70 percent of this to India (Carmel and Tija, 2005:110; Surana, 2011). Some of GE's manufacturing would be difficult to offshore, such as military equipment and especially jet engines (Stevenson, 1992). However, a large amount of electronic manufacturing was offshored to Asia, and GE recorded record profits on these items, especially large appliances (refrigerators, washers, ovens, etc.). In 2011, 154,000 of GE's total workforce of 287,000 workers were in China and Asia (Uchitelle, 2011).

Walmart as an Offshoring Merchandiser

Walmart is the world's largest merchandising firm, which means that their main task is to purchase goods from other manufacturers and then resell them in a retail store. In 2010, they had over 2,100,000 employees (CNN-Fortune, 2013). Since they do not produce any physical products (other than the big box buildings), their manufacturing story is nil. The only aspect of lean production that Waltonism uses is principle 2 of the four components of this theory – the supply-chain network. Walmart's is perhaps the most effective just-in-time supply-chain management system in the world, with their own satellites (Vidal, 2010; Kharif, 2007). By the turn of the century Walmart was the largest corporation in the world in terms of employment.

Our main concern about Walmart is the bargaining process that occurs in their supply-chain management system. This process offers a big payoff for suppliers – a national and even worldwide contract for producing millions of units – and a major downside for them – supplying these products at an extremely low price. Walmart has a reputation for being relentless in pursuing these low prices and this has caused them to largely abandon suppliers in AICs and instead pursue low-wage production in LDCs, especially China (Walton and Huey, 1993; Abernathy et al., 1999; Lichenstein, 2006, 2009; Fishman, 2006; Gereffi, 2005; Gereffi et al., 2005).

Walmart invites suppliers to Bentonville, Arkansas, or to centers in Asia to negotiate the prices that suppliers will be paid for the goods they would like to sell to Walmart. The incentive is huge since suppliers can gain access to markets all over the world (e.g., Walmart sells more in one day than Lowe's, a major hardware store and lumber supplier, sells in a year). However, the price-cutting pressure that Walmart exerts on these suppliers is massive. Walmart even engages in "reverse auctions" (a more intense form of competitive bidding) that pit a number of suppliers against each other in forcing down prices. The PBS show *Frontline* (2005) tells the story of how Rubbermaid, a major supplier of US kitchen and household ware, refused the Walmart price pressure and were almost put out of business. At the opposite end, Vlasic, a producer of pickles, accepted a deal to sell a gallon of Kosher Dills for $2.97, which is less than the average price of a quart of these same pickles (Fishman, 2006:79–83).

Walmart's use of the just-in-time philosophy extends not only to inventory but to labor. Walmart's computerized scheduling and labor optimization system makes employee work schedules much less regular and predictable for workers (Maher, 2007). The software improves efficiency for the store and short-term profits by determining how many employees are needed based on demand and store traffic. But employees get the short end of the deal as they will be "on call" and have to come into work when business surges, or sent home when there is a lull. For the low-paid hourly employees at Walmart, reductions in hours and sporadic work schedules increase stress and financial burdens. This is a stark contrast to Toyotism, where employees are kept and trained for the long term and given competitive wages and benefits. But for Walmart, the pressure to cut labor costs is due in part to its low-cost business model. The low margins that they receive on sales and the high volumes required to make a profit necessitate cutting costs elsewhere, so labor costs need to be kept at a minimum (Vidal, 2010). With the massive numbers of employees they have, Walmart effectively sets the minimum wage for the US (Vidal, 2010; Hamilton, 2006).

Walmart's treatment of its employees both in the US and abroad has been a constant source of criticism. US employees are rarely if ever organized into quality teams with effective input into the merchandizing process (Fishman, 2003; Harney, 2008; Vidal, 2010; Ingram et al., 2010). Foreign employees are subject to constant human rights violations that the company supposedly corrects, but which they constantly tolerate. The team-work elements of production by foreign subcontractors are sometimes advertised but not actually implemented. When pushed to the extreme, workers made unemployed by their employers being forced to go offshore would find it increasingly difficult to buy products no matter how low the prices. All in all, there is a strong element of immiseration in Waltonism. However, despite the maltreatment of employees at home and abroad, our main point here is that Waltonism does not employ principles 1 and 4 of the lean production model. Additionally, low-level employees at Walmart are not empowered for problem solving (principle 3) as they are in Toyotism.

Consequences for Lean Production and Donut Corporations

While management and economics are not particularly concerned with the consequences of lean production and offshoring, other than how these improve the profitability of various corporations, sociologists are concerned with three major aspects of the development of lean production, especially as it has moved away from Toyotism.

First, the use of computers in just-in-time inventory and supply-chain management, a technique used by all three types of lean production, results in greater between-firm productivity differences, which then lead to greater between-firm wage inequality (Faggio et al., 2010). This means that the more firms interact in modular networks, the more they produce inequality in wages between firms. This is the result of a "core competency chain" that creates a cascade of profitability and wages. The OEM or parent firm takes the most productive core competency (e.g., design and assembly) and subcontracts out the less productive core competencies (e.g., making component parts like shoe soles or pistons) to other firms. The first-tier subcontractor subcontracts less profitable items to a second-tier subcontractor that has a less productive core competency (e.g., making bolts and fasteners), and so on until core competency loses its meaning and the third- or fourth-tier subcontractor just does what is left (e.g., providing boxes and pallets). Each firm higher on the production ladder sheds tasks that are less profitable and yield lower incomes for workers. This is especially the case for offshoring where costs of production may be reduced by a factor of ten and the process is foreshortened (e.g., actually manufacturing moves to the third tier more quickly). The additional costs of transportation exist but with the technological development of large container ships, although the profitability factor may be reduced from ten to nine, this still allows a sizable difference in costs. The end result in an AIC where production is subcontracted within the country is a major increase in income inequality. If inequality were to be computed for the entire supply chain or value chain, which includes foreign countries, it would be even larger (Acemoglu and Autor, 2010; Autor and Dorn, 2009; Autor et al., 1998, 2005; Acemoglu, 2002).[7]

Second, much of this discussion is about manufacturing because this sector is very important in a country's overall economic health (Smil, 2013). As shown in figure 2.2, the US balance of trade for goods production went from being positive in the 1970s to over $100 million in deficit by 1984.

Deficits dominate the positive aspects of service exports. The conclusion that we must reiterate is that in the face of massive US purchases of manufactured goods from abroad, the ability of the service sector to generate enough exports to balance manufacturing or goods production is minuscule. The US cannot generate enough services to make up for the amount of manufactured goods from China that Walmart and Best Buy sell to the American consumer. The government debt situation is derivative of this deficit in goods production. This balance of trade deficit does not exist for a few countries like Germany, Sweden, and Japan, but they are the exceptions that prove the rule. In late 2011, Germany had a positive $14.9 billion balance of trade, and Sweden had a $1.5 billion balance. Japan had $5.9 to $8.9 billion positive balance of trade before the disastrous tsunami in 2011.[8] All three countries have maintained strong manufacturing presence within their borders, so their balances of trade are positive despite their heavy dependence on foreign oil imports (OECD, 2011a, 2011b). As shown in figure 2.2, services do little to improve the balance of trade because they are difficult to export. Consequently, manufacturing and material goods production (including agricultural products) are the main determinants of a surplus, with too little being a deficit. As such, the decline of manufacturing in the US is the American Achilles heel.

The labor process of how work is done in these three models shows that LP-1 is much more favorable for workers in AICs while simultaneously producing some jobs in LDCs. It uses a labor process reliant on quality control circles, which are teams with a bit less empowerment than self-managed teams from the socio-technical perspective. They make up for producing in higher-cost countries with much overtime and the use of temporary workers, generating secure and generally loyal employees. LP-2 uses semi-autonomous teams in the creative aspects of its engineering and marketing departments in the US and other AICs, but teams disappear overseas, where Foxconn and others largely use Fordist principles with 18- to 28-year-old female employees. LP-3 is notorious for low-wage employment with few benefits in the US, and also employing many workers part-time so that the organizations can avoid providing benefits. These organizations are largely unconcerned with the labor process among their offshore industries, which also use largely Fordist assembly principles paying incredibly low wages. On the whole, the labor process in this new global division of labor utilizing lean production principles is highly conducive to wage inequality and exploitation.

Third, FDI is both inward and outward, and it has three components: sizable investments in equity capital that are over 10 percent of the purchased company's stock, reinvested earnings in a foreign plant or joint venture, and intracompany loans (UNCTAD, 2010a, 2010b). We argue that outward FDI is an imperfect measure of offshoring and that the measure we would really want is investment in plant and equipment. For instance, buying stocks and bonds is not going to increase a company's job creation capability, and if it leads to a merger, you can be sure that many employees will lose their jobs. Further, this chapter has shown that Toyotism increases jobs while Nikeification and Waltonism reduce jobs. So ideally, in predicting unemployment we would like to have a separate FDI variable for each type of lean production. However, this is not possible at the moment, and we can only look at some suggestive studies.

Sociologists Matissa Hollister (2011) and Alison Davis-Blake and Joseph Broschak (2009) argue that outward FDI reinforces inequality and devastates manufacturing. Economists Mihir Desai and colleagues directly measure two aspects of FDI. In one study (2005) they show that FDI in the 1980s and 1990s reduces domestic investment in 19 out of 20 countries. In another study (2007), they show that FDI increased employment in 600 US firms in 1982, 1989, 1994, and 1999. This seems to refute our claim until you see that employment increased only 2 percent (a mean of .0193), while wages for these very few employees increased by a factor of four (mean $82,321). So Apple may have increased their Cupertino design employees by 1.9 percent while the potential manufacturing employment of iPods, iPads, and iPhones was sent to Foxconn in China, where employment tops a million. We find this data incomplete, but even with the evidence we have, employment growth is disappointing.

Fourth, how far can offshoring go? To address offshorability, Alan Blinder poses three questions that if answered "yes" indicate that an occupation is not offshorable: (1) does the employee need to be physically close to a specific US work location? (2) does the employee need to be physically close to any work unit? and (3) does the work unit need to be at a US location? (Blinder, 2006, 2007; OECD, 2007a). This can be revised into five categories of jobs.

Offshorable jobs:
1   jobs that make anything that can be shipped or boxed (most assembly jobs in factories and even ship-building); and
2   jobs that generally involve computer or electronic communication that can be sent anywhere in the world (call centers, programming, evaluation of tests, accounting, etc.).

Safe jobs:
3   jobs involving bodily contact that require an employee to be physically close to the client or patient (e.g., medical services, child care, wait staff at a restaurant, haircutting professions, and primary and secondary teaching);
4   jobs involving proximal contact, including some that require that employees be close for geographical reasons (e.g., police and fire, utilities, home and building construction, or garbage pick-up) and some sales jobs (e.g., high-end sales generally requires personal contact and trust); and
5   jobs that involve symbolic values and authentic locations that must be done in country (e.g., elected politicians, judges in courts, or professional athletes representing a team like the Boston Celtics or Los Angeles Lakers);

Blinder's articles were quite influential because estimates of offshored jobs were lacking or flawed. His results did not estimate the number of jobs offshored, but showed that hundreds of thousands of American jobs could be offshored quite easily. This vulnerability produced some heated discussion.

Conclusion

While no database exists that provides a comprehensive assessment of how many workers have lost their jobs to off-shoring, the impacts in the destruction of the manufacturing sector have been clear just in the number of US products now being produced abroad (Levine, 2012). Just one firm in China that makes most of Apple's products – Foxconn or its parent company Hon Hai Precision – now has over a million employees. The evidence for services being offshored is more ad hoc, but also important (e.g., call centers in India). Out of the three types of lean production that have consequences for employment in AICs, clearly LP-2 with Nike and Apple and LP-3 with Walmart produce the most offshoring.

On the positive side, LP-1 or Toyotism produces a large number of jobs in the US both for individual originating equipment companies and for their suppliers. The focus is on market share and this leads to internalizing profits for the long-term expansion of the firm. While not the darlings of Wall Street, since they reject shareholder value strategies, Toyota, Honda, and similar firms create a large number of American jobs and as a result reduce inequality and the balance of trade deficit in the US.

On the negative side, LP-2 and LP-3 produce very few high-quality jobs in the US, and a large number of semi-skilled jobs generally done by young girls aged 18 to 28 in China. As a job creator, Nikeification results in an employment vacuum for manufacturing workers in the US. It creates a "donut hole," which is more or less American unemployment. Waltonism creates a large number of low-pay jobs with stingy benefits in the SLAM sector. Like Nike and Apple, its thirst for low prices drives further offshore production with foreign workers having to endure sweatshop conditions. It eschews all of the principles of lean production except for the just-in-time supply-chain management, and generates large numbers of low-wage and low-skilled jobs in the US and elsewhere. Its massive pressure for offshoring creates even more of an employment vacuum than Nikeification. Further, both these forms of lean production – Nikeification and Waltonism – lead to a wider spectrum of suppliers and parent firms, which increases the divergence of wages. One can conclude that the more one outsources and offshores production, the greater the overall inequality in society.

This change in organizational structure also contains a contradiction between being open and closed. The modular structure leads to more open networks of multiple subcontractors that can lead to firm secrets being revealed to competitors. While computer technology has allowed a monitoring of supplies and production to a degree not previously possible, it can also create the situation of greater leakage of important proprietary information. Toyotism avoids this problem with its more closed firm boundaries and by enclosing its network of suppliers within its boundaries with loyalty-based membership (i.e., subcontractors are not allowed to produce for competing firms). Foxconn, the subcontractor that produces for Apple and many competing corporations, must present Apple with many security problems.

Even more serious, Andy Grove, the former head of Intel for many years, warned in a cover article of *Businessweek* that subcontracting production to offshore sites gives those firms a technological advantage in dealing with the product (Grove, 2010). Eventually, the subcontractor moves upstream, develops their own R&D laboratories, and then produces their own branded products. Many Chinese firms seem to be aimed in this direction (e.g., see the case of Boeing sharing its production secrets; Nolan, 2009) with joint ventures giving way to Chinese-based firms (Atkinson and Ezell, 2012:95–6, 107–8).

Finally, former IBM executive and Sloan foundation president Ralph Gomory states that "the fundamental goals of the country and of our companies have diverged" (Kochan, 2011:2). While Thomas Kochan doesn't refer to lean production, his description of "America's human capital paradox" refers to "fewer good jobs for the middle-class" since the number and quality of jobs are permanently lower. Donald Jackson (box 3.1) knows full well what much of this means as he was laid off for good at IBM due to outsourcing production, and now IBM does not do any actual manufacturing in the US. Kochan says that a major part of the jobs problem is American management's "destructive obsession with total shareholder return" (2011:2). It is becoming painfully apparent to American workers and to many academics as well that American corporations are little concerned about the number and quality of jobs in the US. However, the most important point leads back to bringing "the fundamental goals of the country and of our companies" back together.

4

Technological Change and Job Loss

> In the official Guidebook of the [Chicago Technology] Fair appeared the sobering Motto "SCIENCE FINDS – INDUSTRY APPLIES – MAN CONFORMS."
>
> Leo Marx (1983:9)

"King Ludd" signed a workers' manifesto condemning new technology in the late seventeenth century. King Ludd may have been modeled on Ned Ludd, who destroyed two large stocking frames in England in 1779. The crown soon mandated heavy penalties or even execution for frame-breaking, and the use of a false name like "King Ludd" was probably wise if one did not want to be arrested. The subsequent Luddite movement was an organized action by stockingers that first began in 1675, but its most important phase occurred in the early nineteenth century when the hardships of the working classes peaked, from 1811 to early 1813, near the end of the Napoleonic Wars (Binfield, 2004). The Luddites met at night on the moors around small towns, and then destroyed a number of wool and cotton mills. Following large battles between the Luddites and the military in Middleton and throughout Lancashire, the Luddites were crushed by overwhelming force by the British crown, which sent over 11,000 soldiers to stop the violence and protests. At the peak of the violence, there were more British troops fighting the Luddites than in Europe fighting Napoleon. Machine-breaking was soon made into a capital crime by the Frame Breaking Act, seventeen men were hung in 1813, and many others were "transported" to Australia. After this, Luddism waned.[1]

To those sympathetic to the working classes, the Luddite movement can be seen as leading to the rising protests of the English working class and its later incorporation into the Labour Party, especially after World War II when Labour prime minister Clement Atlee and the economist and social reformer William Beveridge sculpted the welfare state and the National Health Service. To those somewhat unconcerned with the working class (e.g., Sale, 1996), "Luddite" is an epitaph hurled with a laugh at someone stupid enough to oppose the inevitable march of progress through labor-saving machines (Thompson, 1966). Implied in this view is the thought that technology will increase the number of jobs for workers who might be displaced. And one can go back in history to view these improvements as the result of the industrial revolution producing rising economic growth and employment.[2]

But if one goes back to the early 1800s to see what happened to the Luddite communities, it is important to ask whether these workers actually got jobs with the new technology. While some did, Jeremiah Brandeth in 1817 led the unemployed Nottingham stockingers in the Pentrich Rising to protest against unemployment and the poor living conditions that accompanied the new technology. In the four years after the executions of Brandreth and others involved in the rising, most workers did not find new jobs that would lead to increasing prosperity. In short, when the Luddites were replaced by machines or had their wages lowered by new technology, these workers were left much worse off. So were they wrong or irrational to oppose their future of immiseration? When new technologies replace workers, these specific workers are most often overlooked by technological apologists. Those with poor employment prospects are little comforted by the long-term prediction that eventually more jobs will be created.

So we can ask the question whether new technologies cause structural unemployment, create new jobs, or have any other significant impact on the labor market. This issue has received significant attention since the early 1990s, especially after major recessions in 2001 and 2008 (Brynjolfsson and McAfee, 2011; Cappelli, 2012a; Ford, 2009; Kelly, 2010; Rifkin, 1995). Contrary to the claims of many media articles and some recent books, this question is complex and difficult to answer. However, even though the debate over the role of technology in employment remains controversial, we must still ask whether innovation and new technologies (1) *increase* employment; (2) *decrease* employment; (3) *restructure* employment (eliminate jobs in one sector but add jobs in another) with no change in absolute amounts of employment; or (4) have minimal impact on overall employment levels. Depending on the industry, new technologies probably do a number of these things.

These questions can be divided into two parts according to one's perspective on time. In the long term, new technologies undoubtedly lead to efficiencies that create more production, which enables lower prices for products. As volume increases, owners of capital, including managers, major stock owners, and even some pension investors, receive greater profits. Some of these profits and lower prices will eventually lead to greater demand and production of other items through multiplier effects. The end result over the long term of 10, 20, or 30 years may contribute to greater economic growth. Perhaps this growth will lead to greater employment over time, but there will be major lags on both the employees' and the investors' side.

In the short term, displaced workers have to deal with these major lags. There is little delay to be tolerated in paying next month's utility bills, mortgage payment, car payment, or grocery bills. In areas of high unemployment, it is difficult to sell your house and move to find work elsewhere, businesses are generally loath to move into such an area, and the existing businesses in the community then have lower and lower sales, which leads to their distress and the possibility of more lay-offs. The problem is that employees and workers live in the short term. They cannot wait for the boom that may be coming 10–20 years from now. As an individual's duration of unemployment grows, employers avoid them. While much of this can be rhetorically placed on the victims' backs – get retrained – the reality is that many older workers in their 50s or 60s will have very restricted possibilities of employment even after retraining because firms often prefer younger and newly trained workers. And many younger workers without experience languish as well. The basic fact is that we all live in the short term of months and years, not the long run of decades and centuries, in which "we are all dead" (Keynes, 2000:ch. 3).

So the question about technology in explaining structural unemployment (i.e., the process of unemployment then leading to downward mobility through segmented labor markets) is not what happens in the long term. It is instead, what happens in the short term when people actually need work and have to pay the bills. Consequently, this chapter will be about how technology leads to structural unemployment while in the long term it may lead to revenue and profit growth and possibly employment growth.

We will view this in three parts. First, we will outline how some disciplines and theories have looked at technology and unemployment. This has largely been a contentious literature and there is little agreement on the results other than that "people lose their jobs" in the short term. Second, we look at important changes in technology that have led to job losses, which can occur in a number of ways. One type of change in technology directly replaces a worker – a welding robot replacing a welder on an assembly line. Another change in technology transforms many industries simultaneously such that direct replacement is not always clear, since so many people are affected. For example, computers infuse many businesses so that it is unclear that any direct replacement has occurred, but business is nonetheless totally transformed (e.g., the web replacing newspapers or computers replacing physical files, resulting in the disappearance of file folders and bureaus). And finally, offshoring technology can move jobs to other countries with lower wages and infrastructural costs – the container ship industry allows manufactured goods to be shipped at very low costs back to the country that once produced them. These three technological forces – direct replacement, indirect replacement, and offshoring displacement – contribute to structural unemployment in the short-term no matter what their long-term effects might be with the uncertain investment of profits. And third, after the major sections of this chapter, we look at some direct evidence on the impact of computer technology on labor.

Theories of Technology and Structural Unemployment

A number of disciplines have looked at the impact of technology on the labor market, and we will consider economics, business, and sociology. There are four basic ways to frame technology that roughly correspond to these disciplinary approaches: (1) macro-process approaches that are typical of economics and adhere to mathematical modeling; (2) micro-process approaches as utilized by most business and organizational perspectives on firms, and their internal dynamics and interrelationship with external entities and processes; (3) Marxist approaches to technology that focus on management manipulation of technology; and (4) historical-institutional approaches that draw upon both macro- and micro-perspectives but attempt to engage the various other important variables that are integrally intertwined with the economy, labor, and society.[3] Again, while there are some overlaps between these four approaches across disciplines, more often each of the various fields examines technological processes from its own disciplinary view, which determines the unit of analysis, scales of assessment, and methodological adherence to quantitative, qualitative, or mixed methods.

Economic theories

Technology entered into this area with the exogenous and then the endogenous growth theories. First with exogenous growth, Robert Solow found that about 67 percent of economic growth is driven by capital and labor, and that the residual 33 percent of economic growth is driven by technological advances. Much of this neo-classical model was used by Edward Denison in *Why Growth Rates Differ*, and the amount of technology or "contributions to knowledge" sub-sequently went up to 38 percent (Denison, 1969, 1980). However, the Solow model did not directly measure technology. It assumed that the residual of a regression equation (unexplained variance) was due to technology, new products, quality or process improvements, or other increases in efficiency. Thus, technological progress was indirectly theorized, which was not very convincing (Romer, 2012:6–45, 47–8).

Endogenous growth economists in the 1980s proposed a second approach where technology would actually be measured and put in the equation. This was done in two ways: (1) continuously changing levels of R&D expenditures, employees engaged in R&D, or investments in human capital such as higher levels of education, or (2) a simple "shift parameter" not unlike a dummy variable (e.g., zero for a time and then one for holding patents or having computers at a certain point in time) (Romer, 2012:103, 126). More recently, these studies have found that industry-funded R&D has been more effective than government R&D, so the implication is that government policy should focus more on tax credits to support industry-led measures to increase innovation.[4]

Endogenous theory often assumed a constant saving rate and some studies relied on perfect competition; however, they later used imperfect markets and optimized R&D leading to technological progress (Romer, 1990; Aghion and Howitt, 2009). Technology could also lead to an interaction with human capital. Endogenous growth theory implies that countries that embrace openness, competition, change, and innovation will prosper. Countries that restrict or slow change by protecting or favoring threatened industries or workers will stagnate. Thus, the richest nations among AIC countries that benefited from the industrial revolution allowed the painful results of what Joseph Schumpeter (1950) termed "creative destruction." According to this concept, economies that avoid the march of technology are destined to suffer weak economic growth (Acemoglu, 2009).

Two significant components of "creative destruction" (Schumpeter 1950:63–4) come into play. Schumpeter argues that creative destruction is an instrumental part of capitalism, and as such is dependent upon (1) *crises*, or economic down-turns that produce cyclical unemployment, which are then followed by (2) *innovation* in terms of R&D, new technology, and more effective management. This changes various business processes as well as the development of new or enhanced products. According to many economists and business leaders, this crisis-driven change plays a healthy role in any growing economy, and without these crises, innovation would be stymied along with prosperity.

Creative destruction is not generally well accounted for in most of these models. However, it largely remains deterministic toward unemployment. Those subject to creative destruction (Laurie Galston in box 4.1) must get out of the way by

Box 4.1:   Employees whose employment was threatened by technology

Laurie Galston graduated from high school and is 26. She worked as a temporary worker for two years in a major Japanese transplant factory in Ohio, and was told that she did a very good job. However, when more robots were brought into the paint shop she was let go. While other permanent workers were reallocated within the firm, all of the temporary workers were permanently dismissed. She looked for another factory job but instead started working part-time for UPS in the package sorting facility. Her pay at UPS is only half what it was at the transplant due to its being part-time and the wage rate actually being much lower. Laurie has considered a job at the Amazon.com warehouse because it is full-time, but she heard that the starting pay is only about $12 an hour.

Maddie Parlier graduated from high school in South Carolina and is 23. She started work as a temporary worker at Standard Motor Products but did such a good job for the auto parts maker that she was taken on permanently. However, she only has a high-school degree and can only follow instructions as a level 1 employee rather than independently doing precise machine work. The manager says that she is hanging on to her job by a thread and will likely be replaced by automated equipment. Maddie is single with two young children, which means that she cannot realistically go back to school for further training. Most likely, she will soon be unemployed (Davidson, 2012).

Winston "Stone" Wilson worked in technology design doing CAD/CAM in Houston, where his friends called him Stone after a wrestler he was fond of imitating. He worked on the parts for pumps that were used to eliminate water in oil rigs overseas. He is single and 32 years old. He finds that his CAD/CAM skills can easily be replicated by designers in other parts of the world, so he is considering upgrading his AS degree from the local community college to a BS degree in mechanical engineering. However, this will take at least two years of study. Stone is currently looking for jobs in CAD/CAM and thinking about going to school part-time.

Luke Hutchins says "I am good at math." He went to a technical school for two years, has six semesters of machine tooling, and has five years of experience. He can do a form of practical calculus and trigonometry, which is needed to run a Gildenmeister-7 axis-turning-machine that costs $500,000. While the machine operates largely by itself, Luke has to adjust it roughly ten to twenty times an hour to meet the rigorous specifications of fuel injectors. Although Luke says he would like to learn more metallurgy, he is now a level 2 operator and Standard Motor Products in South Carolina says he has job security (Davidson, 2012).

Thomas Barnes is 30 and graduated from the Brandeis School of Law in Louisville three years ago. He passed the Bar in Kentucky and is ready to take the exam in other states should an opportunity arise. His brother Alex graduated six years ago and got a position with a prestigious law firm in New York doing legal research and now seems on his way to partnership. But these kinds of jobs have dried up. Tom has heard about but has not used Lex Machina, PACER, RECAP, and the QLP programs for electronic court access and automated legal predictions. Since graduation he has done some temporary work through Robert Half Legal and HireCounsel. He has also applied for a number of legal aid jobs with the government, but these programs have been cut, and they pay peanuts compared to what Alex initially got in New York. And although Tom only has $40,000 of debt, some of his friends, who went to private law schools, have as much as $125,000.

getting an existing job in a more protected sector, or obtaining training in the skills that the newest technologies demand. By and large, economic theories do not see technology as something that can be shaped, controlled or constructed. Technology is deterministic: take it or leave it.

Since the mid-1990s, productivity has been achieving gains not seen since the 1960s. This has been due to the accelerating impact of computers and software throughout many different industries, such as manufacturing with CAD/CAM, electronic banking, web retailing, writing and controlling documents, statistical quality control, just-in-time inventory control, and the general increase in the diffusion of information and communication of ideas. However, there is concern that economic decline, especially in manufacturing, is causing the US to lose out in the "race for global innovation advantage" (Atkinson and Ezell, 2012; Golden and Katz, 2008). All in all, economic models have focused on growth, with less attention toward unemployment, when it comes to technology.

Business or firm theories

Business theories have a more gradualist viewpoint toward technology. Businesses are often in a constant process of developing small improvements in their products, their production processes, and their overall human capital. While businesses may be open to various sorts of fads in terms of decentralizing through divestiture and centralizing through mergers, they are looking for new and better business processes. This is done internally, and it is also done through the diffusion of innovations. The official name for the process that promotes this is currently "benchmarking," which means one should designate the best processes or best practices at other firms as your own organizational goals or procedures. The spread of lean production followed this kind of approach (Cole, 1989; Strang and Kim, 2005).

Shoshana Zuboff (1984) charts the rise of the automated workplace, especially the use of a new, innovative technology, from a more sociological perspective. These new technologies are often in one company. Her work illustrates how even early in the development of a technology now so pervasive in today's world there were significant concerns about its role among individuals and in society. For instance, Zuboff relays the concerns voiced by a pulp-mill worker about the management pushing to adopt new computer technology:

> "The managers want everything to be run by computers. But if no one has a job, no one will know how to do anything anymore. Who will pay the taxes? What kind of society will it be when people have lost their knowledge and depend on computers for everything?" (1984:5)

So even prior to the pervasiveness of the personal computer in the workplace, workers and scholars had growing concerns about information technology, automation, and technological unemployment.

Marxist theories

David Harvey (1990) details the shift in the 1970s and 1980s from manufacturing to service-oriented economies in many of the industrialized nations, asserting that this change should be more correctly affiliated with the shift in production patterns from Fordist activities (e.g., mass production in manufacturing and large-scale industry) to post-Fordist activities in information and financial activities (Krippner, 2011). Following Schumpeter, Harvey (2007) discusses the role of neoliberalism as a form of "creative destruction," detailing how the economic history of capitalism is not one of constructive change, as it is often characterized by economists and business leaders, but one of continual crises, rising inequality, the concentration of capital among the rich, and the immiseration of the working and, now, middle class.

With regard to technology and employment, Harvey follows Braverman's (1974) assertion that new technology does not simply displace workers (even though this does happen), but further restructures labor relations and social conditions, including depressing wages and benefits, forcing workers to be more flexible in their career choices, imposing geographical mobility, and lengthening working hours. This results in forcing many workers down in segmented labor markets to lower-paid and often deskilled jobs in SLAMs. Further, while many workers eventually land in new but often inferior jobs, the short-term consequences of unemployment can be economically and socially devastating (e.g., loss of income, divorce, alcohol and drug use, etc.).

David Noble (1984) shows how management consciously shaped the development of machine tool automation in the US. He argues that computerized numerical control (CNC, and later CAD/CAM) machines were introduced both to increase efficiency and to discipline unions, which were stronger in the US after World War II. These machines that make machines are critical to advanced manufacturing. But management designed the technology to take most of its control away from craft workers and transfer it by way of computer programming to college-educated white-collar employees who did not belong to unions. Noble argues that the separation of blue- and white-collar employees was a failure, but later observers do not agree. The manipulation of technological practice angered union machinists, who felt that their practical skills supplemented by night-school knowledge of applied science were discredited. In response, they allowed the white-collar workers to program the machines and then watched them produce "scrap at high speed." The company relied on the skilled blue-collar workers to fix and sometimes rewrite the CNC software. Eventually, these workers straightened out the more formally trained white-collar workers, but the blue-collar workers lost out in the end when white-collar workers finally learned the job.

While Noble's work is historical and focused on a single industry, its more general claim that technology can be shaped by managers in ways to control workers is an important one. This was a point also made about the early factories that tried to control pilferage by bringing employees working at home into the factory. The factory actually did not increase the efficiency of the production process until much later. The takeaway from this perspective is that the impact and even design of technology can be shaped by social groups. While Noble focuses totally on management as the shaper, he brings a viewpoint on technology that the economists and business theorists do not consider – its social construction.

Historical-institutionalist theories in sociology

While much social science research may "black box" technology, there is a strain that builds on Noble's insight that indicates that the impact of technology is socially molded or even socially constructed. A number of social scientists – especially sociologists – have examined various forms of technological unemployment. Jeremy Rifkin (1995) claimed that automation and information technologies would continue to replace workers, reducing employment and wreaking havoc on the global economy, due in part to the displacement of workers but also as the result of a lack of disposable income as a result of unemployment and underemployment. Some less traditional economists such as Acemogulu (2002), Krugman (1996, 1999, 2011), and others (Cappelli, 2012a; Levy and Murnane, 2004) have argued since the early 1990s that technology is, at the very least, restructuring jobs for both blue-collar and professional occupations, resulting in new forms of stratification. Most of these authors remain mostly optimistic about the role of innovation in long-term economic growth and overall employment.[5]

However, Acemogulu and Robinson (2011) indicate that technology may be delayed or deformed by "extractive" (authoritarian) rather than "inclusive" (democratic) institutions. Noble shows that technology can be shaped in different ways by powerful interests, and a number of sociologists assert that the ultimate consequence of technology and automation has been a downward pressure on wages and benefits which has hurt all workers (Aronowitz, 2005; Aronowitz and Cutler, 1997; Aronowitz and Difazio, 2010; Burawoy, 1979, 1985; Thompson, 1989). As Leo Marx indicates in the quote that introduces this chapter, and as a wide range of critical theorists like Horkheimer and Adorno (2007) have reiterated, the naiveté of assuming science is always good has been severely tarnished by the technologies of war, including nuclear weapons and death drones (Volti, 2010:255–300). And the current and growing consensus on the potentially catastrophic effects of global warming are due to specific technological innovations that we seemingly cannot live without (e.g., the automobile's internal combustion engine and coal-generated power plants) (2010:97–117).

Following Neil Fligstein's work on markets and technology, we go further and claim that all new technologies are socially negotiated, whether fairly to all parties or not. In his political-cultural theory of markets, Fligstein says that entrepreneurs and managers present a "conception of control" or "cognitive frames" that interpret the introduction markets (2001:18). We extend that conception to technological innovation. Technology is not automatically applied to society, as the telephone had to be negotiated with entrepreneurs, investors, and managers, and then by workers, the public, and the state. Organizational fields try to stabilize the concept of a market and this often "depends on the politics in the field and the relation between the field and the state" (Fligstein, 2001:180; Volti, 2010:171–185; Rybczynski, 1985). In a variety of theories (resource dependence, networks, politics and institutional theories), sociologists view this "conception of control" as being negotiated (Fligstein, 2001:176–81). Richard Badham (2005:132–3) terms this a three-dimensional socio-technical interaction between technology and society, and Stephen Barley (2005:386–7) also sees it on three levels: (1) the comparative level (British, French, and American engineers are organized in very different ways); (2) the level of industry effect (technology in different automobiles and semiconductors); and (3) the level of functional aspects of work (production, design, service and R&D engineers and their technologies).

One historical example of such negotiations concerns the "conception of control" in the telephone industry and how it led to tremendous technological innovation with stable markets for workers and consumers. Once the entrepreneurs had sold their "conception of control" to investors in the 1930s, the public through local and state governments directly controlled the rates in each locality and the federal government used the Federal Communications Commission to guide future developments in technology. It did so by requiring AT&T to invest in technological development and make all innovations free and available to the public and industry. This led to the founding of the Bell Labs, which won eleven Nobel prizes for scientific research. Government's creation of the research institution that became the Bell Labs and its funding of a large part of the research led to the creation of the transistor, laser, microwaves, TV, UNIX, cellular phones, radio astronomy, and the photovoltaic cell, to name just a few. Many, though not all, of these discoveries were funded by federal government research dollars, many of which were linked to the Defense Department, including the Advanced Research Projects Agency Network (ARPANET), which created the basis for the internet (Volti, 2010:243–4; Abbate, 1999).

The federal government's initiation of the Bell Labs also led to the development of lean production, with Walter Shewhart heading up their statistical quality control unit in 1924 that led to the World War II quality control unit that was subsequently transferred to Japan via General Douglas MacArthur. As the supreme commander of occupied Japan, MacArthur asked Nippon Telephone and Telegraph for the statistical control charts, but they did not have any. This led to W. Edwards Deming and Joseph Juran traveling to Japan and starting up a movement for quality control out of which lean production was born. The list of achievements at or through the Bell Labs goes on and on, but we will just end with statistician John Tukey and mathematician Claude Shapiro of the Bell Labs discovering the packet bundling theory that made internet traffic possible (not to mention their other innovative contributions to the Institute of Creative Technology and the Industrial Mathematics Laboratory) (Mitra, 2005). Just to show that management would not have done it anyway, when in 2008 state regulation of telephones based on monopoly power no longer existed, and the "conception of control" of the telephone market was radically renegotiated, the Bell Labs pulled out of basic research.

A second major example of how the state can regulate and shape technology concerning employment has to do with the 1862 Morrill Act to establish education that would further the invention and guide the use of agricultural technology at federally funded universities. The reserved Justin Smith Morrill from Vermont authored the act in the House, and the rabble-rousing Jonathan Baldwin Turner, an industrial educator from Illinois, pushed it through. The land-grant universities were furthered by the Morrill Act of 1890 that extended them to the Southern states, and by the Smith-Lever Act of 1914 that established the extension services that developed the concepts of diffusion of innovations much further. The role of the land-grant universities in creating and guiding the use of technology was immense.[6]

So the real question is not the Luddite response that is stylistically framed by management so that "workers conform," but the more historically framed "negotiation of a conception of control" of the use of technology in jobs and markets. And negotiations vary in terms of how favorable they may be to capitalists and workers, but negotiations they are, and this needs to be recognized by social scientists and policy-makers. The more workers' futures are taken into account and the more the adjustment processes are guided by thoughtful policies, the better it will be for society as a whole.[7]

Technologies that Increase Structural Unemployment

While one of the most important changes in social technology occurred after World War II with lean production, in this section we focus on four specific technologies that have had tremendous impacts on structural unemployment in the US: (1) shipping technology with containerization; (2) automation and robots; (3) computer and information technology; and (4) the leap of technology to the professions. Each section shows how these innovations were introduced and what their impact is on employment.

Ocean shipping from stevedores to containerization

Shipping across the seas had long been reliant on stevedores to load and unload a variety of boxes, crates, and containers by hand. In the 1950s, the shipping industry introduced large interlocking containers, which would revolutionize the movement of goods throughout the seas (Levinson, 2006). The containers were transported by the SS *Ideal X*, a former World War II oil tanker that had been converted to carry them (see row 1 in table 4.1). With this event, the movement of goods worldwide expanded dramatically, restructuring global trade and leading to the tremendous growth of manufacturing over the course of the next sixty years. While an early form of container technology had been around over one hundred years ago on railroads in England, the new shipping container design allowed longshoremen to load and unload the cargo in a fraction of the time previously necessary (Cudahy, 2006; Levinson, 2006). The largest container ships can now carry 18,000 "twenty-foot equivalent units" (TEUs), and the Panamax ships with a capacity of 10,000–14,500 TEUs can now fit through the recently widened Panama Canal. At the same time, the largest automobile carriers, called roll-on, roll-off (RORO) ships, can carry 8,500 vehicles (Belson, 2012). Coupled with advances in crane technology, standardization of the size of containers, and information technology used to track both the containers and their goods, the result was a dramatic increase in total global trade by reducing the time for loading and transporting cargo from multiple months to just under three weeks (Levinson, 2006). Further, the design of the containers allowed for seamless transfer of goods between ships and rail or trucks without having to unpack the containers. This greatly reduced one of the biggest costs of overseas trade during the 1950s, when in 1956 it cost \$5.62 to move a ton of loose cargo compared with only \$0.16 per ton using containers (*Economist*, 2006, 2013; Smil, 2010).

One of the biggest changes to further revolutionize shipping was in logistics, especially related to changes in information technologies (e.g., computers, software, handheld scanners, etc.). The most important element in the logistics of consumer goods is getting the correct amount of goods to a particular market (i.e., a store) to meet demand but not oversupply them. Since producers often overproduce when attempting to anticipate future demand, the movement of surplus goods to alternative markets becomes of equal importance. According to Womack et al. (1990), this tenuous yet imperative linkage between supply and demand – in

Table 4.1: Technological changes, 1950–2013

Years Crises	1950–9 Growth	1960–9 Boom	1970–80 Two oil crises	1981–9 Recovery	1990–9 Boom	2000–7 Up and down	2008–13 Deep recession
1 Ocean shipping	*Ideal X* converted tanker ship in 1951	Atlantic Container Line in 1969	*Svendborg Maersk* in 1974	*Marchen Maersk* in 1988	*Sovereign Maersk* in 1997	*Emma Maersk* (ULCV) in 2006	Maersk orders three Triple Es
(1) Size	52 TEU	700 TEU/RORO	1,800 TEU/RORO	4,300 TEU/RORO	8,000 TEU/RORO	15,000 TEU/RORO	18,000 TEU/8,500 RORO
(2) % of non-bulk (not oil or grain)	1%	30%	50%	70%	80%	85%	90%
2 Robotics, automation, and NC	Individual machine tools, & conveyors, Research on NC	Crude automation, beginning use of NC in defense industry	Automation, some robotics, advancing NC in economy	First automated factory in Japan, NC becoming strong	Increased automation, NC and CAD/CAM dominant	Automation dented by offshoring, NC and CAD/CAM further dominant	CAD/CAM dominant with automation becoming more and more sophisticated.

3 Computers/IT

(1) Micro-capacitor and Hertz/byte	Vacuum tubes and card sorting	Intel 4004 in 1969, 4 bit CPU, 740 kHz	Intel 8086 in 1978, 16 bit CPU, 500–1,000 kHz	Intel 8386 in 1985, 32 bit CPU, 12,000–40,000 kHz	Intel Pentium II in 1997, 64 bit CPU, 500,000,000 kHz	Intel Core i5 in 2007, 64 bit multiple cores, 2 GHz	Intel Core i7-9x in 2011, 64 bit multiple cores, 1,300 GHz
(2) Storage	Cards and tape	Cards	5" floppy disk	3½" floppy disk	CD	Stick	Stick/cloud
(3) Internet	Non-existent	US Defense ARPANET	US Defense and universities	Beginning of public access	Widespread US public access	World public access	World public access
(4) Web	Non-existent	Non-existent	Non-existent	Non-existent	Initial business applications	World wide web, growing business	World wide web, strong business
(5) Phone/TV	Black-and-white TV, party-line telephone	Color TV, individual-line telephone	Cable TV, first crude portable phones	First cable TV, cell phones widespread	Cable and satellite TV, initial smart phones	Web, cable, and satellite TV, smart phones common – texting and tweeting	Web, cable and satellite TV, smart phones dominant – texting, tweeting, and syncing

CPU = central processing unit; that portion of a computer that carries out the instructions of a program as opposed to storing data or results.

NC = numerically controlled machine tools.

RORO = roll-on-roll-off vehicle carriers.

UVLC = ultra-large container vessel that cannot go through the new Panama Canal.

For other abbreviations, see list on pp. x–xii.

terms of both the point of sale and the supply of materials or products needed for various forms of production – led to innovations such as lean production and other approaches using information technology to facilitate supply-chain management.

By the mid-1960s, stevedores and their union leaders began to recognize how new technologies such as containers adversely affected their jobs. Edna Bonacich and Jake Wilson (2008) argue that the linking of new information technologies – especially computer technology and inventory software – with container shipping created a logistical revolution that moved production and distribution from Fordist mass production to post-Fordist lean production. This eventually resulted in a power shift away from manufacturers to retailers in consumer goods markets.[8] Bonacich and Wilson go on to discuss how these changes – as shifts from Fordist to post-Fordist flexible and lean production regimes – led to numerous changes in the conditions of labor (2008; Finlay, 1988). For instance, automation and new logistical technologies increased the power of retailers, who then made an even stronger push for further cost-cutting to reduce prices (e.g., Walmart). This included extensive reliance upon logistics for better delivery and stocking of products to reduce the overall costs of labor (e.g., wages and benefits).

This resulted in an increasing reliance upon contingent labor that reduced the permanent workforce and moved labor around as needed as the human part of "just-in-time" production. Since automation reduced the overall need for workers and pushed efficiency by temporalizing work, this resulted in a less stable workforce, dwindling union membership, and decreasing financial and political support for unions. The other significant change facilitated by increased automation but directly driven by new logistical operations in shipping was the offshoring of production in manufacturing to various overseas locations. The consequences of this shift not only had a dramatic effect on the number of jobs directly lost but also had an equally important effect on the quality of jobs, resulting in a "race to the bottom" with regard to wages, benefits, and labor standards. Winston Wilson and Maddie Parlier (both in box 4.1) show how these factors affect real people.

Artificial intelligence in robotics and numerical control

The use of machines to enhance or substitute for human labor existed long before Henry Ford implemented the first fully operational assembly line to manufacture automobiles in 1908. Centuries before, the printing press, the cotton gin, the loom, the agricultural threshing machine, and the more generally transformative steam engine all had dramatic consequences in spurring on the industrial revolution. Automation – the substitution for human labor of self-operating machinery – relied upon a more complex set of human inventions, such as control systems, information technologies, and reliable forms of energy such as electricity (see row 2 in table 4.1).

A number of more recent works have attempted to detail the negative role of technology in structural unemployment. Erik Brynjolfsson and Andrew McAfee (2011) assert that even though many companies have seen a return to profitability follow the recession, most are not hiring new workers. The reason that the authors give is simple – machines are replacing workers. They argue that innovation-spurred changes in technology have infiltrated nearly every job sector. Technology either increases the individual productivity of workers, thereby reducing a company's need to hire additional workers even while it expands in terms of economic output, or directly displaces workers (see Laurie Galston in box 4.1).[9]

Going even further, Martin Ford (2009) discusses the role of information technology in the market and concludes that we are currently on the road to *technological singularity*. Ford predicts that automation will continue to take jobs away from people, eventually forcing society into staggering rates of unemployment – 75 percent of people will be out of work. This massive joblessness will be devastating. Ford goes on to say that government could tax companies that rely heavily upon automation in order to re-employ this huge group of displaced people as workers in the public and nonprofit sectors to rebuild society. Ford's concept is similar to Ray Kurzweil's more optimistic view of *singularity* (2005) that states that due to Moore's law of exponentially increasing computer capabilities, not only will work disappear by 2040 but human minds will merge with machine-based minds.[10] But Kurzweil's scenario does not deal with the consequences of the withering away of work and is also a bit far-fetched at the moment.

The over-reliance upon automation and similar technologies pose dangers for society. And while some of these dangers have not yet materialized, automated technologies have had destructive consequences in many instances for workers and society. One example involves the introduction of automation to the cockpit and flight controls in commercial aviation. Cockpit automation has had an effect on pilots by reducing the need for the "flight engineer" as a third crew member in larger, multi-engine jet aircraft. However, some critics of automation have pointed out that a pilot's increasing reliance upon an automated cockpit environment can have dangerous, even deadly, consequences. In one instance in 1995, a pilot's reliance upon the onboard computer for navigation resulted in two experienced pilots flying a Boeing 757 directly into a mountain just outside Cali, Columbia, killing 151 passengers. In another example, at an air show in Mulhouse, France, one of Air France's premier pilots flew the company's new "fly-by-wire" Airbus 320 directly into a forest, killing three of the 130 passengers. According to testimony by the pilot, the new computer system overrode inputs by the pilot in his attempts to fly the plane to a higher altitude.

Automation has also been blamed for a number of industrial accidents, including contributing to the Three Mile Island nuclear plant meltdown in 1979 as well as British Petroleum's Texas City oil refinery explosion in 2005. However, the issue of automation and unintended consequences goes beyond industrial accidents and disasters to extend to (1) changes in economic structure, including a loss of jobs from labor-saving technologies; (2) increased control by management over workers; and (3) the decreasing efficiency and effectiveness of workers in completing their jobs (Tenner, 1997; Perrow, 1984).

Automation continues to have an impact on unemployment, and the full impact of many technologies remains to be felt. From Clarence Saunders' initial weak attempt in 1937 at an automated grocery store (Keedoodle) on, new technology has been used in retail grocery stores, including moving belts, motorized hand carts, data warehousing, and barcode scanning (Goeldner, 1962). The self-service kiosk with U-Scan technology even goes beyond deskilling to eliminate the need for human cashiers at all. As a result, the number of cashiers per store has been drastically reduced even though the total number of cashiers has gone up because of the expansion of large supermarkets and warehouse stores throughout the US (e.g., Walmart, Kroger, Safeway, Aldi, Costco, and Sam's Club). The new technology has allowed these major chains to expand while reducing their costs per worker and thus increasing their profits.[11]

In parallels to the automated technologies of grocery stores, Yamazaki Mazak, a Japanese robotics manufacturer, has created a robotic factory; Amazon has advanced the use of robotic retrieval systems in warehouses; and in London, the 2012 Olympic games used three robotic Mini Cooper vehicles to retrieve items used for track and field. Since the London Olympics workforce was primarily volunteer, the Mini Coopers did not directly replace paid workers, but the robotic vehicles demonstrated an approach to displacing laboring in a high-profile venue. And more commonly, most automobile factories now use robotic welding and painting technology, and banks use automated tellers for receiving and dispensing money.

But automation and job losses are not just an issue of labor and class but also one of racial and ethnic politics, according to Rifkin (1995). African-Americans and Latinos are seeing the consequences of the restructuring and reduction of manufacturing jobs due to automation as well as their replacement by low-paying service-sector employment. This change in automation coupled with changes in information technology has reduced the number of decently paid jobs in important urban areas in the Northeastern and Midwestern cities (see Trish McFadden in box 3.1). This disproportionately affects black and Hispanic communities and leads to the large structural differences in unemployment rates for people of color and whites seen in figure 1.4 (Wilson, 2012).

The impact of computers on unemployment

Computers are a transformative technology that has impacted numerous other technologies. Following Moore's law that computer capacity increases exponentially every four years, computers have gone from vacuum tube technology and the size of a floor in a building, to chips having capacities of only 740 kilohertz in the 1960s, to chips with capacities now over 1,300 gigahertz (see row 3 in table 4.1). Memory has similarly expanded by leaps and bounds. In some cases, computers and related software – especially personal computers – directly drove innovation through the enhancement of design techniques as well as making specific operations easy that were previously laborious or even logistically impossible. But the most significant impact of computer technology has been the application of computers to facilitate, enhance, or extend existing logistical operations. For example, computers helped shipping and containerization to a dramatic increase in the volume of goods that were shipped, a major decrease in the time to ship the goods from factory to market, and a reduction in the amount of labor necessary to complete the process. On the voyage, developments in information technology enhanced the use of containers through better tracking systems for transit, the weight distribution technology on board ship to allow for increasing amounts of cargo, and storage on larger and larger ships. At the destination, computers led to greater ease of unloading, movement to storage facilities, and delivery to retailers, warehouses, or production facilities by truck or rail. This created a multiplicative change in shipping capacity and speed.

New forms of computer and informational technology have transformed the manufacturing of parts, from its being done by semi-skilled machine operators to requiring operators trained in CAM and with AS degrees. For instance, while managers are impressed by high-school graduate Maddie Parlier's work (box 4.1), she is hanging on to her job in an auto parts manufacturing firm by the skin of her teeth. Meanwhile, the community-college-trained Luke Hutchins looks like the employee of the future with his CAM programming skills (box 4.1; Davidson, 2012). Beyond production, computers also transform the process by which engineering design takes place through more efficient processes, reduced costs, and increased productivity. For instance, innovations in high-speed processors and memory in CAD software have altered (1) who is involved in design, with a shift from designers to experts in information technology; (2) what type of training and skills designers must have, with the addition of CAD skills and computer programming; and (3) the amount of labor necessary in the design process. As a result, designers, entry-level workers, and even interns trained in color drawing, rendering, and producing documents are being replaced by a few skilled workers from anywhere in the world who can "do it all" using multifaceted software. This type of displacement has happened in many professions including civil, architectural, and structural engineers; mechanical, electrical, chemical, aerospace, nuclear, and petroleum engineers; and biomedical engineers in the life and medical sciences.

The influence of computer and other informational technology has been significant in many design fields outside of architecture and engineering, such as interior design, clothing design, industrial and process design, scheduling and logistics, and transportation. As a consequence, semi-skilled or low-skilled workers are often displaced by increases in efficiency through labor-saving enhancements on the production side. For instance, computers and software now not only effectively design the aircraft, with human input and direction, but also provide logistical input into the machinery used in production by making use of sophisticated software to run it. Computers using CAM direct the use of laser technology and nanotechnologies to produce the parts and assemble the aircraft (Manyika et al., 2012:88–95; Scheer, 2011; Finkelstein, 2011; *WSJ*, 2013). Especially important is additive manufacturing based on creating objects through 3-D printing technology – "selective laser sintering" that fuses multiple powders into one object, "fused deposition modeling" that layers new products, and "stereolithography" that uses optical fabrication (Manyika et al., 2012:89–90). These manufacturing technologies build up objects rather than subtracting materials from them (e.g., drilling and cutting subtracts material from the original object). In apparel design and production, computers and software speed up the process of design and can calculate with precision the most efficient use of materials and thereby reduce costs; on the production side, innovations in manufacturing have reduced the need for semi-skilled and low skilled labor.

The Bravermanic leap to the professions

In this section we show how, just as Braverman pushed Taylorism or scientific management (i.e., the application of extreme rationality and time-and-motion studies to increase the efficiency of workers) into the white-collar professions, so technology and offshoring have been extended into the higher levels of the labor market. Computer information technologies – including computer hardware, software, technological networks, and the internet – all played an important role in the movement of many forms of work to other countries. Offshoring and computers also apply to work that relies on knowledge-based skills or techniques, which generally falls into the area of the professions (e.g., OILM and OLM labor market segments). We look at two professions – doctors and lawyers – to see how this has occurred.

First, a widely reported example is the offshoring of the reading of X-rays by US physicians and hospitals to countries such as India (Pollack, 2003; Friedman, 2005; Levy and Goelman, 2005). For instance, hospitals can save money by hiring much lower-paid radiologists abroad since X-rays can be easily sent over the internet. Hospitals can also speed up their results by taking advantage of international time differences since radiologists in India can do their work during the day while most American radiologists are asleep at night. The consolidation of radiological readings among consultant companies increases these cost savings through economies of scale.

However, these services can have significant costs in that outsourcing and offshoring can have dangerous consequences. In one instance, a young woman had her intense headache and debilitating pain misdiagnosed as a tumor, whereas in fact it turned out to be a very dangerous abscess that would eventually rupture (Eban, 2011). In this case, the Pennsylvania hospital sent the patient's X-rays to an outsourced consulting firm headquartered in Minnesota, who employed a radiologist in Hong Kong who had no direct communication with the doctors treating the patient in Pennsylvania. The loss of medical context prevented the correct diagnosis. Yet despite these problems, the number of medical facilities offering outsourced teleradiology (i.e., within the US, and including the Cleveland Clinic) and offshored radiological services (i.e., in India and elsewhere) is slowly growing (Levy, 2009; Yu and Levy, 2010).[12]

Other medical fields are equally vulnerable to the role of labor-displacing technology. For instance, robotics continue to be effectively used in some forms of surgery including ones requiring repetitive precision and micro-surgical techniques. Some medical facilities (e.g., health maintenance organizations (HMOs), hospitals, medical centers, and large medical practices) are turning to automated processes using complex algorithms encoded in software to read computerized tomography (CT) scans and magnetic resonance imaging (MRIs) (Manjoo, 2011; Volti, 2010:118–34) (see row 3 in table 4.1).

Since the early 1990s, robotics including micro-processes have been used in a number of surgical sub-areas such as orthopedics, urology, and gynecology. The first robotic techniques were used in cardiology and neurology, including the first robotically assisted heart bypass in 1999. Surgeons using these robotic methods completed the procedure without having to open up the patient's chest cavity, thereby reducing many risks of traditional heart bypass operations. Micro-surgical techniques are used now in a number of difficult procedures but typically these operations only involve enhancing a surgeon's abilities as opposed to replacing surgical labor.

The automated reading of CT scans and MRIs started in the 1990s when the Beckton-Dickinson Company developed software to be used in screening pap smear slides. More recent clinical studies indicate that automated screening results in better identification of abnormalities in both pre-cancerous and cancerous cells. Further, through automated screening – in conjunction with a human examiner – nearly

170 slides can be examined per day compared to around 80 to 90 per day for human screeners alone (Manjoo, 2011). Currently, automated analyses of test results are being used in examining mammograms to detect breast cancer. This has allowed physicians to skip the "double reading" approach in which two independent physicians analyze the same mammogram to independently verify each other's results. The claim is that the use of just one physician in conjunction with independent automated software screening results in an even greater degree of accuracy in determining abnormalities than the two independent physicians approach. Some argue that this will result in one of two changes: either salaries will be reduced as physicians become more dependent upon automation and robotics, and thereby reduce the skills necessary for their work; or automation will continue to widen the growing wage divergence between highly educated and skilled physicians and their skilled support staff running the technology (e.g., medical technicians, screeners, nurses, and nursing assistants). Whether this will translate into fewer physicians or free up physicians for other procedures or patient care is difficult to say.

Second, young lawyers have been negatively affected by technology. Becoming an attorney is an arduous and expensive proposition. Once finished with law school – and often saddled with student loans – most new graduates in the past often took jobs as team researchers to help track down information, review and summarize case precedents, and write briefs to be used in cases by major law firms. These entry-level jobs gave young lawyers a chance to learn from experienced attorneys as well as to see how the law works in the US system. Most of their work involved laboriously poring over court decisions and law journal articles in legal libraries and firm offices. But despite being entry-level jobs, the pay for this was usually quite high at the major law firms.

However, these jobs have largely disappeared. By 2000, law firms cut costs by reducing their firm's more expendable employees (see Thomas Barnes in box 4.1). To do this some firms began to use temporary lawyers or consultants to outsource much of the legal research to overseas companies.[13] Offshoring is a bit tricky because legal systems vary a great deal, and some regulations in the US as well as the bar association rules require that much of this work must be supervised by attorneys who have passed the state bar examination in the US (Crawford, 2008; Brooks, 2011). So while this trend seemed to grow through the early part of the decade, it has not become the dominant approach due to the many constraints on the offshoring of legal research.

Instead of offshoring, legal firms turned to computer software that can search, find and collate information, and even produce written summaries by synthesizing massive amounts of legal data through the use of complex algorithms (Markoff, 2011). With this software, law firms no longer need armies of young law graduates and paralegals to do this work. In fact, the evidence indicates that computer software is more efficient and more accurate than young lawyers. Since this is a relatively new and expensive technology, many smaller firms have not yet chosen to adopt it. Consequently, there is very little data on the link between this software and its effect on employment among young lawyers, paralegals, and legal assistants. However, the implications are clear for new graduates and their unemployment rates have risen.

Assessing the Impact of Technology

While economic studies have been more concerned with efficiency issues, sociologists have studied the impacts of technology on income inequality. Tali Kristal (2013) does this by examining the amount of national income that goes to labor and capital, disaggregating the data for 43 industries over 38 years. She finds that by comparison with the 1947–60 period, labor's share of national income has declined 6 percent, with 5–14 percent declines in construction, manufacturing, and transportation, and smaller decreases of 2–5 percent in finance and service industries. She shows that the causes of this overall decrease of 6 percent are investments in computer technology (short-term in rates of change and long-term in annual levels) and the indirect impacts of declining union density and unemployment. The impacts are greatest for manufacturing and other core industries, and less for trade, FIRE, and service industries. The impact was also greater from 1988 to 2007 than from 1967 to 1997 (at least 30 cases are needed to run the pooled methods so the overlap in years is necessary). Thus, Kristal finds two impacts: (1) factor-biased technological change (FBTC), in which capital benefits more because of cheap and labor-replacing technology producing unemployment; and (2) class-biased technological change (CBTC), in which technology reduces labor's power by weakening unions through unemployment, and "management's greater control due to the computer revolution empower[s] employers and management, allowing them to use more legal and illegal anti-union tactics" (2013:369). While economists assume that society benefits from technology since high-skilled workers are paid and employed more, Kristal finds that high-school workers are hurt the most in the US, college graduates make slight gains, but overall American capitalists (non-workers) gain the most since both types of workers lose 6 percent of national income over the time period. Kristal also finds that import penetration as an indirect measure of offshoring has a significant effect on manufacturing workers but not on non-production employees (2013:table 4). She finds similar effects in a study of over 18 advanced industrialized countries (2010). And this decline in labor's share even includes the 39.2 percent salary explosion of CEOs. Kristal concludes that with the advent of computerized technology, "capitalists have grabbed the lion's share of income growth over the past three decades" (2013:383).[14] And this fits with our view of structural unemployment that begins with unemployment and is then followed by a descent into secondary labor market segments with lower pay. So is computer technology biased toward capitalists? The answer based on this evidence is "yes!"

Conclusion

Even though Leo Marx dismisses the deterministic view of technology in the quote at the beginning of this chapter, "Science finds – industry applies – man conforms," we demonstrate how technology has changed employment while at the same time we point to how technology is debated, molded, and shaped as a "conception of control" by entre-preneurs, managers, workers, and state regulators (Fligstein, 2001). Technology is applied through negotiation, and one very effective negotiation strategy of management is to get workers, employees, and even the state to believe in a deter-ministic view of technology. While there are no guarantees about these negotiations concerning outcomes, one should recognize that the process is not dichotomous – "take it or leave it." There are many outcomes and compromises, and we should pursue those that minimize negative impacts on workers and employees.

Nonetheless there are two caveats. First, although we argue along with Fligstein and many social constructionists of technology that technologies are negotiated, we are not saying that the parties involved, especially labor but even the state, are equal in their bargaining power. Firms whose technologies are making profits have an advantage in obtain-ing what they want (as per Noble, 1984), but in a number of ways (e.g., the Bell Labs and the Morrill Acts), the state and society can guide, channel, and influence the framing and subsequent implementation of technology. In the case of nuclear power, for instance, societies and governments effectively hemmed in power generation technology so that new plants were not constructed for over three decades.

Second, we are not arguing that new technologies only destroy jobs. Clearly, new technologies create many new jobs both directly and indirectly (Volti, 2010:174–5). However, there is a "crossover replacement" of workers whereby many who lose their jobs in a specific area do not become the candidates for the new jobs that are created with nascent technologies. The skills gap prevents this directly and indi-rectly (e.g., the assembly line worker does not become a CAD/ CAM operator in an auto plant or a genetics counselor in a hospital). Consequently, the jobs that are created by new technology rarely go to the people who are replaced, which means that they will most likely be unemployed for a long time. These unemployed workers then may get a downscaled job at Walmart or another low-skilled service employer, or may go on unemployment and into training for a new line of work where they may obtain new employ-ment after completing the training program. This is what we refer to as structural unemployment as defined in our first chapter.

As indicated by Sam Grobart (2012), "The ratio of jobs created to jobs eliminated . . . ultimately winds up entirely dependent on how workers, business, and policy makers prepare for this new area" (i.e., technology). This "preparation" or "negotiation" then becomes a question of politics and inequalities of bargaining power.

5

Global Trade, Shareholder Value, and Financialization as Structural Causes of Unemployment

If you're paying $12, $13, $14 an hour for factory workers and you can move your factory South of the border, pay a dollar an hour for labor, hire young – let's assume you've been in business for a long time and you've got a mature work force – pay a dollar an hour for your labor, have no health care – that's the most expensive single element in making a car – have no environmental controls, no pollution controls and no retirement, and you don't care about anything but making money. There will be a giant sucking sound going South . . . "Why won't everybody go South?" They [the experts] say, "It'd be disruptive." I said, "For how long?" I finally got them up from 12 to 15 years. And I said, "Well, how does it stop being disruptive?" And that is when their jobs come up from a dollar an hour to six dollars an hour, and ours go down to six dollars an hour, and then it's leveled again. But in the meantime, you've wrecked the country with these kinds of deals.

Ross Perot (1992)

Presidential candidate Ross Perot, in response to a question about trade, said that "We've shipped millions of jobs overseas" and "We have got to stop." He laid out a 20-year scenario from 1992 to 2012 that describes much of what has happened. In his stark statement, Perot correctly critiqued the process of the "giant sucking sound" from 1992 to 2012; however, the dominant direction was west to China, not so much south to Mexico.[1] Most of it was in electronic equipment rather than automobiles, though cars have followed. The promised labor standards in the North American Free Trade Agreement (NAFTA) deal were weakly attempted with Mexico, but when it came to China and India, they were not even seriously put on the negotiating table. In fact, there really wasn't much in the way of a treaty. The agreements were largely joint ventures, supply-chain agreements with third party producers (e.g., Foxconn), or joint ventures backed by the state (i.e., China) and the OEM (or the US company that would market the product). After the first President Bush and Clinton administrations got NAFTA passed, it wasn't much of a step to offshore production to China and India.

In this chapter we illustrate what impact financialization has had on unemployment, and why globalization, in the form of trade liberalization, outsourcing, and offshoring, was so easily sold to US politicians and the American public as well as to the rest of the industrialized world. To illustrate this process we will look at two historical developments: (1) the early development of financialization, which leads to forces that would enable structural unemployment, and then how these changes served to exacerbate economic cycles making unemployment and downward social mobility more frequent; and (2) how the process of negotiating these treaties and trade relationships involved the financial aspects of globalization but ignored the re-setting of international labor standards. But let us first look at what we mean by financialization and then examine how it plays a role in increasing unemployment.

The Growth of Financialization

Financialization is the intensification of financial institutions including stock markets in the economy, and this can consist of five different facets. First, financial markets have been the initial economic institutions to globalize with instantaneous communications between stock markets, banks, and investors. This expands markets for financial products from nations to the world. Second, with globalized markets, profits and investment funds have shifted away from goods manufacturing and personal services to banks, hedge funds, pension funds, and other institutional investors. This has led to new financial pressures and has created instruments of tremendous complexity and risk. Managers are being pressed by owners to generate increased profits, which results in progressively riskier investments. Some of these instruments become automatic, and often opaque (e.g., financial derivatives), and offshoring has been strongly encouraged (i.e., stock prices spike when companies announce offshore ventures). Third, exceptionally high bonuses and wages have been set for CEOs, market deal makers, and brokers, which then diverts talent from the sciences and engineering into financial innovation and risk assessment (e.g., PhDs in physics become Wall Street traders because the pay is so high) (Boeri et al., 2013; Khurana, 2002).

Fourth, speculation has increased exponentially as loans, debt, and leverage expand because credit is given out to increasingly riskier consumers and firms (e.g., subprime, toxic mortgages in the 1990s and 2000s). And fifth, regulation by the securities, environmental, and labor agencies was de-clawed under the Reagan administration, and the Clinton administration repealed the Glass-Steagall Act. Meanwhile, replacement regulations have been delayed, hobbled, or watered down (e.g., much of the Dodd-Frank Act has been delayed and there is much talk of repealing the Sarbanes-Oxley Act).[2] The result has been the increasing frequency of financial bubbles and the "great recession" of 2008 (see the time-lines in table 5.1). These five factors have increased structural unemployment and we discuss them one by one below.

Global financial markets

Global financial markets grew and then exploded. When the oil crisis created a flood of petrodollars from the newly formed Organization of Petroleum Exporting Countries

(OPEC) nations in the mid-1970s, investment brokerage firms attempted to take advantage of the expanding global market. With manufacturing on the decline in industrialized nations, and concomitantly expanding in many developing nations, opportunities to invest in manufacturing facilities were shrinking in AICs. Consequently, investment strategists continued to seek out new forms of investments, primarily through the development of new, complex financial instruments such as derivatives.

However, financial markets were truly globalized after a number of important political changes: the fall of communism in the early 1990s, the signing of NAFTA, the increasing reality of the EU, and the advance of the global free trade regime under GATT and the WTO (see row 1 in table 5.1). The increasing use of computers accelerated globalization by providing the real-time pricing of stocks and bonds to worldwide markets of purchasers, sellers, and policy makers. Trades could be posted within seconds from nearly anywhere in the world. This change occurred within a decade-long bull market of rising stock prices. As a result, there was a time compression unheard of in earlier periods due to these instantaneous informational technologies. One new development – automated informational networks – concerns the nearly automated performance and interactive processes of markets with institutional investors, investment banks, and stock exchanges. As a result, decision-making for buying and selling is automated with outcomes that sometimes cause huge declines in market value. With or without automated decision-making, global financial markets operating with instantaneous information would make the business cycle more pronounced.[3]

Profits and investments flowing to financial services

These growing financial firms inhaled profits and investment funds. In the early 1950s, manufacturing accounted for 34 percent of US GDP, while the FIRE industries accounted for only 12–13 percent. By 2008 this relationship had reversed, with the share of manufacturing dropping to 12 percent and FIRE rising to 23 percent (Krippner, 2011:3–24; OECD,

Table 5.1: Economic cycles and the development of structural financialization, US, 1960–2013

Years / Crises	1960–9 Boom	1970–80 Two oil crises	1981–9 Recovery but first financial failures (S&L scandal, 1986–9)	1990–9 Boom but second financial failures (LTCM 1998; dot.com, 2000)	2000–7 Up and down with third financial failures (9/11 crash, 2001)	2008–13 Deep recession with fourth financial failures, bailout of banks and autos (2008)
1 Scope of operation changes from local to global.	Banks are within states; international WB and IMF become influential	Banks expand to national level; WB and IMF become important	National banks become international; WB and IMF are strong	Globalization of finance with internet, and GATT tariff reductions	Complete globalization of finance, free trade regime (GATT and WTO)	Financial sector wounded but still global
2 Financial innovation changes from mundane to exceedingly complex.	Initial globalization constrained by Cold War and conglomerates	Mutual funds and M&As begin for the wealthy	Increased mutual funds (401k, 403b), and M&A with junk bonds	Search for greater profits in M&As, HF, outsourcing, and speculation	Beyond mutual funds to CDS, ABS, CDO, HG, SPV, derivatives, and high speculation, plus outsourcing	TARP bailouts and profit without regulation; new conservatism
3 Trader/dealer incentives increase astronomically.	Somewhat conservative: loans charge 6%, deposits pay 3%	Changing with downsizing and milking; higher pay for CEOs.	Traders love M&A and outsourcing for bonuses and profits; CEO pay increases	Traders receive very high wages and bonuses for deals; CEO pay skyrockets	New financial products (derivatives) result in extremely high bonuses; CEO pay astronomical	Many traders laid off but bonuses still high; CEO wages still high
4 Cycle of speculation becomes excessive.	Low (insider trading common); credit cards hard to get	Increasing speculation; credit cards easier to get	New and moderate speculation (insider; trades); credit cards very easy to get	High speculation; credit cards given away; mortgages sold	Highest speculation; credit card abuse with predatory interest; mortgage abuse	Banks become more conservative; financial collapse curbs abuses
5 Financial regulation disintegrates.	Glass-Steagall Act, but deregulation	Glass-Steagall in effect, but SEC gutted	Deregulation; SEC regulations weakened.	Gramm-Leach-Bliley Act repeals Glass-Steagall; SEC regulations very weak	Sarbanes-Oxley Act to prevent more Enrons; SEC regulations very weak.	Weak reform in Dodd-Frank; attacks on Sarbanes-Oxley Act

For abbreviations, see list on pp. x–xii.

2008, 2011c). Showing an even greater difference, Krippner points out that the percentage of profits going to FIRE has gone from 10 percent to 45 percent (2011:33). Overall public and private debt in 1960 was at 146 percent of GDP, but after the financial crisis of 2008 it rose to 380 percent in 2009 (dropping to 350 percent in 2013).[4] This increase in debt was especially due to the baby boom generation using credit cards and buying houses with mortgages in the 1980s and 1990s, which they could not afford to do in the 1960s (household debt going from about 35 percent to 62 percent). But it was also due to a tremendous growth in banking and other financial debt rising from 6 percent to 61 percent (Weisenthal, 2013). Both forces contributed to the creation of complex financial instruments with innovations like mutual funds, 401k and 403b pensions, hedge funds and derivatives. Meanwhile more and more private corporations that have gone out of business have dumped their pension obligations on the federal government in the form of the Pension Benefit Guaranty Corporation (1998–2012), which provides pensions for retirees stranded by corporate bankruptcies. And finally, the frequency of financial bubbles and economic downturns has increased from the two recessions in the 1950s to the major downturns since 1999 (see row 2 and "Crises" in table 5.1).

We have to do a considerable amount of separating of the more immediate effects of the financial market, which involves the short-term operation of the business cycle, from long-term structural changes in financial markets in considering the impact of market declines on employment (see (4) in figure 1.6). The business cycle has been an integral part of capitalism for a very long time, but in making a structural argument, we demonstrate that today's global financial markets have some permanent, long-term features that were not previously involved with structural unemployment.

Under new conditions, management was pressed to generate more profits. Firms operating within this new global scrutiny of investors all over the world have a great deal of pressure to perform. Investors are looking for the highest return, and participating in global financial markets gives them the expectation that they can find higher-performing corporations with greater profits and thereby greater returns on investments. Consequently, corporations are constantly seeking those higher profits. Walmart exerts similar financial pressure on their suppliers to provide the retailer with items at increasingly lower costs, which of course makes it more difficult for these firms to hit their own profit growth levels. This pressure eventually leads each firm to ask for the "China price," or what is the absolute lowest cost that can be achieved through offshoring production. These conditions often result in an emphasis on short-term fiscal goals of quarterly reports, dividends, and rates of return, but do not adequately consider the long-term perspective, and this can have significant deleterious effects on innovation and workers (Atkinson and Ezell, 2012:66–8). Further, in some instances this viewpoint can lead to fraudulent practices (e.g., Ponzi schemes)[5] which are attractive to companies in their efforts to hit often otherwise unattainable levels of profits.

Exceptionally high wages and bonuses

After massive new investments, CEOs and Wall Street deal makers pocketed inflated salaries. Following agency theory, which tries to tie CEO rewards very closely to corporate performance, boards of directors began to add stock options to CEO compensation packages. The results were that CEO wages and benefits began to increase exponentially even when corporate performance was poor (Boeri et al., 2013). Bonuses for brokers and investment bankers began to reach multimillions of dollars for putting together large deals (e.g., initial stock offerings and corporate mergers). Box 5.1 indicates some of the high salaries – over $20 million for CEO Jaime Dimon – and extravagant retirement perks, such as those for Jack Welch. The comments by Bernice Walston show that this even applied to smaller firms. Meanwhile wages in the US economy as a whole continued to stagnate (see row 3 in table 5.1). One direct consequence of this has been the drawing of physics, math, and engineering PhDs from research and innovation fields to finance so they can design and operate the sophisticated quantitative financial models used in derivatives and similar markets. Particularly galling to the American public was that even when these models failed and the federal

Box 5.1: Experiencing unemployment or exemplifying top wages under financialization

Bernice Walston is 61 years old and has worked for the Durham Gas company for 42 years. Her job is secure. When she started work in 1971, Sam Wilson was the president of this small, multi-state gas company, and in her opinion he took care of his workers. As Bernice gained experience in the accounting department, she became an internal auditor during a period in the 1980s when a lot of people were let go. But the employees who stayed were effectively doing two jobs, which entailed too much overtime. Her job gave her access to information about higher management's wages and stock options. She couldn't believe how much money these new types of managerial cost-cutters were getting in stock options, bonuses, and salary increases, while the other employees were being squeezed.

Jack Welch received a PhD in chemical engineering in 1960 and became GE's youngest CEO in 1981. He retired in 2001, and in his first year of retirement received $2.5 million in in-kind benefits. This included his personal use of the GE private jet, the use of a $50,000-a-month New York City apartment, a chauffeured limousine at his beck and call, and office space in both New York City and Connecticut. This information was not available from corporate reports, and only became available when his first wife filed for divorce.

Jaime Dimon, the CEO of Citibank, has a banking pedigree. His father and grandfather were stockbrokers at Shearson Brothers, and his other grandfather was a banker in Athens. His father, who became a vice-president at American Express, passed one of Jaime Dimon's essays on to Sandy Weill, the CEO of the company. Weill persuaded him to join the firm rather than go to Goldman Sachs, which offered more money. Dimon followed Weill to Citibank, and has had a star-studded career since then. He made about $23 million in 2012, and much of this came from stock options. He is only one of over a hundred CEOs in *Businessweek*'s annual review of executive compensation who was paid more than $20 million in a recent year.

Zachary Rustin is 24 and graduated from the University of Illinois two years ago. He has been looking for a job in communications after shooting a few local documentaries and a short movie. Zach currently delivers pizzas for Dominos and lives at home. He has applied for entry-level jobs at advertising agencies, television stations, and many corporations, but the job market has not been kind. He has looked into forming his own company but needs much more money than he now has. Zach is waiting it out at his parents' home, hoping for things to get better.

Linda Johnson is 36 and worked as a highly paid drug sales representative for Abbott Labs. She called on doctors for a number of years and entertained them at Chicago's top restaurants. She even organized a number of trips to Las Vegas for her top clients. However, in 2008 this came to an abrupt end as she was laid off. Pressure on the industry had begun earlier with the new Medicare drug laws passed under George Bush and the corporate tax laws that laid waste to the three-martini lunch. Linda has since looked for work in the medical area but has not found anything. After two months on unemployment compensation, she took a job as a sales representative for Office Max at a 40 percent pay cut.

Gary Mullen is 47 and worked for First Union Bank (FUB) in the 1980s in North Carolina. He did well and thought he was on the way up in the company. In 1986, FUB merged with Wachovia. In 2001, Wells Fargo bought Wachovia and their managers got the good jobs. Gary was transferred to a rural branch to supervise small mortgages and car loans. After 9/11, the bank laid off 20 percent of its staff, and consolidated its rural offices. Gary was lucky since his office absorbed another. But in the "great recession" of 2008, the bank closed his office and let him go. He worked as a financial consultant, but found that he needed some retooling especially compared to new finance grads. He finally was able to get a job managing a large upscale restaurant. It was a 30 percent pay cut but at least he was still in management.

government bailed out firms, the investment banks and other financial organizations claimed that they had to continue to pay staggeringly high wages and bonuses or they would lose this talent pool – even going as far to say that these financial wizards were the only people who could save the collapsing world economic system.

Increases in speculation

As this flurry of investment and high salaries swirled, ever more new and risky attempts were made to make even more money. As the economy recovers from downturns and proceeds into moderately good times, there are opportunities for net investment and inevitably various forms of speculation (see row 4 in table 5.1). Investors' time horizons vis-à-vis risk-reward opportunities vary significantly and the economy as a whole can be subject to different combinations of these opportunities. Back in 1986, Hyman Minsky viewed these variable positions on investments as involving three different viewpoints of risk-reward, starting with the more conservative and going to the more radical. He saw an economy that "oscillates between robust and fragile financial structures" (2008:230–38). First, the *hedge-financing approach* involves an expectation that "the cash flow from operating capital assets . . . be more than sufficient to meet contractual payment commitments" for the present and the near future.[6] Investment and commercial banks will keep the volume of debt rather low, with conservative investing and a reasonable expectations of profit (e.g., the humorous description of the 1950s banking approach as 6–3–3: charging 6 percent interest, giving 3 percent on savings, and being at the golf course at 3:00 p.m.). Second, the *speculative-finance approach* expects that cash flows from investments will be less than receipts in certain periods, which requires the refinancing of some debt. As a result, this strategy pursues more risky investments with greater volumes of debt, but it expects a higher volume of profits. Last, the *Ponzi-financing approach* is similar to the speculative approach but the financing of debt is greater, and it then becomes incumbent upon these investors to "capitalize interest into their liability structure"

(Minsky 2008:231). This level has the lure of very high returns but it is inherently unstable, which then leads to crashes beyond the usual business cycle. Minsky's point is that finance under the pressure of increasing profits often progresses from "conservative to risky to rash investments," creating booms and crashes.

Government deregulation

Finally, in the midst of this vortex of finance, government regulation stepped back from the fray. Some of the government regulations that tried to prevent the more risky extensions of speculative finance were repealed. Regulation began to erode in the 1990s in various ways (e.g., the repeal of Glass-Steagall Act liberalizing the investments of banks, the repeal of restrictions on bank size and interstate operations, and the inventions of derivatives that go largely unregulated and uncharted) (see row 5 in table 5.1). Minsky's choice of "Ponzi" to describe this third stage of this approach is not intended to say that this strategy is illegal, but it is clearly much riskier than the other approaches. Using Minsky's terminology, the inference is generally made that the boom of the 1990s to 2008 resulted in too many financiers using "Ponzi-scheme strategies" toward risk. The result was an extremely serious recession in 2008. This is one major explanation of why this deeper cause of unemployment is termed structural, because it depends on institutional changes and the acceptance of much higher risk than the more conservative risk-reward strategies of "hedge financing."

Accepting Global Trade and Offshoring

The story of how the American public – especially the labor force – came to accept the highly uneven deal under globalization involves five rather complex steps. The first one is the "bait" and the other four are "switches." These steps are (1) welcoming lower consumer prices for American workers; (2) the selling of comparative advantage; (3) a shift from a concern about global labor standards to saying that low wages and bad working conditions are simply the comparative advantages of LDCs; (4) a shift from the social sharing of international profits to global corporations hoarding profits, with little allegiance to any society; and (5) a shift from developing countries with little or no bargaining power to one particularly savvy developing country – China. So the "bait" of low prices led to the "switches" of biased comparative advantage, deteriorating labor standards, the hoarding of corporate profits, and a unique LDC that is now the second largest economy in the world.

Lower prices as irresistible bait

First, the American public and other consumers were offered consumer products at greatly reduced prices as the first and immediate installment of the overall benefits of trade with the people in all the countries involved. The production of various high-value-added products from automobiles to consumer durables would make the deal very affordable to American consumers. It would also put somewhat of a lid on inflation, which could at various points in time eat away at each worker's pay check. The outsourcing of production in manufacturing was already occurring by the 1970s, with non-essential services being performed by third party vendors in the US (i.e., copying, janitorial services, cafeteria services, etc.). It was also being offshored from the union-friendly states (e.g., the East and West coasts, and the Midwest), where the United Automobile Workers (UAW) and other unions were strong, to the "right-to-work" Southern states, where traditions were politically, legally, and culturally hostile toward unions.[7] Although American auto companies would remain unionized, their suppliers could avoid unionization and costs could be reduced. The Japanese transplants would avoid unions in their Southern locations, and in many other industries in the South a unionized workforce could be entirely avoided. However, for most workers in the North, the reasons for outsourcing and offshoring were quite clear – offshoring reduced a company's wage and benefits liabilities for its workforce and thereby served to help increase profits.

An analogous argument can be made for the EU, which brought free trade to the Eurozone, and then expanded this model to the world at large through the push for globalized trade. After German reunification in 1990, the German left and trade unions were able to get West German wage regulations applied to the newly added Eastern *Lander*. But many viewed this victory as a long-term defeat because corporations avoided investment in the Eastern provinces, to invest instead in Poland, the Czech Republic, Slovakia, and Hungary, where wages remained extremely low for a comparably skilled labor force. With Germany having the highest wage rates in the world (save some oil-rich kingdoms in the Middle East like Kuwait and Dubai), it was ripe for offshoring production, and German corporations were the first into China with Volkswagen. The UK had just emerged from years of strikes that Prime Minister Thatcher used for her neo-liberal push for freed-up investment and capitalist expansion. The political left and labor representatives were clearly aware of the implications of these changes, but their influence was in decline at a time when neo-liberal regimes took power in the 1980s and thereafter (Prasad, 2006). However, Germany never went as far as US and UK corporations.

Biased comparative advantage

Over the past few decades, many white-collar workers, some intellectuals (especially economists), prominent editorialists, and nearly all conservative politicians believed that international trade operated according to the principle of "comparative advantage." They argued that whatever small losses might be endured in one industry were more than made up for by the beneficial effects for the economy as a whole. Many economics texts will state this principle as the one truly dependable "law" of economics. According to David Ricardo (1821), the theory says that two countries being self-sufficient in the production of wool and wine can benefit from each country specializing in one or the other and then trading till their demand is satisfied. Ricardo formulated the law and gave the example of how England would be better off specializing in wool, and Portugal would be better off specializing in wine, and then they would engage in trade. The climates of each country would enable better efficiency and labor productivity for each good and each country would be better off. To make the example work, one needs to have geographical and cultural advantages that are generally less available in our more technologically advanced world.

More modern theories of comparative advantage, like the Heckscher-Ohlin theory, show how advanced industrialized economies with more trained workforces have a comparative advantage over LDCs (Wallerstein, 1974). Since the late 1970s and 1980s, we now have "new trade theory" (NTT), advanced by the Nobel Prize winner Paul Krugman. Assuming that constant returns to scale are relaxed, some nation-states could use protectionist measures to develop a large industrial base in important industries that would allow them to dominate or be an important player in emerging and even developed world markets.[8] While "protecting new industry" was certainly not new, NTT used rigorous mathematical theory to model returns to scale, and the network effects on suppliers and industrial regions. These quantitative models supported the case for protectionism for national specialization in particular industries more similar to monopolistic competition. Ha-Joon Chang (2002) argued that the Japanese auto industries of the 1950s would not have survived free trade, and Japanese tariffs and regulations on imports were important protections for these industries from foreign competition. While economists could argue that Japanese consumers suffered from having to buy inferior vehicles in the 1950s, this suffering has certainly disappeared as they now have a world-leading auto industry (Denison, 1980). China's policy of state-run capitalism (neo-mercantilism) is not far removed from this example.

However, despite these sophisticated theories, some of which justify some protectionism, most politicians and the business-oriented public generally believe in the benefits of free trade coming from Ricardo's original formulation. World and national economies do better if they have freer trade rather than protectionist trade. And the overwhelming thrust of international relations from 1992 to 2008 was to reduce trade barriers through the GATT rounds, the WTO, the IMF, and the World Bank.

There are several deficiencies in the theory of comparative advantage. From the development perspective, more advanced countries tend to take advantage of LDCs in their terms of trade. Often the advantaged production is rather forced upon the LDC with unfavorable terms of trade (e.g., as described by world systems theory). But in many cases, this relationship may be reversed, as when the ostensibly less-developed country has workers who are well educated, disciplined, and highly motivated to work. In this case, the advantage is nearly absolute over AICs for many industries. This relates to Adam Smith's concept of "absolute advantage," which economists are less fond of citing (1776; Watson, 2005). So as comparative advantage seems elusive for many American workers, academics and pundits still encourage workers to get more education in an effort to obtain some sort of employment-based comparative advantage.

Declining labor standards

Labor regulations and labor standards have continuously declined with free trade. American and other AIC workers were assured that there would be a level playing field with regard to wages, benefits, and distribution of jobs. Foreign workers were never told that management will pay them one tenth the wages, give them no benefits, and threaten them with all sorts of punishments if they do not entirely comply with all that we ask, including polluting their environment. Arguments at the NAFTA accords instead focused on how labor standards and working conditions would be equal and fair between the three member countries. A proposal for rigorous labor standards was developed by the International Labor Office (ILO), which has legitimacy in Europe, but among American politicians and businesspeople the ILO is typically ignored. In the actual NAFTA negotiations, labor standards were gradually reduced and left as a possible area for "further negotiations" after the main treaty was passed (e.g., labor side agreement). However, these labor standards were ineffectively negotiated and numerous problems developed, such as those concerning *maquiladoras* and other low-wage manufacturing plants within Mexico.

However, in the largely "non-negotiations" with China and to some extent also with India, labor standards were more or less a matter of national sovereignty and their own labor laws, which often entail dual unions appointed by the government and which are typically solely concerned with overall production quotas. As with Japanese and German auto transplants in the US, each of the American or European firms sought a non-union environment in China with fewer rather than more regulations.

The labor standards of offshoring corporations fell into two types. First, for companies that offshored and outsourced their production, like Apple and Nike, the control of management practices and labor standards was outsourced to another corporation (e.g., Foxconn for Apple). For instance, managers at Foxconn making iPods and iPhones demanded that young women aged 14–30 must work six days a week and up to 10- to 12-hour days. Though the legal employment age in China is 18, Foxconn and other major factories working with multinational corporations have been unable or unwilling to verify the age of a large number of 14- to 17-year-old employees. Wages were much more than these workers had earned in the rice fields of the countryside, but they are still very low. Workers live in dormitories with 10–14 roommates and travel outside the factory walls only one day a week on their day off. The second type of offshoring arrangement involves firms run as joint ventures with Chinese and AIC corporations. Most often, the AIC partner knows very little about the actual production process and how Chinese workers are treated. In some cases, poor labor conditions have led to intolerable conditions, such as at Foxconn, which saw a number of workers commit suicide by jumping off the top floors of their factory buildings.[9]

Even though the issue of labor standards has been a concern of the ILO for nearly a century, in the past decade or so, the Fair Labor Association (FLA) has been the most prominent player in human and labor rights issues with clothing manufacturers (e.g., Nike, Liz Claiborne, Reebok, Patagonia, etc.). Started in 1997, the FLA often operates by what we call *regulation by scandal*, in which the politicians react to media reports of labor abuses by instituting new forms of labor rules or standards – but often these new rules are merely half-measures, ineffective, and usually unenforced. The FLA process – a contemporary form of "muckraking" – usually starts with a reporter visiting a factory or meeting with the workers of a multinational corporation and collecting their stories of abuse and exploitation. Naturally, these workers are taking quite a risk to talk to these reporters, but many cooperate. The reporters then write stories and supply pictures to document abuse and exploitation to American and European media audiences on television, radio, or the web. Apple didn't enter into agreements with the FLA until its scandal with Foxconn intensified in 2010.

The FLA is mostly financed by its corporate members, but some money also comes from universities because their apparel licensing contracts can be quite lucrative (e.g., Oregon, Michigan, etc.). The FLA's tripartite board is composed of corporations protecting their product image, university administrators protecting their school logos on T-shirts and sweatshirts, and the non-governmental organization (NGO) itself, which is actually interested in protecting workers. The ultimate power in the relationship is the corporate brand's leverage to discipline subcontractors. But the process requires generating media publicity, so that reporters can shame the parent corporation into working with the FLA in its investigation to correct the abuse of workers in the international production of their highly successful products.[10]

There are huge deficiencies in the FLA's "scandal" approach to labor standards. First, the FLA is supported by employers (i.e., multinationals) and certain retailers (i.e., universities that sell athletic apparel), which more or less makes the FLA somewhat of a "captured" agency. When news outlets occasionally report the findings of the FLA, this puts public relations pressure on multinational corporations to discipline their subcontractors. Without this publicity, enforcement can be ignored. Second, the firm voluntarily complies with the proposed resolution and in order to find out whether or not it is followed, the FLA or other organizations have to investigate periodically.

Third, China, Vietnam and a few other countries have laws against collective bargaining and strikes by organized labor. Consequently the state enforcement of employee protection does not have pressure from labor. In a few cases in China, foreign companies have been forced by the Chinese government to treat Chinese employees better (e.g., the aftermath of Toyota and Honda strikes in June and July 2010 with the government encouraging wage increases). But for most workers, there is little or no impact on internal labor standards. Fourth, the pressures brought about by reporters are highly episodic and this means that most labor violations are ignored and unregulated. And fifth, many corporations do not belong to the FLA and place little emphasis on enforcing labor or human rights. In sum, labor standards exist mainly to protect corporate reputations, especially when they are exposed to public scrutiny. Labor regulations at the national level have actually declined in recent years, and the UN, while supporting the ILO, has provided little guidance or leadership in this area (Anner, 2012).

While labor standards have a moral and justice component that is very compelling, they have a flip side in terms of offshoring and the disadvantages of AIC workers who face unemployment. Whenever offshoring is mentioned in AICs, most throw up their hands and say nothing can be done. However, if labor standards were raised there would be a more level playing field. As the WTO has done with unfair trade concerning dumping, a similar mechanism could be applied for unfair labor standards. If a corporation did not live up to labor standards, a case would then be filed at the WTO, and if found guilty of not adequately monitoring suppliers or their own plants, the corporation would pay a fine and/or face tariffs. This is not against free trade because free trade also involves free workers who are treated as having human rights. If these rights are abused, the corporation should be penalized. Corporations will argue that they are not responsible because they have used offshoring or outsourcing as a buffer for worker responsibility, but obviously these mechanisms are not a buffer against gaining profits. The sanction would be proportional to the damage. Walmart and clothing companies would pay a surcharge or tariff for the Tazreen fire that killed 125 workers (November 2012), and the Rana Plaza building collapse that killed 1,129 workers in Bangladesh (April 2013), that would be more than Apple would pay for Foxconn working conditions and suicides

(Yardley, 2013). The private, company-dominated FLA would be abandoned in favor of this stronger and enforced investigation system led by the WTO. It could be additionally enforced by negative publicity.

Concentration of profits for private gain

Exaggerated economic benefits led to a channeling of profits to corporations and stockholders. The companies engaging in offshoring and outsourcing earn greater profits since they pay very low wages and provide few if any benefits to their workers in foreign countries. This process masks the situation of structural unemployment in three important ways: (1) offshoring increases profits but the problems with trade deficits and unemployment are most often ignored; (2) these profits from offshoring then lead to increased investment, but large portions of it go offshore; and (3) the offshoring companies tend to avoid taxes. On the first of these points, the reports of stock market "fundamentals" such as earning or profits reports boost the price of the stock of these companies (Frydman and Goldberg, 2011). The more companies are engaging in offshoring the higher profits they are reporting. As a result of large amounts of offshoring, the economic and business press reports that markets are booming and American companies are making very high profits. This news tends to overshadow any subsequent reports of poor job growth in the US or Europe. Thus, the gloom of structural unemployment is masked by the corporation's good fortune in increased revenues, higher stock prices, and generous stockholder dividends, giving the overall impression that the economy is on an upswing.

Analysts, economists, and corporate financiers often provide a number of reasons why high stock prices and overall stock market expansion benefit a wide swath of American households, claiming that large proportions of workers own stocks through their 401k or 403b funds (rather than fixed pensions) and so directly benefit from these high stock prices. The control average workers have over these funds makes them in many ways think like investors and capitalists. But these arguments are partial at best since only 40 percent of workers who are eligible for 401k or 403b benefits actually take advantage of them. In large part, the replacement of fixed structured pensions programs with mutual funds or individual retirement accounts has been disappointing in its coverage. In the end, the 60 percent of workers who do not have 401k or 403b plans see little benefit from the buoyancy of the stock market that may be due to offshoring and outsourcing. But even the 40 percent who have invested of late have seen relatively poor returns from their pension funds and retirement savings due to the effects of the recession of 2008 and bear markets before that (Hacker, 2002; Pierson and Hacker, 2010).

Proponents of global trade claim that the profits then lead to greater investment in US jobs. However, for offshoring companies, further investment is more likely to go into offshore plants and equipment, not domestic plants. As a result of this second masking point, the profits from overseas production lead to additional investments in offshoring so that greater profits can again be made. Why would corporations invest in the country with lesser prospects for making profits? Undoubtedly there are small percentages of profits that might go to domestic investment, but we argue that this percentage pales in comparison to the percentage going into international and offshored investment. Rubin (2012) shows that $1.2 trillion in profits are held overseas by 70 US-based companies (e.g., GE, Pfizer, Apple, Google, Microsoft, and others), and that these offshore accounts increased by $187 billion in 2011–12.

Beyond the second masking point that corporate profits generated by offshore production do not readily facilitate the creation of jobs, the third point is that offshoring companies have been increasingly effective at avoiding US taxes. And much of this lost revenue could be used to increase training and site-selection processes to bring overseas industries back to the US. For instance, the corporate tax rate has been whittled down from 50 percent in the 1950s and 1960s to 35 percent. Through loopholes and other tax-shelter strategies, there are numerous legal opportunities for corporations to avoid paying domestic taxes. Some of these strategies are (1) *double Dutch* and *double Irish*, whereby corporations claim to receive their revenues in another country, which then in turn allows them to utilize offshore tax havens such as the Cayman Islands or Bermuda to pay as little as 5 percent of their income as corporate taxes (e.g., Google); (2) *Internet companies* being exempt from sales taxes (e.g., Amazon. com); and (3) *hedge funds* being able to pay taxes at a much reduced rate due to the secrecy of the actual operations, and, as a consequence, their interest income often being taxed at only 15 percent, which is well below the current corporate tax rate of 35 percent.[11]

Consequently, even a reduction in the general corporate tax rate from 35 percent to 25 percent, while increasing corporate profits within the US, may not lead to job creation, for two reasons: (1) opportunities to invest overseas may have more profit potential than in the US, and corporations would just continue to invest offshore because of lower wages, financial incentives, and fewer regulatory standards; and (2) many corporations want a tax holiday on profits held overseas with no taxes paid at all, and the federal government is not likely to do this (see Steve Jobs' comments in Isaacson, 2011:200–1, 546). The argument for more offshoring then becomes lower wages, lower regulations, foreign incentives, plus not having to pay US taxes on the profits. Instead, given current tax rates, corporate profits will most likely continue to fund greater job creation overseas.

Not your average third world country

With regard to globalized trade and international manufacturing, China is a large and unique case. Much of the process of globalization of investment in the US follows the example of the UK in its decline in providing jobs and domestic investment (Ferguson, 2004; Atkinson and Ezell, 2012). Investors largely operate according to the principle of the potentially largest domestic markets rule. In the British Empire from 1850 to 1950, investment went into the colonies (e.g., Indian railroads) but especially into the US because it had the largest potential for a very large domestic market to sell goods. As a result, the twentieth century saw the rise of the US economy to become the dominant hegemonic power (despite a rocky start including the great depression of the

1930s). Now, China appears to be poised to become the world's largest domestic market. As such, successful corporations must be in this market, even though this doesn't necessarily mean that it will particularly benefit US workers or the domestic economy.

Two factors make the Chinese situation particularly compelling. First of all, Chinese workers are particularly well disciplined and, in some cases, properly desperate in terms of having to perform factory and other types of jobs or go back to low pay in their home villages. Some have pointed to a Confucian work ethic in explaining how hard Chinese men and women apply themselves, in a sort of "Orientalized" application of Max Weber's "spirit of capitalism" argument (1958). However, the Maoist Chinese leadership has certainly put a damper on any Confucianism in present-day China. Whatever the underlying motivation of Chinese workers, they seem ready and willing to participate in capitalist development. Second, China as a nation-state is certainly flexible but it is also quite sensitive to giving too much control to foreign corporations within its own borders. As a result, its insistence on joint ventures and technology-sharing mechanisms set it apart from the other third world countries that cannot enforce these measures. China could model its development on the rise of US prominence in the world economy, in which American political leaders were able to separate themselves from European and British ownership (e.g., bankrupt railroads that made it easier for the next wave of investors and companies with domestic ownership) (Gibson, 2012:30–1).

To reiterate, the answer to the question of how American citizens accepted this economic bargain comes in five parts. First, prices did come down on many manufactured goods as Walmart became the leading commercial corporation to sell low-priced Chinese goods. Second, comparative advantage as a relatively old theory was sold to the public. Third, labor standards overseas were quickly taken off the agenda due to limited political will at the national and global levels. The scandal-driven pressure from the media and public to make changes resulted in only limited and sporadic enforcement. Fourth, while profits came to US companies, actual investment made with those profits was disguised and, most often, had little effect in supporting US workers. Any jobs that were created typically occurred in the service sector and led to workers cascading downward into lower labor market segments in terms of pay and benefits (e.g., from FLMs and OLMs into SLAMs). Finally, the labor conflicts in China's growth processes have been disguised by their new and growing role in the global marketplace. While this growth engine has its own logic, it doesn't really generalize into a growth model for other developing countries, and it certainly doesn't provide a model for the US. As a result, the relative acceptance of this situation of structural unemployment has been the result of incentives (lower prices), obfuscations (comparative advantage and investment leakages to an emerging world power), and failures in assimilating a new global system of labor standards.

Financialization Becoming Part of the Structural Process

We separate the operation of the business cycle from structural changes in financial markets in considering the impact of market declines on employment. While the business cycle has been with capitalism for a very long time, structural financialization makes cyclical declines much deeper, more devastating, and increasingly frequent. This move to financialization and the resulting structural unemployment comes, in part, from the increasing frequency of financially driven crises. This change has come about through three strategies.

Shareholder value strategy

The first strategy was the negative reaction to stakeholder theories of the firm that emphasize a firm's responsibilities to the community, their employees, and the nation-state as a whole – whoever could be conceived of as a "stakeholder." James Davis and Tracy Thompson (1994) and Neil Fligstein (2001:84–6, 147–69) show that a shareholder value strategy emerged out of this clamor for participatory management and the crisis of "financial managerialism" of the late 1960s to narrow the focus to only the stockholders. Intense competition from Japan and low profits in the 1970s led to a distinctive strategy that instructed top managers to (1) sell off overvalued and otherwise diversified assets, (2) take on debt from banks to minimize shareholder interferences and "keep firms disciplined" toward their own goals, (3) flatten hierarchies by removing layers of middle management in order to save money and improve communication, (4) buy up or merge with competitors, and (5) offer very high wages and bonuses to CEOs and top executives (Fligstein, 2001:85; Davis, 2009). This is not a clear production strategy as it involves higher-level management decisions and does not directly concern the actual organization of production processes. However, this Wall Street-focused theory is responsible for intensifying "short-term management thinking" concentrated on stock prices, and thus being antithetical to the "long-term thinking" that characterizes the Toyotism type of lean production.

In fact, shareholder value theory directly contradicts many of the major points of Toyotism. Within the shareholder values framework, production can be severely strained by (1) the infighting of disruptive mergers, (2) processes of being divested from a parent company, (3) being milked by managers not approving needed maintenance on plant and equipment, and (4) generally ignoring long-term investment and employee loyalty. In some ways, it is an intense backlash to older "stakeholder" and newer "corporate citizenship theories" that try to show that corporations should operate with a much wider-angled lens of participation. But despite criticism, shareholder value strategies caught on with boards and CEOs, often with the prompting of institutional investors.

Exploding consumer debt to correct for underconsumption

A second strategy was to sell "debt." As inequality increased by 23 percent from 1969 to 2008 (recall table 1.2), the workers' share of GDP declined 6 percent (Kristal, 2013), and real wages only increased from $11.37 to $11.75 an hour over nearly 20 years from 1988 to 2007 (i.e., before the "great recession" of 2008). The income of the lowest and second-lowest 20 percent of the population declined by 0.7 percent and 2.2 percent respectively, while that of the corresponding top fifths increased by 5.7 percent and 7.2 percent over 36 years from 1970 to 2006 (Leicht, 2012:200–3). If employers had shared all of the productivity gains they made during this period, average hourly wages would have been $4.24 more, and if they had merely shared half of the gains, average wages would have been $2.04 more. This presents a problem for mass consumption in the US because if people stop buying products and services, the economy will go into a tailspin.[12] There are three ways that employees can respond to reduced wages in order to keep consumption high: (1) stop saving money for a rainy day; (2) have an additional family member work, add overtime, or take a second or third job; and (3) borrow money. The cuts in savings and the addition of overtime both occurred. But the third strategy has a direct relationship to financialization because it increases consumer debt in terms of credit cards, car loans, payday loans, student loans, and house mortgages (Leicht, 2012:204).

Further, financial innovations during the housing bubble even allowed people to borrow on their own mortgages as the value of their house went up. Other innovations targeted the retired by allowing reverse mortgages whereby elderly people could get cash as they effectively sold their own house off during retirement. Kevin Leicht (2012) makes the point that overall debt and a more standardized measure of the debt-to-asset ratio went up between 1980 and 2007 in two ways that benefit capital: (1) households were able to maintain the economy through high levels of consumer spending, and (2) banks under a new regime of deregulation were able to reap further rewards through the high interest rates of credit cards, automobile loans, and housing loans. Creative use of interest rates such as low initial rates followed by very large balloon payments got more people into the mortgage markets. As interest rates went down, yielding lower profits, the large fees of refinancing became a way of recouping profits by churning the mortgage market.

Leaving high financial risk and derivatives aside, the point of this section is that fueling high consumer debt was a functional equivalent of a Keynesian demand management policy, only instead of paying taxes for government spending, financial institutions could inflate the economy through debt and reap numerous financial benefits for themselves. Leicht compares the pre-deregulatory economy to full deregulation in order to make the statement that this debt explosion could not have occurred in the pre-1970s environment. In the 1930s, Henry Ford said to Walter Reuther that he was going to replace workers with robots, and Reuther replied: "Then who is going to buy your cars?" The deregulatory response to Reuther's question is: "Debtors will buy the cars." And as corporations have denied workers the fruits of productivity increases through higher wages, the main way that they have responded is with "debt bankrupting the middle class" (Porter, 2012). Obviously, this is not a stable and long-term solution, so crises were inevitable.

Wall Street financialization

The third strategy was moving from the actual corporations producing goods and services to the investment banks and brokers on Wall Street with globalized investment strategies. This change diverts productive capital from job creation and product innovation to highly leveraged and risky financial investments (e.g., derivatives like credit default swaps, and mortgage-backed securities). The high wages and bonuses offered by Wall Street created a major diversion of talent from the PhDs in the physical sciences and engineering into financial innovation and risk assessment on Wall Street, because they had the specific mathematical skills to operate the sophisticated models that became popular in the 1990s (e.g., the Black-Scholes option-pricing model). Financialization combines with the shareholder value theory to emphasize mergers where capital is unconcerned with job creation and is instead solely focused on generating higher returns on investment. But most importantly, financialization intensifies financial pressures on corporations to increase profits and boost stock values, which in turn leads to pressures to offshore production and outsource services (Fligstein, 2001).

This process of capital market financialization has often resulted in major booms (e.g., speculative profits coupled with economic growth and increased employment); however, often these periods are soon followed by major crises – the savings and loan (S&L) crisis in the 1980s, the WorldCom and Enron crises of the early 2000s, the Long-Term Capital Management (LTCM) crisis of 2001, the "dot.com bubble" of 2002, and the derivatives and toxic mortgage crisis of the "great recession" of 2008 (see the "Crisis" row in table 5.1). Each one caused the contraction of markets, the freezing of capital liquidity, and increased unemployment. The business cycle of about three to five years is expected in capitalism, but recent market failures have seriously threatened the long-term economy and inhibited job creation. This acceleration of down cycles – including their increasing severity – has resulted in the need for a number of significant bailouts to stabilize capital markets and avoid catastrophic failure (e.g., the S&L government bailout, the LTCM bank-organized bailout, and the Troubled Asset Relief Program (TARP) government bailout). So the resulting crises that can be attributed to these new forms of financialization outlast the short-term disruptions that are a normal part of the business cycle. Instead, these crises are taking on long-term, structural characteristics that precipitate "jobless recoveries."

Even more speculative aspects of short-term trading involve currency or commodity arbitrage, which seeks to exploit very short-term differences in pricing of commodities or instruments between markets (Frydman and Goldberg, 2011). For instance, one might recognize the different prices of the Euro versus the dollar when some critical information is known that the dollar might decline (e.g., insider information on the failure of negotiations on a debt ceiling and the refinancing of US Government Treasury bonds) or the temporary price differences between types of oil such as West Texas light oil and Brent crude (Carollo, 2011; Lambert, 2010). This information can then be used for material gain. Carollo shows that world trading institutions have to be very careful about deliberate manipulation of markets for arbitrage purposes, such as deliberately holding back oil supplies till prices rise and then quickly selling this oil at the higher price before the market reacts (2011:89–90, 123–30). These opportunities often lead to more speculation and large booms, which are then followed in a few years by major crises. The business cycle is a reality in capitalism, but these intensified market manipulations seriously threaten the global economy and often drain job creation efforts.[13] These financial crises now go beyond the business cycle and take on structural characteristics that exacerbate structural unemployment and jobless recoveries. Former Federal Reserve Chairman Alan Greenspan's admission that he had "found a flaw" in the ideology that financial markets limit their own excesses confirms this (Frydman and Goldberg, 2011:217). The result may be that the structural but excessive swings in markets could be kept within bounds so that they do not compound trends found in the other three processes that cause structural unemployment (i.e., mismatches, offshoring, and technology). This does not mean that the other factors will disappear, but at least this fourth factor would be kept from intensifying the other three.

Conclusion

Not all of finance is directly connected to structural unemployment, but the combination of shareholder value theories within the corporation, the increasing financialization of global markets, including the creation of new and risky derivatives and other financial instruments, and the globalization of free trade all led to an exceptional emphasis on profits at the expense of other societal goals such as growing labor markets and a stable economy.

Just as Gary Mullen lost his job in a combination of mergers and the "great recession" of 2008, many young workers like Zachary Rustin cannot get a job to match their educational credentials (see box 5.1). Shareholder value and financialization's tendencies toward speculation have squashed the dreams of decent employment for many. The end result has been a substantial contribution to high structural unemployment, in combination with the other three forces discussed in the previous chapters. As financial instability is the new normal, should Gary and Zachary just expect that employment will ride down into a structural valley of low pay? These declines in segmented labor markets and losses for the middle classes in jobs, homes, and stable family lives, as happened to Linda Johnson (box 5.1), can be covered up by low prices and the rise of stock prices in between the crises. But even as crises peak with government bailouts, arguments are mounted by conservatives that we need to tax corporations less and give Wall Street more freedom. Often these arguments are pushed forward by elites who possess some control of the media and are influential within society, so the collective memory of these crises is short or at least extremely malleable. How else can we explain a major-party presidential nominee coming close to being elected while essentially proposing more financialization and shareholder value policies and less regulation after the "great recession" of 2008? And all of this in the name of job creation. The bait of low prices and the four switches detailed earlier in this chapter explain how this is accepted. The connection between financialization and structural unemployment is too often ignored, but Linda Johnson, Garry Mullen, and Zachary Rustin, whether or not they recognize the causes, are clearly forced to deal with the consequences of financialization.

6
Fixing Structural Unemployment

> Right now, countries like Germany focus on graduating their high school students with the equivalent of a technical degree from one of our community colleges. So those German kids, they're ready for a job when they graduate high school. They've been trained for the jobs that are there . . . We need to give every American student opportunities like this.
>
> Barack Obama (2013)

These four causes of structural unemployment – mismatches, offshoring, new technologies, and financialization – harm graduating students and employees with more experience in the labor market. Fred Block indicates that we need not only an economic sociology of "economic dysfunction" but also one of "financial reconstruction" (2010:384). Not only does the "chopped-up and incoherent American system of human capital development" need change (Osterman, 2011a:502, 2011b), but it needs to be done on a large scale in "thinking in terms of millions" of people (Mourshed et al., 2012:11). The approach we take here will be mainly focused on reconstructing labor markets. So we will look at a wide variety of government policies and institutions that help counteract these employment difficulties before and after unemployment becomes a problem. Governments vary in how they try to reduce unemployment through active labor market policies and regulation of investment and trade. Our approach will be to provide more targeted programs for job training, job creation, job placement, and encouraging investment.

Situating Workers in Labor Markets Undergoing Volatile Structural Changes

Individual employment strategies in AICs are becoming complex. We use a canoeing metaphor to delineate three types of labor markets: (1) the *upstream model*, with high-paid jobs with high benefits in industries that are constantly producing high-value-added products, where workers can expect employment security and promotions; (2) the *downstream model*, where wages and benefits are low, especially since the company competes on the basis of low price and of necessity low cost; and (3) the somewhat newer *white-water model*, based on highly skilled workers being paid well but with little expectation of job security.[1] The white-water model is gaining ascendancy where skilled employees are constantly upgrading their skills at their own expense and moving to new opportunities before firms lay them off. But for workers in SLAMs, this movement is more like a trap. Thus, the labor market has moved from the placid model of stable and life-long careers – the upstream model of continuous education in one career, like the 1960s IBM training model – to the white-water labor markets where there are many unexpected twists and turns. Individual reactions to these structural changes will be difficult for workers subject to the major social forces of structural unemployment, especially for older, minority, and less-skilled workers. This is why a structural view of unemployment is necessary to provide possibilities for governmental and institutional responses to embrace a larger percentage of the labor force.

Government Policy Responses

There are two long-existing and diametrically opposed approaches to cyclical unemployment: pure Keynesian spending policies to stimulate demand, and conservative tax cuts to stimulate investment. A variant of the conservative policy is the more libertarian position of removing the Federal Reserve System and all guarantees for bank deposits (Dowd and Hutchinson, 2010), but this is not likely to happen. However, both policies may simply increase offshoring – US workers buy more Chinese-made goods at Walmart with Keynesian demand stimulation, and US corporations use tax cuts to invest more in China with neo-liberal tax cuts. As a result, neither of these policies will have much of an impact on structural unemployment in AICs, though they may alleviate some cyclical unemployment. What is needed is a policy that will lead toward an increasing market share approach, generally following the active state model. It should be kept in mind that profits may not be reinvested in AIC countries and hence outward investment in LDCs reduces job creation inside AIC countries. Waiting for 30 or more years for US and Chinese wages to equalize taking into account transportation costs (i.e., economic market equilibrium) will take far too long. It is tantamount to sacrificing a generation or two of graduates. Consequently, these two approaches are much more cyclical than structural, so we remove these recommendations from consideration in this chapter.

We use an approach that is more short-term than the equalization of wages and more structurally targeted than fiscal policies to get the US economy into a more competitive position. It is oriented toward the application of policy to reconfigure labor and economic institutions, and it consists of three parts. First, it concerns major changes in education and job training programs. In chapter 2 we showed that the horizontal structure of the US education systems is seriously flawed for the 40–50 percent of students who will not go on to college (Hoffman, 2011; Halpern, 2006; Mourshed et al., 2012; Thelen, 2004; Janoski, 1990; and see Finegold et al., 2010, for 12 contributions on this topic). This system leaves large numbers of students with non-specific and watered-down training that produces unskilled workers for what is supposed to be a labor market for advanced skills. The German apprenticeship system that integrates high-school-age workers into the labor force and gives them much more specific training is often given as an example of an improved approach (OECD, 2007b). While the German system has some disadvantages concerning early labeling and inequality, the liberal education system in the US definitely needs a much more targeted approach, especially since its current record on inequality is not exactly stellar. For example, one could simply put American "non-college-oriented students" into community college programs when they are juniors so they can directly learn a set of job skills.

Second, the US needs to be much more concerned about creating jobs in, and targeting investment to, itself rather than sending them offshore. A number of other policies will be necessary to keep investment into American jobs growing. More specifically, a National Infrastructure Reconstruction Bank (NIRB) will be needed to quickly fund interstate highway construction, needed bridges and dams, and other infrastructural projects, perhaps including high-speed rail projects. Connected to this is the repatriation of profits that would provide both tax revenue for job creation and private investment funds to be used within the country to stimulate the economy. President Barack Obama's "American Jobs Act" proposed in 2011 was intended to make a clear distinction between small businesses, which invest more within the US and could grow many jobs, and larger corporations, which have a very strong predilection toward offshoring, like Apple and GE.

Clearly, structural unemployment is increased when the state subsidizes offshoring, and decreased when subsidies are targeted toward those who actually increase jobs in the US. This brings up the larger issue of the relative power of nation-states that seek to protect their citizens, and multinational corporations that are concerned with overall profits and not worried about the citizens of any particular country. The multinationals GE and Exxon are crystal clear about responding to the interests of their stockholders, and not to the labor force of any particular country (Rothkopf, 2012; Coll, 2012). But if government is to influence job creation within its borders, it needs strong tools it can use including subsidies, regulation, and taxes.

Employment concerns including short-term displacements causing unemployment also need to have a much more prominent place in the WTO, the IMF, the World Bank, and the

UN (Langille, 2005). A more finely tuned approach below fiscal and tax policy can target the application of policy to reconfiguring training and economic institutions. Especially important is recognizing the importance of labor standards in all countries throughout the world. This was originally part of the NAFTA, but as production has shifted to China and elsewhere, labor standards have been ignored by official policy makers who pay meticulous attention to free market issues. In other words, international organizations that promote trade need to also be concerned about unemployment and the unfair treatment of employees that comes about as a result of free trade!

Now to a certain degree the short-term improvement in labor markets also depends for the most part upon revenues. We will make a large number of tax recommendations oriented toward tax havens, tax avoidance, and international financial transaction taxes that will improve the ability of the US government to finance these ventures.

Active Labor Market Policies

Active labor market policies (ALMPs) have been recommended as a major way to attack unemployment since the 1960s. ALMPs can get the unemployed into identity-preserving jobs and those in insecure jobs into new jobs with more of a future (Bonoli, 2010; OECD, 2011a, 2011d; Kalleberg, 2011; Martin and Grubb, 2001; Calmfors, 1994; Janoski, 1990, 1994). A cross-national study of 17 countries served to confirm the positive relationship between ALMPs and employment levels (Bradley and Stephens, 2006). More recently the OECD has indicated that ALMPs have a vital role to play to boost job creation and support long-term labour supply (2012a, 2012b, 2012c; Kalleberg, 2011:184–92; Boeri and van Ours, 2008; Bradley and Stephens, 2006).[2] By design, ALMPs aim to increase the employability of jobless workers and reduce unemployment, regardless of whether the economy is in an upturn or a downturn. In practice, however, the effectiveness of active policies may vary with the business cycle. The US has been a laggard in this policy area while

Table 6.1: Public expenditure on ALMPs for seven countries, as % of GDP, 2002–11

Year	US	Canada	UK	France	Germany	Sweden	Spain
2002	0.2	0.4	0.3	1.1	1.3	1.6	0.7
2003	0.2	0.4	0.4	1.1	1.2	1.2	0.7
2004	0.1	0.4	0.5	1.0	1.1	1.2	0.8
2005	0.1	0.3	0.4	0.9	0.9	1.3	0.8
2006	0.1	0.3	0.3	0.9	0.9	1.3	0.8
2007	0.1	0.3	0.3	0.9	0.7	1.1	0.8
2008	0.2	0.3	0.3	0.8	0.8	1.0	0.8
2009	0.2	0.4	0.3	1.0	1.0	1.1	0.9
2010	0.1	0.3	0.4	1.1	1.3	1.1	0.9
2011	0.1	0.3	–	0.9	0.8	1.1	0.9

Long-term unemployment (% of unemployed over 12 months unemployed):

2010	29.0	12.0	32.6	40.1	47.4	16.6	45.1

Total government debt (% of GDP):

2011	61.3	36.1	85.5	67.4	44.4	33.8	51.7

Source: Compiled with data from OECD (2011c) for ALMPs and (2011e) for unemployment and government debt.

Sweden and Germany have spent more on these job matching, job training, and job creation programs. In table 6.1, we can see that from 2002 to 2011, Canada spent two to three times as much as a percentage of GDP on ALMP as the US, depending on the year, while Germany and Sweden generally spent seven to ten times as much as the US.[3]

In general, ALMPs result in better outcomes. In 2010, figures show that Germany, Canada, and Sweden had unemployment rates of 2.6 percent, 1.7 percent, and 1.3 percent less than the US, and in Sweden and Canada the duration of unemployment was 12.4 percent and 17.0 percent lower than in the US (but the duration of unemployment was higher in Germany). Youth unemployment was 17.0 percent and 10.4 percent lower in Germany and Canada than in the US, but 6.8 percent higher in Sweden. While the results are not a perfect correlation between higher ALMPs and labor market performance, the countries with higher expenditures on ALMPs have much better outcomes in seven of nine comparisons, with the lower unemployment rates being consistent across all three countries. Meanwhile, ALMP expenditures divided by GDP are quite small compared to other social programs: ALMPs were 0.2 percent at their high point for the US, while social security, medical care, unemployment compensation, and disability payments were from over five to twenty times higher at 4.2 percent, 4.0 percent, 1.6 percent, 2.5 percent, and 1.1 percent of GDP. While passive expenditures such as unemployment compensation are also needed, in many cases ALMP programs can replace some of these. On the face of it, many of these ALMP programs work, but later we will discuss some evaluation studies of these more active programs. In contrast to passive policies, the focus of ALMPs is to increase the employability of unemployed workers. Besides ALMPs, other types of policies need to be enacted concerning innovation and stability.

Consequently, the next four sections look at (1) job training in secondary, tertiary, and interventionist systems; (2) job creation including incentives to create jobs, government-created jobs, and supported employment for the challenged and disabled; (3) job placement, job search assistance, and planning for new work opportunities; and (4) recommendations for trade and economic stability policies. The history of ALMPs concerning the first three items is in table 6.2, and we will review each one.

Training through Vocational Education

The first area of ALMPs consists of job training programs that primarily focus on vocational training for the unemployed or those who are at risk of losing their jobs. These programs build on a vocational base in countries such as Germany, Austria, and the Netherlands so that a reasonably high and sometimes very high level of skill can be taught. However, in eight different country studies, the OECD shows that American students are not enrolled in upper secondary schools that have specialized vocational education

Table 6.2: Employment legislation, ALMPs, and financial taxes, US, 1960–2013

Years	1960–9	1970–80	1981–9	1990–9	2000–7	2008–13
1 Job training	Startup of MDTA with some job training; Job Corps	CETA – strong job training; Summer Youth Employment program	JPTA – small job creation plus TAA; Job Corps	JPTA – small job creation with employer councils; TAA; Job Corps	WIA – small job training with some councils; TAA; Job Corps	WIA – small job training with some councils; TAA; Job Corps
2 Job creation	Weak: MDTA – doesn't do job creation (1962–70)	Strong: CETA – large job creation and youth jobs (1973–82)	Weak: JPTA – no job creation but extended UEC (1984–99)	Weak: JPTA – no job creation but extended UEC, NJTC	Weak: WIA – no job creation but extended UEC (2000–12), WOTC subsidies	Restart but weak: WIA with boost from ARRA for economic stimulus (2009–11), WOTC subsidies
3 Job placement	USES reform separates placement from unemployment benefits	USES reform	USES reform but state and cities stronger	USES morphs into One-Stop for all labor market services	One-Stop USES becomes stronger	USES reformed with One-Stop and internet
4 Financial tax	None	None	None	Discussion of Tobin or global tax	Discussion of Tobin or global tax and VaR	Discussion of Tobin or global tax and VaR

For abbreviations, see list on pp. x–xii.

programs (OECD, 2007b:60, figure 2.2; Hoffman, 2011). This systematically denies about 40 percent of US secondary school students the opportunity of a technical education that would give them the skills to do a higher-level job and escape SLAMs.[4] For instance, Trish McFadden could have been a licensed practical nurse out of high school (see box 3.1). Most European countries and especially Anglo-Saxon countries are now emphasizing or strengthening these kinds of higher-skilled vocational programs. Subsequent ALMP retraining programs can build on this strong vocational base.

But the US does not recognize this fundamental weakness in its education system. As a result, many US job training programs are aimed at disadvantaged workers who do not have basic skills, and some training may even be in how to become job ready and have some initial discipline (e.g., soft skills like interviewing, using an alarm clock, dressing for the job, etc.). Connected to this type of training may be remedial training for reading and arithmetic, often leading to a General Education Development or high-school degree. Sometimes these programs may be connected to job-finding clubs where people give each other mutual support while they are out in the job market. For instance, many Job Corps programs and adult training programs in the US would fit these descriptions, though some further vocational training may be added at the end. Some of the intent of the Job Corps was to remove trainees from their environment so they would have fewer distractions, but these programs have fallen out of favor. While remedial training may be needed for many workers or those who have never worked a conventional or legal job, Janoski has criticized the US system for its very low level of skilled training (1990, 1994; see also Mourshed et al., 2012; Kalleberg, 2011:199–200; Thelen 2004; Hamilton, 1990; US-JEC, 2011).

European job training programs are much more oriented toward giving specific and sometimes advanced skills that are in demand to smooth the transition to new employment. For example, the German government operates extensive training programs that include several types of interventions. These include so-called "further training" (*Fortbildung*) aimed at technical development and advancing the careers of trainees, as well as retraining programs (*Ausbildung*) that support up to two years of education toward a new vocational education degree or certification. Training may also include grants to firms for general staff training and incentives to employers to recruit apprentices or train workers from targeted groups. Training programs most often make up the largest share of ALMP funds.

There are a number of other innovative programs in this area. One is Mozilla Open Badges, which offers credentialing for mastery of Java script using "tightly focused courses" with strong standards. Another is the Automotive Manufacturing Training and Education Collaborative (AMTEC) involving Toyota, other automotive subcontractors, and the community college system. It is a modular certification program for 110 critical skills sets that develops high-performing technicians for the auto industry with the intention of spreading to multiple states (Mourshed et al., 2012:68, 72–3).[5]

Training seems to be the policy of first resort since it fits so easily with the job mismatch theory discussed in chapter 2, and it is hard to argue with improving people's skills (US-JEC, 2011). Yet there is a wide range of variation in this large category of active policies, especially in terms of the quality and depth of this training. Further, if a policy is really active, much of this training could occur one to two years before someone actually becomes unemployed. This amount of "vision" or "predicting a probable career trajectory" is most often lacking in the US. However, in countries like Germany, works councils are legislated and exist in firms with over 15 employees.[6] One of their major duties is to construct a "social plan" with management concerning workers whose jobs are most likely threatened by technology, downturns, or offshoring. Some such plans can be negotiated in the US where unions and employers come up with retraining programs in the face of cutbacks (e.g., auto companies and UAW joint training programs), and in areas that have county or community planning councils. One of the stronger though limited planning programs with extensive training involves the Trade Adjustment Assistance (TAA) program. However, on the whole, social plans are most often neglected in the US, mainly because they are seen by conservative politicians as government interference. The US needs an early warning system for retraining that moves quickly to help those about to lose their jobs, especially in its growing non-union sector.

Job training needs a system that includes vocational and technical areas. This would provide adult training for manufacturing at national, state, and community levels. We should also integrate community college and workforce development by getting community colleges and local businesses to cooperate in providing training for work, which is in a number of ways similar to what happens in Germany and Sweden. The plan we propose here is somewhat parallel but goes much further. It is based on the principle that secondary education for the roughly 40–50 percent of the student population aged 14 to 18 who don't go to college is largely a waste of time for them. They want jobs and the skills that can provide jobs. Quite frankly, the American horizontal system does not provide these (Van Horn et al., 2012). Instead these students get a watered-down college prep course, and spend their time on sports, socializing, or getting into trouble. The American system of education for the 40–50 percent of students not going to a four-year college needs to be restructured in four aspects.

The first restructuring aspect involves non-college-bound students. Robert Halpern states that "it is time to re-think the nature and organization, if not the purpose, of high school" (2006:62; Cullen et al., 2013). We could send non-college-oriented students for the junior and senior years of high school directly to the community college in the area where they can take a range of vocational courses that will give them an associate's degree and certification to do a specific job. This would not consist of college courses per se, but rather would be apprenticeship, vocational, and technical education. For instance, it could be in web design and information technology or CAD/CAM and numerical control of machine tools, or it could be a Licensed Practical Nurse program or even a two-year Registered Nurse program. The instruction in school would then be combined with practical learning on the job in a work setting.

The second restructuring aspect involves creating apprenticeship partnerships with employers so that academic or classroom instruction can be combined with on-the-job training, as in an apprenticeship at the employer's place of work. This is because having schools try to simulate actual work situations is going to be inefficient. Employers need to be directly involved in the education. In Germany this is called the "dual system" because it involves state-based schooling and employer-based practical learning (Halpern, 2006; Hamilton, 1990, 1999; Thelen 2004). These apprentices get paid a small salary while they are in secondary schooling. Halpern gives the example of the Wisconsin Youth Apprenticeship Program that started in 1991. Apprenticeship programs begin in the junior year with "individualized curriculum maps." Programs exist in areas such as computers, printing, CAD/CAM, and graphic arts (Halpern, 2006:69–73). Other examples include the Urban Boat Builders in Minnesota; Berkeley Biotechnology Education, Inc., in California; Apprenticeships in Science and Engineering in Oregon; and Rocking the Boat and Careers in Culinary Arts in New York (Halpern, 2006:65–8, 118–26). But generating widespread employer cooperation in the US will be a real challenge.

As a third aspect of restructuring, testing and perhaps even licensing need to come at the end of this vocational education. In Germany and much of Europe, testing is given at the end of the two years to certify that the student is a fully trained worker. If you don't pass the test, you don't get the certification. In the US, testing comes more often than not at the beginning of a schooling career to determine whether someone should be admitted. Testing must come at the end in order to have a serious certification program where employers really believe people have learned important skills.

And the fourth aspect of restructuring is that the classroom has to be brought to the workplace. The state-based schools bear the costs of buying equipment for classroom training when the employers already have state-of-the-art equipment. It makes sense to eliminate the costs of buying duplicate equipment by doing training in the workplace. The state could pay for some or all of this training, but the important point of doing training in the workplace is that employers get more directly involved and equipment does not have to be duplicated. The state may subsidize the stipends if it is an apprenticeship, but short of that, the government would provide the costs of training but not purchase expensive equipment.[7]

Subsequent retraining would be based on the discipline and skills that are learned in the initial vocational training at the community college. This training would be oriented toward two goals: (1) retraining for an entirely new job, and (2) advanced training to enable workers who are certified at level 1 to be certified and level 2 and then at Masters level. Some of the advanced training would be in modules so that workers could engage in lifelong learning at their specialties or new trades. The idea is to keep these workers flexible and ready to learn new ideas and technologies. It should be kept in mind that many firms create inflexibility by not providing new and challenging training.

While not currently feasible due to their expense, "serious games" are clearly in the future of vocational education. Video games are very popular with young adults as they have become more and more realistic. The serious-games industry now provides training via serious gaming in 135 of the Fortune 500 companies. IBM has developed "INNOV8" to teach its employees business process management and over 1,000 universities around the world have downloaded it (Mourshed et al., 2012; 72, 94; IBM, 2012). There is evidence that serious games result in 9 percent more information retained, 11 percent higher factual knowledge levels, and 14 percent more skill-based-knowledge than classroom or web-based training. Students using an electrostatics program called "Supercharged!" showed two to five times more understanding than students in interactive lectures and classroom demonstrations. While developing these games is expensive ($50,000– $500,000), one can see that they are on a learning curve to reduce costs and it won't be long before complex instruction will be taking place on tablets around the world.

Past arguments against vocational training have been that these types of education reinforce class divisions and prevent students from going on further.[8] This criticism has been made about the German education system, where those who choose apprenticeship programs at the age of 12 cannot get into other, more academic tracks later. In large part this is true since the German vertical system makes it difficult to switch. But our plan uses the last two years of high school for more advanced training, and it would still confer a high-school degree. Students would then find jobs more easily and could work at a job that paid well while going to college (i.e., rather than working in the library or flipping burgers). Thus, an adapted tracking system would not be as restrictive as the German vertical system, since this new type of American training would retain openness to later university studies. For instance, a student who was trained as a licensed practical nurse, millwright, electrician, or webmaster could earn a decent salary and then go to university for any number of majors and hopefully not have to take out large student loans.

This list of job training possibilities and existing programs sounds good but actual programs need to be ramped up. As Maureen Conway, Amy Blair, and Matt Helmer indicate, "Industry-specific or sectoral workforce initiatives . . . have shown promise, but these initiatives typically have remained very small scale" (2012:6). This scale needs to be exponentially increased.[9]

Job Creation and Entrepreneurship Programs

The second part of ALMPs consists of job creation programs. They are often the more controversial programs in the ALMP mix. During the depression in the US, the Works Progress Administration (WPA), the Public Works Administration (PWA), and the Civilian Conservation Corps (CCC) all provided hundreds of thousands of jobs for unemployed workers. They especially created large construction and transportation projects like massive dams and even small projects like WPA murals in post offices and other public buildings. In the 1980s during the oil crisis, the Comprehensive Employment and Training Act (CETA) provided funding to keep many public sector and police jobs, but many economists accused them of fiscal substitution (state and city governments transferring their budgets to the federal government).

To misquote *A Tale of Two Cities*, job creation policies are the best of programs and the worst of programs. Direct job creation in government programs (e.g., the WPA and

PWA in the 1930s, and CETA in the 1970s) undeniably created jobs for unemployed workers. But there are a number of concerns about substitution effects (Janoski, 1990). Even the lowest estimates find that one new job is created for the two that might be financed by other means (i.e., one of the two jobs might have already existed without government assistance). The highest estimates may go up to eight jobs actually created for every ten that are financed. The more that these programs are oriented toward the disadvantaged, the more effective the job placements. If federal job creators can get unbiased estimates of police and teacher jobs lost in cost cutting, then these types of job creation programs for surely needed public workers can be effective. But to some extent, state and city officials have an incentive to displace their employment costs onto the federal government (fiscal substitution) and then have money to finance other endeavors. The more successful these state and city officials are in simply shifting some of their costs to the federal government, the fewer new jobs are created. The much-criticized CCC and WPA leaf-raking and low-productivity work would involve few displacement effects since few organizations would pay for this work. And major infrastructure projects like building bridges and dams would have few displacement effects, though their main disadvantage is that a great deal of planning and negotiation goes into building such projects, and few of them are what is now referred to as "shovel ready." This means that unemployed workers who ultimately would benefit from these jobs have to wait two to three years before the projects are ready.

Governments can create jobs that are temporary until the economy recovers. Some of these created jobs may be for police, teachers, and nurses who may be let go due to true downsizing or austerity measures. Some jobs may be created for disabled or mentally challenged citizens. These jobs are most often in the public or nonprofit sector. A good example is "Jobs for Young People" in France, which targets long-term unemployed or groups that are difficult to place in other types of jobs. It subsidizes fixed-term contracts for young people in government and NGOs (OECD, 2009, 2012b).

Many of the new employment incentives that are part of job creation efforts do not involve direct government creation of jobs. Instead, they are temporary payments either to employers to create new jobs or to employees to supplement the low wages that they might receive in a new job. Neumark (2011) refers to employer subsidies to hire workers as "hiring credits." His examination of a large number of studies shows that hiring credits are cost effective if they focus on the recently unemployed and provide incentives for jobs that are actually new. As with state and city employers, there is often a cat-and-mouse game about whether jobs are new. But if adequate time is spent to determine whether jobs are new, then these subsidies can be well worth the effort. These employment incentives can also be made to influence employers to maintain employment in threatened jobs during restructuring. In this sense, the policy moves from job creation to job maintenance, and accurate and truthful information from the employer is essential about whether any particular job might be threatened. However, one should keep in mind that "active" labor market policies are supposed to be preventive in some ways, and this is the type of policy that would be most "active."

Subsidies that go to employees allow firms to pay rather low wages, and workers can then avoid poverty through additional wages coming from the federal government. Often, these types of supportive employment can go for employing disabled workers with lower rates of productivity, such as injured workers having finished vocational rehabilitation or citizens with intellectual challenges. Such programs can also benefit disadvantaged workers, and Neumark (2012) finds that single mothers from low-income families especially benefit from these kinds of programs, which may help to reduce Temporary Assistance for Needy Families (TANF) or other payments. In general, employment subsidies are less effective when unemployment is widespread during a major recession because there are large numbers of workers who are unemployed and targeting criteria are harder to discern.

The US had a large number of programs for disadvantaged young workers such as the Summer Youth Employment Program in the 1970s, but these were largely dropped with the other of job creation programs when the Reagan administration came into office in the 1980s. These programs are helpful in preventing or at least competing with alternative income from drugs and crime. However, with high unemployment for young workers, one can easily envision federal subsidies to create paid internship programs in private industry. To make these programs more effective, training and some regulation might be quite useful to have interns avoid menial tasks. As a result, taking into account scrutiny of job candidates and employers for substitution effects, there are many programs that can be effective.

Specific job creation programs focus on the NIRB and various types of work subsidies. The NIRB would help build bridges, tunnels, and roads that have fallen well behind the standards of a highly developed country. These programs must avoid the substitution pitfalls of replacing state and local budgets (Janoski, 1990), but given that, there is much infrastructural work that needs to be done. Recall the Minneapolis I-35 West Bridge collapse in 2007 that killed 13 and injured 145, and the poor state of the I-75/71 Brent Spence Bridge from Kentucky to Cincinnati. These kinds of repair and rebuilding programs could provide work experience and skills for those who have little or none, like young workers looking for a job. The NIRB would administer job creation programs as an independent financial institution owned by the government, with a board of directors from a wide range of government, industry, academic, labor, and other persons knowledgeable about labor market needs. It would provide for a broad range of infrastructural initiatives through public and private capital.

The NIRB would be financed from an increase in existing funds from general revenues that are allocated for ALMPs, and also from existing interstate highway systems for road expansion and improvement (Gerard and Hindery, 2011). President Obama, one Republican, and five Democratic senators proposed this in the bills known as the "American Jobs Act."[10] The funds for this job creation could also come from two new revenue sources. A new form of American bonds much like the US Savings Bonds program (Series E and I) is proposed, built on similar programs in the 1960s based on national defense. And related to this, a cost-sharing guarantee from the federal government could be provided for state and municipal bonds for the states and cities that desire greater infrastructural projects and jobs.

Another specific recommendation consists of a variety of employer tax credits that would fund new jobs. WOTC subsidies would subsidize jobs in different industries. The main area would be in supplying construction jobs for infrastructure improvements, building on the work of President Dwight Eisenhower's Interstate Highway System to update, replace and expand upon the existing highways, bridges, and roads that need improvement. The presence of expanded financing for construction would then stimulate the training of skilled workers in this area. A wider range of jobs would be subsidized in specific firms with the WOTC, which needs to be broadened beyond its current focus on veterans' employment (a laudable but too narrow focus on the unemployed). Finally, jobs would be provided for disadvantaged workers with two programs. The Summer Jobs Program for In-School Youth would recreate summer jobs that existed in 1960s and 1970s programs, and a Dignity Voucher Program for disadvantaged young adults is another way to provide jobs for modestly skilled workers in their own home or nursing homes, to help older and disabled citizens (Gerard and Hindery, 2011).

These three ALMP programs – NIRB, WOTC, and summer programs – have evaluation studies showing that they work. Job placement and training programs have been considered more successful in raising wages, but job creation programs create jobs and training programs do not. In most cases, the former produce at least one net job for every two that are funded. We cannot review the diverse findings of these evaluation studies, but one can see the many different results in the US and Europe from the following sources: Card et al. (2010), Forslund and Krueger (2008), Nie and Struby (2011), and Bonoli (2010).

Innovation, entrepreneurship, and technology

Job creation can also be encouraged through technological innovation and entrepreneurship programs. President Obama has said that "innovation is what America has always been about" (Obama, 2013). Here we make recommendations about technological innovation and entrepreneurship. As new technologies in entrepreneurial firms are the engine of growth for new industries, countries have to invest in innovation in order to gain an advantage in the new global economy (Litan and Schramm, 2012). Government finance of R&D in the US has gone from 2.20 percent of GDP in 1965 to 1.40 percent in the mid-1980s to 0.85 percent in the mid-1990s (OMB, 2012). While private industry R&D has gone up from 1.4 percent to 1.69 percent in the same period, much of its effect may be more in evidence in offshored industries than in US continental production (NAS/NSF, 2013). Governments need to finance innovation to promote job creation, and such financing can also make firms more amenable to promoting jobs and sharing innovation rather than hoarding it for commercial profits (OECD, 1998).

Starting a new business requires capital, which an entrepreneur has to provide through savings or loans. If things go well, venture capital firms may loan money, and eventually, stock may be sold to gain more capital through initial public offerings. People may have good ideas but if they do not have capital, a business will not get started. But different positions in the labor market provide different access to wealth. While any labor market segment could produce a major firm, FILMs and OILMs generate more ventures that have growth potential. And each labor market segment can lead to different types of entrepreneurial opportunities (see figure 6.1). However, people differ in their risk tolerance or market segment, so that FLMs, OLMs, and even SLAMs can produce a successful business. There is considerable debate about which types of firms produce the most jobs. Frequently, authors say and data shows that small firms produce the most jobs. On the one hand, small firms increase jobs because entrepreneurs create a firm that stays in business although it does not grow, or one that may grow through outsourcing from a bigger firm. On the other hand, larger firms produce the highest profits and the most growth in revenue. And incidentally, these same large firms produce the outsourcing that creates these smaller firms, and they do more offshoring that takes capital out of the country. Thus, there is controversy about who really creates jobs, and considerable leakage exists with offshore investment.

The Small Business Administration exists to give small businesses a chance to get low-cost business loans and often

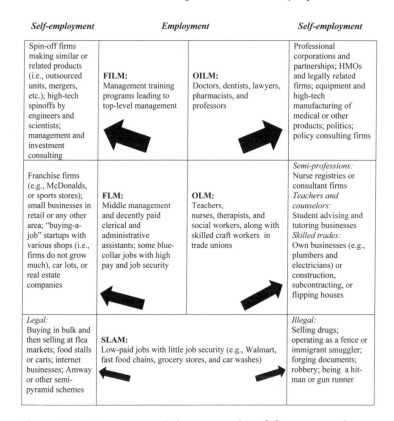

Self-employment	Employment		Self-employment
Spin-off firms making similar or related products (i.e., outsourced units, mergers, etc.); high-tech spinoffs by engineers and scientists; management and investment consulting	**FILM:** Management training programs leading to top-level management	**OILM:** Doctors, dentists, lawyers, pharmacists, and professors	Professional corporations and partnerships; HMOs and legally related firms; equipment and high-tech manufacturing of medical or other products; politics; policy consulting firms
Franchise firms (e.g., McDonalds, or sports stores); small businesses in retail or any other area; "buying-a-job" startups with various shops (i.e., firms do not grow much), car lots, or real estate companies	**FLM:** Middle management and decently paid clerical and administrative assistants; some blue-collar jobs with high pay and job security	**OLM:** Teachers, nurses, therapists, and social workers, along with skilled craft workers in trade unions	*Semi-professions:* Nurse registries or consultant firms *Teachers and counselors:* Student advising and tutoring businesses *Skilled trades:* Own businesses (e.g., plumbers and electricians) or construction, subcontracting, or flipping houses
Legal: Buying in bulk and then selling at flea markets; food stalls or carts; internet businesses; Amway or other semi-pyramid schemes	**SLAM:** Low-paid jobs with little job security (e.g., Walmart, fast food chains, grocery stores, and car washes)		*Illegal:* Selling drugs; operating as a fence or immigrant smuggler; forging documents; robbery; being a hit-man or gun runner

Figure 6.1 Entrepreneurial outgrowths of five types of seg-mented labor markets

advice on how to grow. Numerous states and communities have started Small Business Development Centers or incubators in old industrial buildings or unused schools. The Small Business Innovation Research program consists of 11 federal agencies that provide $2 billion each year to give research grants to small businesses, and they have had positive results (Litan and Schramm, 2012:66, 147; Haltiwanger et al., 2010). Other Proof of Concept Centers – the Deshpande Center at MIT and the von Liebig Center at UC, San Diego, for example – were begun by universities and business communities to show that innovations can become viable commercially (Litan and Schramm, 2012:146–7).

Much of the emphasis on entrepreneurial startups has moved from "the city" from Jane Jacobs' work (1992) to the universities and research parks since the early 1990s. Universities are working hard to develop innovations and new businesses. But patent policies can be a double-edged sword, especially as universities try to capture the fruits of these discoveries. As seen in figure 6.1, this university-centered model would grow out of the OILM labor market, and it would largely shut out the FLM, OLM, and SLAM entrepreneurship possibilities. Often FLM and OLM labor markets can tend toward "buying-a-job" startups but these do not scale to large job producers. Even when there are a large number of small businesses, they often represent the duplication of outsourced businesses (i.e., the work was already being done in a corporation so no net jobs are produced) or just hang on to supply a living for those who run them (Hurst and Pugsley, 2011). FILMs often have good access to venture capital and most often have few problems in getting started. But even small startups from humble beginnings can prosper and produce jobs. For instance, Chobani Yogurt started with a Turkish immigrant and a Small Business Administration loan, and by 2013 had generated over a billion dollars and had 1,300 employees (Gruley, 2013). The critical problem to be solved, of course, is to find which businesses will scale, and this requires a lot of research.

An entirely different model comes by "importing entrepreneurs" through an immigration policy that gives entrepreneurs and wealthy foreigners privileged entry and citizenship in the US if they invest in businesses that will create jobs in America. This is also connected to offering green cards to foreign students who get PhDs or other high-technology degrees at US universities. This forms a high-technology labor pool, and combined with importing wealth from abroad, it can create the means to start major new businesses (Litan and Schramm, 2012:116–22). Again, this targets the OILM and FILM segments. The trick is to find the right mix of these strategies and to look for synergies between them.

Finally, negotiating technological innovations should be encouraged in the US. The government, through social responsibility clauses for television (e.g., saving time for public service and news), telephones (e.g., the Bell Labs concerning basic research), and land-grant colleges (e.g., diffusing innovations through the extension service), has done this in the past. It missed an opportunity to do this with computer and internet technology, since it created the web through the defense department, and auctioned off frequency bandwidths. The state could ask industries to do research on the impact of technology on jobs and come up with different ways innovations can be implemented. In changing the role of land-grant universities toward a wider range of technologies, programs could be developed for the implementation of new technologies. President Obama has announced the creation of Centers for High Performance Manufacturing and a National Network for Manufacturing Innovation to advance the development and training for flexible, lean, and additive technologies. Centers have been established in Youngstown, Ohio, and Blacksburg, Virginia. The federal government could also extend the Loan Guarantee Program for Energy Efficiency, speed up the approval process for green manufacturing, extend the Cash Grant Program for Renewable Energy Production, and lengthen the Advanced Manufacturing Tax Credit (Gerard and Hindery, 2011).[11] In a sense, these kinds of programs are a negotiated process, but they could use more emphasis on representing citizens as employees in the implementation of new technologies in businesses. Subsidizing green jobs is an important way to promote new industries and the health of the environment (Kalleberg, 2011:213).

Job Placement Programs

The third aspect of AMLPs involves job placement, which was once the heart and soul of these policies. All AICs have an employment service – the US Employment Service (USES), the Federal Administration for Work in Germany, and the Labor Market Administration in Sweden – to handle job placement activities and dispense unemployment compensation.[12] Job-search assistance includes programs intended to connect employers to the unemployed more efficiently than might have happened otherwise. It includes referrals to available jobs or training, job brokerage services for employers, and financial assistance to help pay for the costs of a job search or relocation to take a job.

First of all, legislation needs to be passed to make it illegal to discriminate against the unemployed. Specifically, firms must not be able to refuse applications for job openings from persons who are unemployed (Peck, 2011; Cappelli, 2012a). A strong message is needed to tell employers to help employ those out of work. President Obama has proposed this in the "American Jobs Act," which was passed only in small part due to Republican opposition.

Second, Title I of the Workforce Investment Act (WIA) of 1998 created the One-Stop service system. Through One-Stop, citizens can obtain a wide range of job placement and training services through comprehensive centers covering all sites, satellite locations, and electronic access locations with minimal staff. The One-Stop system represents 14 different federal programs.[13] The program tries to avoid the bureaucratic runaround by providing all related services in one location. For the most part this has worked well. Nonetheless, social networking with people who know about jobs through social media or simply talking face to face is a most effective way to find work. However, with disadvantaged job seekers, the employment service remains the main connection to employers, whose cooperation is needed in this area. And having pre-existing apprenticeship programs is the best way to ensure this cooperation.[14]

Third, there are a number of programs that can help to make "credible assessments and certifications" (Mourshed et al., 2012:73). Having clear diplomas or certificates that workers can present at interviews or with applications helps, and the programs just discussed with modules do this in specific ways. Where credentials are not available, the "WorkKeys® Assessment System" provides tests for reading, business writing, applied mathematics, team work, listening, and personal interests and values. The ACT, the college testing company, created this system and offers a National Career Readiness Certificate (NCRC) guaranteeing that the bearer is ready to be hired. Forty states now recognize the NCRC and over a million people have the certificate (Mourshed et al. 2012:73; ACT, 2012). Another area where help could be given is with professionals when they move for a job, so that they do not have to get recertified in every state. These are small but meaningful steps toward employment.

And fourth, there is also a group of job maintenance programs that have not been used in the US but are quite prominent in Germany (Janoski, 1990; Bartlett and Steele, 2012). First, *short-time work* is a program that subsidizes jobs in a form of what could be called job sharing. Workers continue to work when there is much less work to be done, and the government makes up the difference in the wages that workers would normally receive. For instance, if there are only 30 hours of work per week for 100 employees (75 percent of the work necessary for a 40-hour week), then the firm would lay off 25 workers to employ 75 full-time workers. However, with short-time work, the government would pay for an additional 10 hours of work for each worker (1,000 hours to add to 3,000 to make 4,000) so that all of them could stay employed and receive a full pay check even though each of them works 30 hours a week. For this to work, the company must show that this is a temporary downturn and that work is expected to go back up to full-time employment. This is a reasonable tradeoff since the government would otherwise have to pay unemployment compensation to these workers, and having them stay on the job maintains their employment skills, self-confidence, and network connections (Kwon, 2012; Reisenbichler and Morgan, 2012). Preserving jobs then connects to creating a social plan for workers to move into new training or employment. Second, *winter work* is a program that is mainly for construction workers who do relatively little work during the winter months. Instead of paying unemployment compensation to these workers, firms get subsidies from the government to cover the additional costs of working in the winter to construct buildings, roads, and houses.

These can be effective policies in the right institutional setting. Short-time work and winter work need careful implementation and monitoring, since many evaluation studies of job maintenance programs show that they can delay firms making necessary changes, and that political pressures from unions and politicians can continue them when they are no longer needed. As a result, care must be taken to show that these policies are coordinated with management strategies to get over a temporary crisis, or that actual planning is going on to move these workers into new settings. While these policies are about as costly as unemployment insurance, they also preserve worker skills and connections to the firm.

Economic Stability Policies Concerning Trade and Taxes

In our fourth area of recommendations, we discuss fair trade policies that offer some protection to national industries from unfair trade, and tax policies that would stabilize and smooth out the business cycle to prevent large recessions.

Fair trade and government offshoring policies

The governmental purchasing decision is actually a rather complicated one. While governments might buy products based on price, they also have to consider quality, service, and dependability, like any buyer. But they have as well some additional concerns, like impacts on national defense, the trade balance, the economy, and American communities. The governments of most sizable countries will not allow their farms to wither and die because they are concerned that their country produce enough food so they will not starve if the international relations situation turns sour. Similarly, there are all sorts of reasons to buy and make military equipment systems within the country under secret contracts. As a result, the Critical Technologies List for Homeland Security clearly focuses on domestically made products (Gerard and Hindery, 2011; AJA, 2011).

A second issue is that the government itself engages in considerable offshoring. The Government Accountability Office found that state governments offshore parts of federal social welfare programs as follows: food stamps, 32 states; TANF, 16 states; child support enforcement, 12 states; and unemployment insurance, 8 states (US-GAO, 2006). Most of the activities are in call centers or information technology work, but these are all jobs that can be done in the US. New Jersey and Arizona prohibit offshoring in state contracts, and they were joined by Ohio in 2010 (Thibodeau, 2010). Taxpayers can demand and have demanded that their own governments not offshore services.

Third, governments should buy domestic products when there are instances of non-reciprocity between trading countries. When another country bars the entry of American products, it is not too much to ask that the government purchase products made in the US to promote the employment of American citizens. These kinds of actions are complicated by trade relations between countries, but some kind of reciprocity can be attempted. Establishing fair global trade enforcement goes along with domestic purchasing. The federal government should establish clear principles and enforcement mechanisms concerning global trade: (1) recognize that trade has clear and measurable benefits for Americans by prohibiting illegal subsidies and currency manipulation; (2) establish measurable progress on labor rights violations involving trade partners; (3) incorporate environmental protections into new trade agreements; (4) impose short-term tariffs on the basis of high trade deficits to protect US manufacturing, which is legal under the WTO; (5) implement a new and independent federal bureau to enforce trade laws; (6) create an unfair trade strike force to prosecute those who violate trade laws by dumping and other unfair trade practices; and (7) prevent or punish the theft of intellectual property rights (Gerard and Hindery, 2011). But there is a large divergence between the interests of US corporations seeking profits and those of American citizens interested in jobs and communities. Getting many of these measures passed would require running the gauntlet of the corporate lobby.

Perhaps we should consider the examples of Sweden or Switzerland, which are small countries. Although each country has many talented people, it wouldn't be too hard to find equally or more talented people in China who could do just about every job in these two countries for less money. Should all the jobs in each country be offshored to China? In other words, is there a limit to the efficiency or low-wage argument – a limit that involves the welfare and survival of the society that inhabits the country that is offshoring its jobs? While corporations might make money in this deal, how would either one of these countries survive? Apple and some other corporations are fond of saying that they are global companies and do not have allegiance to any nation-state. But the members of those nation-states certainly have the right to look after their own welfare. To some degree, this is already happening in public opinion. Even a number of computer manufacturers have repatriated their call centers from India because of customer complaints. The public did not sign the trade treaties, but they did elect their representatives, and those representatives are responding to the survival instincts of many citizens about offshoring public and private services. And we are finding that Apple and GE are slowly responding to public opinion in anticipation that it might turn against them.

Finally, related to this discussion are a number of complex tax questions that cover a wide range of issues. The ability of corporations to keep their foreign earnings overseas and avoid US taxes creates an incentive to offshore. Some corporations go so far as to claim that all their earnings are foreign (or global) so that they can avoid US taxes altogether. This is not good citizenship behavior by a so-called US "person." If a reasonable tax deal could be struck to bring these profits into the US to invest in jobs, it would be worth it. Also, investment tax credits should be established for creating jobs in the US, and conversely, tax credits should be examined for any aid that they give to offshoring, and those that do so should then be eliminated. The government, which is supported by taxpayers, should not be operating contrary to the employment interests of a majority of its citizens. Hence, the tax code should be fixed so that corporations do not have incentives to send jobs overseas increased by the US government's efforts.

Stabilization through taxes and regulation

There are three areas that concern the diminution of corporate taxes (Kalleberg, 2011:200). First, concerning the relatively new world of web corporations, the policy not to tax sales on the web has meant that states have lost revenues as web businesses have replaced stores with physical locations. Just as the world wide web was given the advantage of not being taxed for over a decade, similar privileges were given to worldwide financial operations. These web corporations should be subject to sales taxes just as other corporations are. This has started to change as Amazon.com and others are now required to pay taxes (although unevenly since this has been done from state to state); and this needs to spread to financial institutions, which should pay taxes to match their profits.[15]

Second, corporations have paid fewer and fewer taxes, with various sorts of havens accessed by double-Dutch and double-Irish legal scams. Some of the more dynamic and profitable corporations like Google and Apple have been benefiting from these offshore financial loopholes. As a result, many corporations are paying only about 5–15 percent of profits in taxes rather than the statutory 35 percent rate. The US and other countries have cracked down on secret bank accounts in Switzerland, but further efforts need to be made in offshore tax havens such as Bermuda, the Cayman Islands, and others such as Antigua that actually sell citizenship and passports to people needing tax havens. The basis of the sale is the location of the customer, not an arbitrary designation of cyberspace.

Third, another type of policy addresses market instabilities, which have been on the increase since 2000 due to 9/11, LTCM, the dot.com bubble, and the "great recession" of 2008. It is in the interests of nation-states and the global economy to build a stable world economy in a number of different ways. This section suggests three such policies: two in terms of taxes controlling speculation by generating revenue, and one in straightforward regulation.

Value at risk tax   The US and possibly other countries with large financial sectors should enact a value at risk (VaR) tax to create a brake on speculation. This would strengthen the controls on speculative investment by making tax payments increase when risk goes beyond a certain threshold. Some speculation is good, but once the country as a whole reaches what Minsky (2008) referred to as "Ponzi scheme investments," the country and increasingly the world will suffer from market meltdowns. But new financial instruments are evading many of these issues. A VaR tax rests on an established management tool – value at risk – that would then be progressively taxed as the amount of risk goes beyond a prudential threshold. This is largely similar to requirements that loans not go beyond a threshold of reserves. Rather than simply stop risky speculation, this progressive tax discourages it. The VaR Tax requires reporting on risk, which is helpful in itself, but the tax is really intended not for revenue but rather to prevent excessively risky behavior.

Global investment tax   Global finance has exploded since the early 2000s and has left the social and industrial aspects of globalization in disarray. At the same time, global finance is less stable than ever (as established in chapter 5). Out of the massive sums of money that have been generated by finance, we propose a tax that would target international financial transactions. This would do two things. First, this tax would improve financial stability since it will discourage excessive speculation (parallel to the VaR tax), and would especially hit highly leveraged and high-speed automated trading. The result would be a reduction in the bonuses that traders would receive (Dowd and Hutchinson, 2010:394–95; Conesa et al., 2009). Second, it would generate funds that could be used to improve international labor standards and create institutions that would help the non-financial aspects of globalization catch up with the financial aspects. The funds generated from a very low tax rate (e.g., a hundredth of a percent) would produce considerable revenue because of the very high volume of transactions (Dowd, 2005; Keen, 2011; Bookstaber, 2008; Staddon, 2012). The revenues could be split between AICs that are hurt by offshoring, and LDCs where workers labor under terrible conditions at low rates of pay. The first stream of funds would go to the nation-states involved, and the second stream would go to international nonprofit organizations that would conceivably regulate fair labor standards.

Each one of these three items would be strenuously opposed by Wall Street and the financial sector, but transnational financial and other corporations are now in the driver's seat and most politicians recognize this. Nonetheless, we believe these measures must be enacted despite what Wall Street might want.[16]

Direct regulation of banking   After the repeal of the Glass-Steagall Act in 1999, the Dodd-Frank Wall Street Reform and Consumer Protection Act of 2010 addressed the dangerous instability that often appears in the US financial system. Specifically, Section 619 prohibits banks from using citizens' savings and checking accounts for proprietary trading in risky hedge funds and private equity funds (FDIC, 2013). This section, often called the Volcker Rule (named after Paul Volcker, the retired chairman of the Federal Reserve), has been controversial and may not be implemented until 2014. Nonetheless, we believe that this rule is absolutely necessary to protect citizens from banks using their deposits for excessively risky investments. Although the distinction between commercial and investment banks has been blurred (mainly by mergers), this rule reduces the probability of commercial bank failures in the event of financial crises. It also results in less need for the intervention of the federal government through its federal insurance institutions. Dodd-Frank deals with other risky investment strategies such as derivatives and other financial instruments; however, these banking regulations take us beyond the scope of this book. But the Volcker Rule itself provides basic protection against the wild swings of finance, which have contributed to structural unemployment.

Conclusion

In this chapter, we have made four basic recommendations concerning policy. First, we recommended a major restructuring of job training for non-college students, with more of an apprenticeship system involved with job training, vocational education, and job placement. This, of course, would require an increase in "social capital" involving much more cooperation from employers. Second, we recommended more job creation, especially through the NIRB, accompanied by trade policies much more friendly toward increasing jobs in the US.

Third, we recommended a major increase in R&D and green jobs, which would catch up to the levels of the 1960s and 1970s. And finally, we argued for a menu of tax policies and regulatory changes that would reduce the unstable aspects of financialization and increase economic stability.

The US and other AICs can do quite a bit to improve the lot of the unemployed within their national boundaries. However, there is less concern for the unemployed in the US than in Germany, Sweden, and many other European countries. For these policies to be implemented, the US will have to conjure up both political will and employer cooperation. In our view, Americans must recognize that their job training system, including high school, and their pitiful funding of ALMPs erect a serious barrier to both employers and workers in present-day labor markets. But changing the American high school, that entrenched institution where sports and socialization programs are seemingly in charge in many localities, is very difficult. It is odd that economists who see institutions responding to market needs in so many areas do not seem to have any impact on the American high school. Rigor and testing have been an issue followed by privatization, but the reality is that the high school hasn't changed its structure since the 1920s.

At the same time, most Americans recognize that Wall Street has some serious problems concerning stability, risk, and speculation. It is a very tall order for American society to change these institutions, but it needs to be done. Ultimately, this is the political challenge of the next ten to twenty years. Our plan for a way out of structural unemployment will not be easy to realize, given current political divisiveness, but it offers a meaningful answer to the question of what could be done to reduce worker and family suffering. The final chapter discusses two critical issues in how it might be done.

7

Conclusion: Can We Trust Transnational Corporations?

In each one of our four causal chapters, corporations have played an important and most often negative role. In effect, corporations have given US workers and the state a triple-cross on jobs and investment. First, corporations now dissociate themselves from large numbers of employees through outsourcing and offshoring. They effectively say that while these people make our cars, make our smart phones, or clean our offices, we don't know them or have any responsibility for them. In the US, this insulates the corporation from these workers, absolves them from responsibility for or demands from them, and helps to make the SLAM section of the labor market larger with wages that are smaller and smaller. Overseas, it largely absolves them from scandals that occur in "their" subcontracted manufacturers. Second, corporations dissociate themselves from the nation-state, with some claiming that they belong to no country at all. This has allowed them to escape taxes and amass over $3 trillion in profits that float in tax havens overseas. Third, corporations have gained massive profits with the stock market recovery but they have not been investing these profits in employment or training activities (Asker et al., 2013). Instead, their investments are very short-sighted. Guided by shareholder value theory, they hold large amounts of cash and pay some of it out in dividends to shareholders. This triple-cross destroys the social bond that citizens and states have with the many corporations that behave in this way. Even conservatives such as Prime Minister David Cameron of the UK have had enough. With Apple and Starbucks in mind, he said: "It is time to name and shame multinationals that use creative accounting to avoid taxes" and disarm their "army of clever accountants" (*BBC News*, 24 January, 2013). A mutual plan of expanding market share and job growth is needed when many corporations are more concerned with profits and shareholder value no matter what the impact is on jobs. Kevin Leicht and Scott Fitzgerald answer the question of what the rules should be for corporations by saying that "you should have to take some of us with you as employees" (2007:155).

So what do citizens and societies do with the most important value-generating institutions in the world (created by the nation-state in the first place), which say: "We don't know these workers, we don't know these nation-states, and we have no priorities to invest our profits to produce jobs"? Even the OECD says that the declining share of national income going to wages, increasing inequality since the early 1980s, might "endanger social cohesion" and slow the recovery (2012a:109). Yet these very corporations have inordinate political influence on governments. This final chapter discusses two issues of critical concern for the future of jobs and the broadly defined middle classes in the US and other Anglo-Saxon countries: (1) the increasing independence of private corporations from the multination state and their lack of concern about unemployment and citizen well-being; and (2) the developing of a new social contract between citizens and the twin powers of the state and the corporations. These recommendations are considered separately from those in the previous chapter because they involve much more heavy lifting in politics and institutions.

The first critical issue concerns the status of the transnational corporation and its related investment and large banks, which are a subset of large transnational corporations. As chapter 3 has shown, the interests of major corporations and some private equity firms have become totally dislodged from society. The transnational corporations consider themselves global, with multitudinous rights, but at the same time they have jettisoned any sense of obligation to the multination states from which they were born and the citizens who inhabit these same states. The only exception to their blithe unconcern is for satisfying their stockholders, whose interests in the case of some corporations are subordinated to those of top executives with high salaries and extraordinary performance bonuses (Clements, 2012; King, 1986; Ohmae, 1995; Sassen, 2000; Weiss, 1998; Rothkopf, 2012). But of course, the stockholders could be citizens of any country. If these corporations are "persons," which is firmly ensconced in US law, then they have an odd form of citizenship that provides a one-way connection to various "multination states" and to a number of international organizations. These corporate entities have been very adept at taking advantage of their "rights" to operate, market, and obtain protection from various governments. Their cleverness in evading taxes is also more developed in many cases than that of the government entities that levy the taxes. However, wherever there are rights, there are also duties and obligations (Janoski, 1998). The field of corporate citizenship has developed in the business literature since the early 2000s, but it is not about the corporation as a citizen. Oddly enough, it concerns the corporate employees' citizenship and obligations to the corporation itself. What of the corporation as a citizen with rights and duties?

Financial corporations and stock markets benefitted from a first-mover advantage in being the first global institutions to operate in a worldwide environment. To a large degree they took very effective advantage of these circumstances where multination states and global governance structures were experiencing and still experience institutional lag. The result has been that the transnational corporation has put itself into an aggressive, antagonistic relationship with workers as a whole and with the multination state. Financial institutions including stock markets and banks have also gained tremendous profits and control, but at the same time have done an exceedingly poor job in fostering economic stability and employment growth. So far, much of corporate largesse has created a race to the bottom with low wages, tax-free decades of operation for relocation, extensive offshoring, and other advantageous operating benefits. As Rothkopf summarizes it: "the state constrained, the corporation unbound," with a description of how the Stora Corporation in Sweden became a larger and more powerful entity than the state government of Sweden itself, which gave Stora its initial corporate charter (2012:22, 126, 165). Others detail that highly problematic rise of the corporation over the nation-state (Vernon, 2001; Yergin and Stanislaw, 2002; Micklethwait and Wooldridge, 2005).

But as the political and labor-oriented institutions start catching up with the first movers, two solutions may appear. First, multination states may declare corporations as "non-persons" with fewer rights and more obligations, making incorporation a privilege granted by nation-state or international bodies. These political entities would then refuse the race to the bottom concerning inequality and regulation. For instance, they might take greater control of the international seas and end the registration of the ships of other countries in Liberia and Panama. Or they might seek a larger and more international registration of corporations and not accept those registered in a particularly permissive state like Delaware, where applicants do not even have to supply identification when registering (Clements, 2012; Davis, 2009). Or second, multination states could maintain that corporations are "persons" that not only have rights but also have obligations, and start enforcing those obligations in terms of supporting societies through adequate taxes, treatment of employees according to international labor standards, and not having undue influence on political and regulatory processes. Citizens do not have only one obligation – to maximize return on investment to shareholders. Citizens belong to a multination state or to many multination states and have obligations to a much wider range of other citizens, including workers and other employees. International labor standards and creating new institutions to represent workers' interests are going to be a major part of this movement. While the Occupy Wall Street movement embodies many of these values, there will undoubtedly be a larger political force needed to help push this movement. Neo-liberal forces along with conservatives will oppose these measures, but as the hollowing out of the middle classes goes on, these forces' democratic base will continue to shrink as inequality continues to rise.

Solving this critical issue is not diminished by a small and recent trend away from outsourcing. Most significantly, the CEO of Apple, Tim Cook, has said that production of certain Apple computers will now be done in the US (Tyrangiel, 2012; Satariano and Tyrangiel, 2012). He claimed that two Apple products were being made in the US but those are surely components made by subcontractors (e.g., glass in Kentucky). The Boston Consulting Group (BCG, 2012b) says that, according to their survey, rising Chinese wages, logistics, and a number of other factors are leading a third of large manufacturers to "consider" reshoring to the US. Fishman claims that there is an "insourcing boom" and that there previously was a "herd mentality" about offshoring that sent far too much manufacturing to China (2012:49). He touches on GE's appliance divisions moving back to the US. Jeffrey Immelt, the CEO of GE and chair of President Obama's jobs council, certainly has some conflicts since he is supposed to be creating jobs for Americans but his company still offshores large numbers of jobs. However, whether this is a major trend remains doubtful. One always knew that Chinese wages would rise, but some of the costs also have to do with increasing oil prices for container ships and the difficulties of setting up joint ventures in China, where the government wants to limit foreign production for their internal market in favor of indigenous producers. American workers may find this promising, but it is premature to make any solid assessments of where it will be going. One should keep in mind that production in China involved a labor–technology tradeoff, with China offering more and cheaper labor. Most new manufacturing jobs in the US in the future will involve considerably more investment in robotics and other high technology. This is how labor–technology tradeoffs work. So in the end, this sovereignty discord between nation-states and corporations needs to be resolved.

The second issue involves negotiating a global socioeconomic contract with workers and citizens (Kalleberg, 2011; Webster et al., 2008; Silver, 2003; Rubin, 1996). This area has the largest institutional lag since it is hard to organize workers across boundaries, but it also has the most opposition in terms of global finance and global corporations, which will spend billions of dollars to oppose worker representation efforts that will raise wages, improve working conditions, and reduce the flexibility of treating workers in some countries in an entirely cavalier fashion. In a sense, world labor, most often represented by the ILO, and the largest corporations, represented by the American National Association of Manufacturers and Business Roundtable, never get into the same room together. This is a refusal to bargain on a social contract. Each group is out on its own limb, but on opposite sides of the same tree. Some new integrative institutions need to be built to get labor and capital back to the negotiating table. This could be started with a corporate citizenship tax based on some of the principles of the global investment tax. A global tax that would be distributed to affected multination states would be most desirable because it could also focus on tax havens and eliminate them. This takes us into the area of political will and quite clearly corporations do not see any incentive to move into this area.

It is well beyond the scope of this book on unemployment and the disappearance of good jobs in AICs to provide a blueprint for re-establishing political and social institutions within these countries and throughout the globe. And what we are looking for is not a reversal of globalization, but rather a renegotiation of technology and markets in global institutions. The aim is a global social control that allows workers, countries, and corporations to cooperate in a more stable and just economy. The first movers in globalization have been corporations and financial institutions, and this needs to be balanced by citizen and political institutions. The advent of corporate social responsibility and the use of the Fair Labor Association for 4.2 million workers is a minuscule start since its tripartite structure of corporations, university administrators, and NGOs ignores the voice of workers as a whole. Something more representative within the spirit of civil society will be needed (Anner, 2012; Fransen, 2012).

Notes

Chapter 1   Introduction

1   Our view of sociology relies on historical-institutional and power constellations theory, which combines theories from Max Weber and Karl Marx in using class, status, and power (Huber and Stephens, 2001; Janoski, 2010; Thelen, 1999, 2004; Fligstein, 2001).

2   In the case of Sweden, high wages with little inequality and very low unemployment were the context of what one could call an extremely low natural rate. The solidarity wage policy and neo-corporatist bargaining handled inflation quite well at certain times in history. Similarly, Japan reveals low unemployment and moderate inflation with a different set of institutional constraints. True believers in the natural rate generally avoid these comparisons and assume that capitalism is the same throughout the world. In the end, labeling something as "natural" is politically loaded and simplistic. If there is a relationship between inflation and unemployment at certain times, then let us examine that relationship without such labels.

3   Stone (2013) disputes some of the claims by NPR series. One should keep in mind that disability includes a number of different programs including those for mentally disabled children and adults. Parsing out the causes of the doubling of disability rates will require more detailed and careful study of a national sample of recipients.

4   Economists describe as "hysteresis" the state that develops when the unemployed lose skills and confidence. It may even

be a social psychological depression with symptoms of with-drawal. While these processes do occur, the term hysteresis is not widely used.

5   The Gini index measures the distance from perfect wage equality (World Bank, 2013). While perfect equality is not possible, it provides a good anchor point from which to measure inequality. Figures in the .200s represent high equality, those in the .300s are moderate, and those in the .400s are highly unequal. The state reduces inequality through somewhat progressive taxes, and social security and disability (transfer) payments to the poor.

6   Foreign direct investment (FDI) is too crude a measure to explain offshoring. In chapter 3 we will make estimates of offshoring, but FDI includes too much investment in the stock market, government bonds, and real estate. This wanders too far from investment in plant and equipment.

7   As Harry Braverman (1974) showed in his highly influential book, scientific management or Taylorism made the leap from blue- to white-collar work. We are illustrating a similar leap of offshoring from manufacturing jobs to the professions. The actual term "Bravermanic leap" is our own. For more details on these concepts, see Janoski and Lepadatu (2013).

8   Paul Krugman has rhetorically called structural unemployment a "structure of excuses." He is advocating for government spending to stimulate demand within the context of a major cyclical downturn. We do not disagree with his points, but note that he focuses mainly on cyclical rather than structural unemployment (Krugman, 2010a, 2010b). But his position on trade policy tends to militate against structural unemployment (Görg, 2011:22).

Chapter 2   Shifting from Manufacturing to Services and Skill Mismatches

1   Germany has a better record on high growth and low unemployment than the US. The Hartz reforms, made in four pieces of legislation, reduced unemployment compensation levels in Germany to US levels. While Germany now has more lower-paid jobs than it previously had, the ratio of high- to low-paid jobs is much more equal than it is in the US. The top-income to bottom-income ratios, comparing the top 10 percent to the bottom 10 percent of incomes, are 3.32 in Germany and 4.89 in the US, which means that the very rich make about three

times as much as the very poor in Germany but almost five times as much in the US. Expanding the comparison to the bottom half of the labor force, the top 10 percent in Germany make 1.72 times as much as the whole bottom half of wage earners while the rich make 2.34 times as much as the same half of the labor force in the US (Osterman, 2012:51; Reisenbichler and Morgan, 2012). Clearly, German capitalism exhibits much more equality than American capitalism.

Chapter 3   Transnational Corporations Enthralled with Outsourcing and Offshoring

1   Most factories in the Chinese special economic zones rely on migrant workers from the villages. Because of the *Hokou* migration system, these migrants are semi-legal in the urban areas. Their own health and pension benefits, and schooling for their children do not transfer to urban areas (i.e., their children are not eligible for urban schooling). As a result, they resemble illegal aliens working in the US because of their vulnerability (Lee, 2007).

2   Our definition of lean production uses Liker's (2004) 14 principles outlined in *The Toyota Way*, which itself is loosely based on Deming's (1982) 14 principles from *Out of the Crisis*. Our definition emphasizes teams a bit more than Liker's, mainly because Toyota does so and so does the University of Kentucky Lean Systems Certification Program, which includes a Toyota executive. Liker's points can be grouped into four parts: (1) philosophy (points 1 and 14); (2) supply chains (points 2, 3, 6, and 11); (3) problem solving (points 4, 5, 7, and 12) and (4) strong teams (points 9, 10, and 13) (Liker, 2004:7–41). Morgan and Liker (2008) apply the same principles to product development.

3   For Toyota's more recent difficulties with the 2011 tsunami and quality control issues, see Liker and Ogden (2011).

4   Apple and commentators avoid mentioning Foxconn or Hon Hai Precision. Walter Isaacson's (2011) biography *Steve Jobs* does not mention the company or Terry Gou (Balfour et al. 2004; Balfour and Culpan, 2010a, 2010b). In President Obama's meeting with Steve Jobs and other computer executives, Jobs said that he would bring production back to the US if the federal government trained 30,000 engineers and allowed the tax-free repatriation of all of Apple's foreign profits (Isaacson, 2011:200–1, 546). *Tax Notes* indicates that Apple pays

very little in taxes (sometimes as low as 5 percent) by taking advantage of tax havens offshore. Apple routes its revenues to foreign countries in order to avoid taxes (e.g., double Dutch and double Irish) resulting in a 13–14 percent corporate tax rate, well below the 35 percent rate. It even avoids paying state taxes to cash-strapped California by receiving substantial revenues in Nevada even though Apple is based in Cupertino, California (Goulder 2012a; Duhigg and Kocieniewski, 2012).

5   Six Sigma is a quality control process that was developed by Motorola in 1986. It seeks to improve the quality of products by removing the causes of defects and minimizing variability in manufacturing processes. Each six sigma project is carried out with a sequence of steps with financial targets. Six Sigma refers to six standard deviations from the mean.

6   The GE CEO from 2001, Jeff Immelt, came up under Welch, but Immelt emphasizes basic science research much more (Magee, 2009). Immelt became an advisor to President Obama on jobs, which raised eyebrows. Recently, GE has repatriated the manufacture of some refrigerators to the US and invested in producing a new hybrid water heater in Louisville. But GE had 17,000 employees in Louisville in 1970 and 2,500 workers in 2011.

7   Kim and Sakamoto show that inter-industry wage dispersion may be declining despite overall trends toward inequality in general (2007). Bell and Freeman (1991) show that this was just the opposite in the 1970–87 period.

8   All foreign currencies have been converted into US dollars so that they can be compared.

Chapter 4   Technological Change and Job Loss

1   Neither the Luddites nor the crown were innocent. King Ludd made death threats to magistrates, mill/machine owners, and food merchants. Some industrialists even had safe rooms, and the mill owner William Horsfall claimed that he would "ride up to the saddle girths in Luddite blood" (Sale, 1996:146; Binfield, 2004).

2   Prominent examples of rejecting technological change are Tiberius executing an entrepreneur who had an idea for unbreakable glass; Queen Elizabeth I rejecting knitting innovations; and the Austro-Hungarian Empire rejecting railroads for some time because they would help rebels (Acemoglu and Robinson, 2011).

3   Many other theories exist about science, but we are focusing not on how science operates but rather on the impact of technology on employment (Pfaffenberger 1992: 300, 294; Matthewman 2011: 81–3, 201–2).

4   The comparison is based on elasticities of funding of R&D, which are 0.064 for private industry and 0.049 for government. While total elasticity for all R&D adds the two together (i.e., 0.113), industry-led R&D has had a stronger impact since the early 2000s. Government R&D had greater impacts from 1948 to 1960.

5   Autor et al. (2013) show that rising imports increase unemployment, lower wages, and lower labor force participation in local labor markets.

6   Other examples include the railroads with the Railway Labor Act; efforts to control prices with the International Chamber of Commerce; the interstate highway system with state-required auto insurance, traffic lights, and other safety requirements; the Food and Drug Administration; and the Federal Aviation Administration with the regulation and safety of airlines. Less successful efforts have come with the Occupational Safety and Health Administration and worker safety. There are also many government–university laboratories that promote discoveries (e.g., Lawrence-Berkeley Labs), and the National Science Foundation (NSF) also plays a major role.

7   For instance, the last half-century has seen a negotiation over corporate control concerning theories of shareholder value versus stakeholder participation, with the former winning in the late 1980s (Fligstein, 2001:147–69).

8   Often referred to as a shift from *push* production (e.g., manufacturers) to *pull* production (e.g., retailers).

9   Brynjolfsson and McAfee recommend increasing training and unleashing innovation in response to "the race against the machine." They do not say much about molding or negotiating technology (2011).

10 Gordon Moore, an American inventor and former chairman of Intel, stated that the number of transistors that could be put on an integrated circuit would double every 24 months; later he shortened the time to 12 months (Kurzweil, 2005:56). The law indicates the almost incredible potential for developing artificial intelligence.

11 One significant change since the early 1990s has been the drop in numbers of unionized grocery store employees – in part driven by the rise of Walmart with its clear anti-union stance, and in part by the stagnation or decline in overall wages for

grocery employees due to barcode check-out readers (Lichenstein, 2006, 2009).

12　There are some limits to offshoring. Under federal rules, all medical services to be reimbursed by Medicare or Medicaid must be performed within the US. Further, under many state laws, most medical services – including radiological services – must be performed by individuals licensed within the state in which the examinations and tests are performed (Bradley, 2004).

13　As a result, law school applications went from 100,000 in 2004 to 55,000 in 2013 (Weissmann, 2013). See Hicken and Rogers (2012) for 12 more young and unemployed lawyers.

14　Evidence that capital has grabbed more GDP than employees as a group also comes from Volscho and Kelly (2012), Goldstein (2012), Tomaskovic-Devey and Lin (2011), and Lin and Tomaskovic-Devey (2013). However, these authors do not specially measure technology.

Chapter 5　Global Trade, Shareholder Value, and Financialization as Structural Causes of Unemployment

1　Ferguson (2004), Gibson (2012:77), and Atkinson and Ezell (2012:57–84) compare the UK and US in their periods of crisis and decline. Numerous critics in the UK from 1850 to 1950 "warned that in the long term the maintenance of an open economy in the face of rapidly rising foreign competition would lead to deindustrialization of Britain, the fragmentation of its empire, and the loss of great-power status" (Cain and Hopkins 1987:7).

2　The Glass-Steagall Act built a firewall in the 1930s between conservative commercial banking (savings and checking accounts) and riskier investment banking. The 2010 Dodd-Frank Act is a very wide-ranging securities regulatory act that may do some of what Glass-Steagall intended. After the fall of Enron, the Sarbanes-Oxley Act made CEOs responsible for their financial reports; it penalizes those CEOs who say that they "had no idea what was going on."

3　See Harvey (2010), Preda (2009), and MacKenzie (2009).

4　Debt is larger than GDP because it cumulates for as much as 30 years. For instance, the size of all the mortgage debt in the US is usually larger than GDP in any one year.

5　Ponzi schemes are pyramid schemes that do not actually make money, but pay dividends to older investors from the capital invested by newer investors. As such they are doomed to fail when the pyramid collapses. An example is Bernard Madoff's Ponzi scheme, which collapsed and for which he went to jail in 2009. However, Hyman Minsky refers to Ponzi investment as the most risky type of investment, but not necessarily one entailing an illegal pyramid scheme.

6 Minsky's use of "hedge financing" predates the extensive growth in hedge funds from 1990 to 2012. Consequently, more contemporary hedge-fund strategies should not be confused with his use of "hedge" as a relatively conservative strategy for more or less balancing 3 percent interest-bearing accounts with 6 percent interest-earning loans, typical of bank financing in the 1950s.

7 States primarily in the South have passed right-to-work statutes allowed under the Taft-Hartley Act of 1947. However, debate rages as to whether these laws had an actual effect or whether the states that passed them had already been generally anti-union in many other ways.

8 In NTT, Paul Krugman built on Solow's growth theory. Krugman believed that international economics had ignored *returns to scale* (1996) slightly increasing returns to specialization (1979, 1980, 1981; Krugman and Obstfield, 2009). Instead of a nationally fixed comparative advantage, the mercantilist nation was more or less "creating comparative advantage," which is highly attractive to a developing country. But the empirical results for NTT are mixed, though Japan and China are cited as examples (Harrigan, 2003; Tybout, 2003). One sobering thought for unemployment is that Krugman has said that "Trade policy should be debated in terms of its impact on efficiency, not in terms of phony numbers about jobs created or lost" (1993:25). Economist Holger Görg refers to this as the trade economist's "theoretical straitjacket" on unemployment (2011:22).

9 Foxconn management eventually installed suicide nets near the ground to catch such workers and later instituted various forms of counseling for workers.

10 There were stronger watchdog groups and unions that broke off from the more conservative FLA. The Worldwide Responsible Apparel Production has a stronger monitoring system (see www.wrapapparel.org). The Workers Rights Consortium has also been involved with Nike, the Bangladesh tragedies in 2012 and 2013, and even Apple (see www.workersrights.org). However, the most important multinational corporations, like Walmart, are less interested in using these groups.

11   The US and some other AICs are starting to crack down on tax havens. The US persuaded Swiss banks to provide information on secret accounts in August 2013. How far this crackdown will go remains to be seen (Goulder, 2012).
12   Conservative or monetary economists sometimes imply that any wage increase will increase inflation. And that would be true if there were no productivity increases. But if wages increase in proportion to productivity increases, inflation need not rise. Thus, refusing to give wage increases when productivity increases by a large amount is counterproductive since it depresses consumption.
13   See Stiglitz (2010), Hardie and MacKenzie (2007), Krugman (2009), Levine (2009, 2010), MacKenzie (2009), and Lowenstein (2004).

Chapter 6   Fixing Structural Unemployment

1   The canoeing metaphor combines terms used by Hall (2001; Hall and Mirvis, 1995) and Cappelli (1999, 2008). It also fits the flexibility of the "new economy business model" (Lazonick, 2009). This new model has dramatically changed the terms of employment. "Workers have gone from a modicum of security" to a lack of "commitment, explicit or implicit, on the part of U.S. high-tech companies" to give their workers "stable employment, skill formation, and rewarding careers" (Lazonick, 2009:1).
2   Director for Employment, Labour, and Social Affairs at OECD John Martin also recommends that ALMPs need to be adequately funded even in countries where budget deficits exist. He concludes: "More than ever, these reforms must be pursued vigorously to reduce long-term unemployment and promote better employment prospects for youth" (2011d:11–12).
3   In the European context, these policies are referred to as "flexicurity," which provides a secure base in a safety net along with retraining and retooling for jobs (Atkinson and Ezell, 2012:315–16; Appelbaum, 2012; Kalleberg, 2011).
4   The American high school largely disparages vocational education. Halpern indicates that "the majority of teachers and guidance counselors continue to talk about vocational-technical education in a derogatory way despite the fact that over half of students are on a general (non-college) track" (2006:62). Vocational education is clearly the "Cinderella"

subject to a wicked stepmother of "college for all" in the US high-school system. As Hoffman says, they are the "forgotten half" (2011:14–15).

5 AMTEC is part of an NSF program called the Advanced Technological Education program in its Undergraduate Education division. AMTEC funds over 100 projects in over 30 states for similar programs, including automobiles in Alabama, nanotechnology in California, and marine incubation in Florida. It targets community and technical colleges and could change the face of vocational education in the US. Mourshed et al. (2012) and Halpern (2006) provide many other examples of advanced job training programs.

6 Firms are required to consult with the works council when implementing new technology. In Germany in the 1980s, works councils in research firms opposed the introduction of computers, which might seem self-defeating. But they did this so that computers would be implemented in a way that would not cost people jobs and would ensure that present employees would receive any training that they might need. In the end, the transition to a new technology occurred without job loss and was smoother than it might otherwise have been.

7 Volkswagen, which employs 5,000 people in Chattanooga, invested $40 million in a training program, and their first apprenticeship graduates received their certificates on August 13, 2013 (German Missions in the United States, 2013).

8 African-Americans have faced systematic and structural discrimination with vocational education from the black vocational guidance program in the 1930s to low-level vocational high schools in the 1950s and 1960s – for instance, training to be a janitor or laundry worker in high school and active counseling against going to college even for the most talented students (Janoski, 1990: 59–60). Our recommendations will benefit disadvantaged workers of all sorts; however, every effort should be made to assure that African-Americans have ample opportunities to enter into college-degree programs.

9 The McKinsey Institute estimates that if the US trained 351,000 high-school grads in specific skills by 2020, then the GDP would rise from $5.1 billion to $10.2 billion (Lund et al., 2013:143), taking into account other opportunity costs. Robert Livingston (2013) states that Germany's apprenticeship system has been "one reason why its unemployment, at about 6.4 percent, ranks lowest among European Union countries." He sees interest in such a system growing in the US.

10   The NIRB was proposed in 2007, with President Obama suggesting a $60 billion investment over 10 years and more coming from private investment. The proposal included high-speed trains, clean energy, dams, roads, and bridges. Obama said that the NIRB would create close to 2 million new jobs and would be an independent board that would (1) conduct hearings and issue subpoenas, (2) accept infrastructure projects of more than $75 million, (3) determine the federal share for financing each project, (4) issue general purpose infrastructure bonds and provide direct subsidies, and (5) provide loan guarantees to local governments issuing debt.

11   See Baker (2013) and Dunmur and Sluckin (2010) on how Samsung and LG in South Korea captured the technological lead on lead crystals from RCA's Sarnoff Research Center and others.

12   In the 2003 Hartz reforms, the German *Bundesanstalt für Arbeit* was comprehensively overhauled and renamed the *Bundesagentur für Arbeit*, with a greater focus on providing job search services. It has over 100,000 employees and 178 employment agencies (WCC Smart Search and Match, 2011; Streeck, 2009:62–3).

13   One-Stop includes the Job Corps, Native American services, the US Employment Service, unemployment insurance, TAA and NAFTA transitional adjustment assistance, welfare-to-work, senior community service employment, veterans' employment benefits including Work Opportunity Tax Credit (WOTC), vocational rehabilitation for disabled workers, adult education and English language training, post-secondary vocational education, community services block grant, housing and urban development services, and migrant seasonal farm worker information.

14   The targeted job tax credit for hiring disadvantaged workers also fits into this category. These policies subsidize employers. There are policies that subsidize workers in order to reduce inequality as well. They include the minimum wage, the earned income tax credit, wage subsidies, and wage insurance. This last program would directly attack the slide into SLAMs that comes with structural unemployment.

15   Internet sales taxes are being clawed back by state governments. The cases are often decided by state courts, and a critical issue is whether the internet company has a physical presence in the state (an odd requirement as they claim to have a cyberspace location, not any physical location). So if a state has a headquarters or warehouses located within its borders

(e.g., California and Kentucky), then it can be more successful in getting the internet corporation to pay state sales and other taxes (Wood, 2013).

16   Some recommend that the US lower corporate taxes and create a value-added tax (VAT) that would encourage exports. But a VAT would be regressive. While the actual corporate tax rate in the US is higher than Europe, it is not very effectively enforced. Instead of creating a VAT, corporate tax loopholes could be closed.

References

Abbate, Janet. 1999. *Inventing the Internet*. Cambridge, MA: MIT Press.

Abernathy, Frederick, John Dunlop, Janice Hammond, and David Weil. 1999. *A Stitch in Time*. New York: Oxford University Press.

Acemoglu, Daron. 2002. Technical Change, Inequality and the Labor Market. *Journal of Economic Literature* 40:7–72.

Acemoglu, Daron. 2009. *Introduction to Modern Economic Growth*. Princeton, NJ: Princeton University Press.

Acemoglu, Daron, and David Autor. 2010. *Skills, Tasks and Technologies: Implications for Employment and Earnings*. NBER Working Paper No. 16082. http://www.nber.org/papers/w16082.

Acemoglu, Daron, and James Robinson. 2011. *Why Nations Fail*. New York: Crown.

ACT. 2012. ACT WorkKeys®. http://www.act.org/products /workforce-act-workkeys.

Aghion, Philippe, and Peter Howitt. 2009. *The Economics of Growth*. Cambridge, MA: MIT Press.

AJA (American Jobs Act). 2011. Businessinsider.com. http://articles. businessinsider.com/2011-09-08/politics/30154925_1_payroll -tax-credit-jobs-plan#ixzz22yhWpl75.

Alderson, Arthur. 1997. Globalization and Deindustrialization: Direct Investment and the Decline of Manufacturing Employment in 17 OECD Nations. *Journal of World-Systems Research* 3:1–34.

Alderson, Arthur. 1999. Explaining Deindustrialization: Globalization, Failure, or Success? *American Sociological Review* 65: 701–21.

Alderson, Arthur. 2004. Explaining the Upswing in Direct Investment: A Test of Mainstream and Heterodox Theories of Globalization. *Social Forces* 83:81–122.

Althauser, Robert, and Arne Kalleberg. 1981. Firms, Occupations and the Structure of Labor Markets. Pp. 119–49 in Ivar Berg (ed.) *Sociological Perspectives on Labor Markets*. New York: Academic Press.

Andersson, Fredrik, Harry Holzer, and Julia Lane. 2005. *Moving Up or Moving On*. New York: Russell Sage.

Anner, Mark. 2012. Corporate Social Responsibility and Freedom of Association Rights: The Precarious Quest for Legitimacy and Control in Global Supply Chains. *Politics and Society* 40(4): 609–44.

Appelbaum, Eileen. 2012. Reducing Inequality and Insecurity: Rethinking Labor and Employment Policy for the 21st Century. *Work and Occupations* 39(4):311–20.

Aronowitz, Stanley. 2005. *Just Around the Corner: The Paradox of the Jobless Recovery*. Philadelphia, PA: Temple University Press.

Aronowitz, Stanley, and Jonathan Cutler (eds.). 1997. *Post-Work*. New York: Routledge.

Aronowitz, Stanley, and William DiFazio. 2010. *The Jobless Future*. Minneapolis: University of Minnesota Press.

Arrighi, Giovanni. 2007. *Adam Smith in Beijing*. New York: Verso.

Arrighi, Giovanni, and Jason Moore. 2001. Capitalist Development in World Historical Perspective. Pp. 56–75 in R. Albritton, M. Itoh, R. Westra, and A. Zuege (eds.) *Phases of Capitalist Development*. London: Macmillan.

Asker, John, Joan Farre-Mensa, and Alexander Ljungqvist. 2013. *Corporate Interest and Stock Market Listing: A Puzzle?* Brussels: European Corporate Governance Institute. April 22. http://papers.ssrn.com/sol3/papers.cfm?abstract_id=1603484##.

Atkinson, Robert, and Stephen Ezell. 2012. *Innovation Economics*. New Haven, CT: Yale University Press.

Autor, David, and David Dorn. 2009. *The Growth of Low Skill Service Jobs and the Polarization of the US Labor Market*. NBER Working Paper No. 15150. http://www.nber.org/papers/w15150.

Autor, David, Lawrence Katz, and Alan Krueger. 1998. Computing Inequality: Have Computers Changed the Labor Market? *Quarterly Journal of Economics* 113:1169–213.

Autor, David, Lawrence Katz, and Melissa Kearney. 2005. *Trends in US Wage Inequality: Re-Assessing the Revisionists*. NBER Working Paper No. 11627. http://www.nber.org/papers/w11627.

Autor, David, David Dorn, and Gordon Hanson. 2013. The China Syndrome: Local Labor Market Effects of Import Competition in the United States. *American Economic Review* 103(6):2121–68.

Badham, Richard. 2005. Technology and the Transformation of Work. Pp. 115–37 in Stephen Ackroyd, Rosemary Batt, Paul Thompson, and Pamela Tolbert (eds.) *The Oxford Handbook of Work and Organization*. New York: Oxford University Press.

Baily, Martin, and Robert Lawrence. 2004. What Happened to the Great US Job Machine? The Role of Trade and Electronic Offshoring. *Brookings Papers on Economic Activity* 2:211–84.

Baker, Nicholson. 2013. A Fourth State of Matter: Inside South Korea's LCD Revolution. *New Yorker*. July 8 and 15:64–73.

Balfour, Frederik, and Tim Culpan. 2010a. Inside Foxconn. *Businessweek*. September 13.

Balfour, Frederik, and Tim Culpan. 2010b. The Man who Makes Your iPhone. *Businessweek*. September 9.

Barley, Stephen. 2005. What We Know (and Mostly Don't Know) about Technical Work. Pp. 371–403 in S. Ackroyd, R. Batt, P. Thompson, and P. Tolbert (eds.) *The Oxford Handbook of Work and Organization*. New York: Oxford University Press.

Bartlett, Donald, and James Steele. 2012. *The Betrayal of the American Dream*. Philadelphia, PA: Perseus.

BCG (Boston Consulting Group). 2012a. Skills Gap in US Manufacturing is Less Pervasive Than Many Believe. Boston Consulting Group. October 15. http://www.bcg.com/media/PresReleaseDetails.aspx?id=tcm:12-118945.

BCG (Boston Consulting Group). 2012b. More than a Third of Large Manufacturers are Considering Reshoring from China to the US. Boston Consulting Group. April 20. http://www.bcg.com/media/pressreleasedetails.aspx?id=tcm:12-104216.

BEA (Bureau of Economic Analysis). 2012. US Department of Commerce statistics website. http://www.bea.gov/iTable/iTable.cfm?ReqID=17&step=1.

Beaudry, Paul, David Green, and Benjamin Sand. 2013. *The Great Reversal in the Demand for Skill and Cognitive Tasks*. NBER Working Paper No. 18901. http://www.nber.org/papers/w18901.

Bell, Daniel. 1973. *The Coming of Post-Industrial Society*. New York: Basic Books.

Bell, Linda, and Richard Freeman. 1991. The Causes of Increasing Inter-Industry Wage Dispersion in the United States. *Industrial and Labor Relations Review* 44(2):275–301.

Belson, Ken. 2012. Around the World with 5,500 Cars. *New York Times*. July 13.

Benner, Chris, Laura Leete, and Manuel Pastor. 2007. *Staircases or Treadmills?* New York: Russell Sage.

Berggren, Christian. 1992. *Alternatives to Lean Production*. Ithaca, NY: ILR Press.

Binfield, Kevin. 2004. *Writings of the Luddites*. Baltimore: Johns Hopkins University Press.

Blinder, Alan. 2006. Offshoring: The Next Industrial Revolution? *Foreign Affairs* 85(2):113–28.

Blinder, Alan. 2007. *How Many US Jobs Might Be Offshorable?* CEPS Working Paper No. 142.

Block, Fred. 2010. The Future of Economics, New Circuits for Capital, and Re-Envisioning the Relation of State and Market. Pp. 379–88 in Michael Lounsbury and Paul Hirsch (eds.) *Markets on Trial, Part B*. Bingley: Emerald Group.

BLS/CPS (Bureau of Labor Statistics/Current Population Survey). 2013. Databases, Tables and Calculations by Subject. Labor Force Statistics from the Current Population Survey. http://data. bls.gov/timeseries/LNS11300000.

Bluestone, Barry, and Bennett Harrison. 1982. *The Deindustrialization of America*. New York: Basic Books.

Boeri, Tito, and Jan van Ours. 2008. *The Economics of Imperfect Labor Markets*. Princeton, NJ: Princeton University Press.

Boeri, Tito, Claudio Lucifora, and Kevin Murphy. 2013. *Executive Remuneration and Employee Performance-Related Pay*. New York: Oxford University Press.

Bonacich, Edna, and Jake Wilson. 2008. *Getting the Goods*. Ithaca, NY: Cornell University Press.

Bonoli, Giuliano. 2010. The Political Economy of Active Labor Market Policy. *Politics and Society* 38(4):435–57.

Bookstaber, Richard. 2008. *A Demon of Their Own Design*. New York: Wiley.

Bradley, David, and John Stephens. 2006. Employment Performance in OECD Countries. *Comparative Political Studies* 40(12): 1–25.

Bradley, William. 2004. Offshore Teleradiology. *Journal of the American College of Radiology* 1:244–8.

Brady, David, Jason Beckfield, and W. Zhao. 2007. The Consequences of Economic Globalization for Affluent Democracies. *Annual Review of Sociology* 33:313–34.

Braverman, Harry. 1974. *Labor and Monopoly Capital*. New York: Monthly Review Press.

Brooks, Robert A. 2011. *Cheaper by the Hour: Temporary Lawyers and the Deprofessionalization of the Law*. Philadelphia, PA: Temple University Press.

Brynjolfsson, Erik, and Andrew McAfee. 2011. *Race Against the Machine*. Cambridge, MA: MIT Press.

Burawoy, Michael. 1979. *Manufacturing Consent*. Chicago: University of Chicago Press.

Burawoy, Michael. 1985. *The Politics of Production*. London: Verso.

Cain, P., and A. Hopkins. 1987. Gentlemanly Capitalism and British Expansion Overseas II. *Economic History Review* 39:501–25.

Calmfors, Lars. 1994. *Active Labour Market Policy and Unemployment*. Paris: OECD.

Cappelli, Peter. 1999. *The New Deal at Work*. Boston, MA: Harvard Business School Press.

Cappelli, Peter. 2008. *Talent on Demand*. Boston, MA: Harvard Business School Press.

Cappelli, Peter. 2012a. *Why Good People Can't Get Jobs*. Philadelphia, PA: Wharton Digital Press.

Cappelli, Peter. 2012b. The Skills Gap Myth: Why Companies Can't Find Good People. *Time*. June 4.

Card, David, Jochen Kluve, and Andrea Weber. 2010. *Active Labor Market Policy Evaluation: A Meta-Analysis*. NBER Working Paper No. 16173. http://www.nber.org/papers/w16173.

Carmel, Erran, and Paul Tija. 2005. *Offshoring Information Technology*. New York: Cambridge University Press.

Carollo, Salvatoro. 2011. *Understanding Oil Prices*. New York: Wiley.

Chang, Ha-Joon. 2002. *Kicking Away the Ladder: Development Strategy in Historical Perspective*. New York: Anthem Press.

Chen, Jinzhu, Prakash Kannan, Prakash Loungani, and Bharat Trehan. 2011. *New Evidence on Cyclical and Structural Sources of Unemployment*. IMF Working Paper WP/11/106.

Clements, Jeffrey. 2012. *Corporations Are Not People*. San Francisco: Barrett-Koehler.

CNN-Fortune. 2013. Fortune 500: Top Companies. http://money.cnn.com/magazines/fortune/fortune500/2011/performers/companies/biggest/employees.html.

Cohen, Dov, and Robert Lawless. 2012. Less Forgiven: Race and Chapter 13 Bankruptcy. Pp. 175–91 in Katherine Porter (ed.) *Broke: How Debt Bankrupts the Middle Class*. Stanford, CA: Stanford University Press.

Cole, Robert E. 1989. *Strategies for Learning*. Berkeley: University of California Press.

Coll, Steven. 2012. *Private Empire: Exxon Mobile and American Power*. New York: Penguin.

Conesa, Juan, Sagiri Kitao, and Dirk Krueger. 2009. Taxing Capital? Not a Bad Idea After All. *American Economic Review* 99(1): 25–48.

Conway, Maureen, Amy Blair, and Matt Helmer. 2012. *Courses to Employment*. Washington, DC: Aspen Institute.

Crawford, Beverly. 2008. Introduction: Globalization's Impact on American Government and Law. Pp. xiii–xl in Beverly Crawford (ed.) *The Impact of Globalization on the United States. Vol. 2.* New York: Columbia University Press.

Cudahy, Brian. 2006. The Containership Revolution: Malcolm McLean's 1956 Innovation Goes Global. *TR News* 246:5–9.

Cullen, Julie, Steven Levitt, Erin Robertson, and Sally Sadoff. 2013. What Can be Done to Improve Struggling High Schools? *Journal of Economic Perspectives* 27(2):133–52.

Daly, Mary, Bart Hobijn, Ayşegül Şahin, and Robert Valetta. 2012. A Search and Matching Approach to Labor Markets. *Journal of Economic Perspectives* 26(3):3–26.

Daniels, Peter W. 2007. A Global Service Economy? Pp. 103–25 in J. R. Bryson and P. W. Daniels (eds.) *The Handbook of Service Industries*. Cheltenham: Edward Elgar.

Davidson, Adam. 2012. Making it in America. *Atlantic*. January/February:58–70.

Davis, Gerald. 2009. *Managed by Markets*. New York: Oxford University Press.

Davis, Gerald, and Tracy Thompson. 1994. A Social Movement Perspective on Corporate Control. *Administrative Science Quarterly* 39:141–73.

Davis, Steven, R. Faberman, John Haltiwanger, and Ian Rucker. 2010. Adjusted Estimates of Worker Flows and Job Openings in JOLTS. Pp. 187–216 in K. Abraham, J. Spletzer, and M. Harper (eds.) *Labor in the New Economy*. Chicago: University of Chicago Press.

Davis-Blake, Alison, and Joseph Broschak. 2009. Outsourcing and the Changing Nature of Work. *Annual Review of Sociology* 35:321–40.

Dedrick, Jason, Kenneth Kraemer, and Greg Linden. 2010. Who Profits from Innovation in Global Value Chains? *Industrial and Corporate Change* 19(1):81–116.

Dedrick, Jason, Kenneth Kraemer, and Greg Linden. 2011. The Distribution of Value in the Mobile Phone Supply Chain. *Telecommunications Policy* 35(6):505–21.

De Lange, Deborah. 2011. *Cliques and Capitalism*. London: Palgrave Macmillan.

DeLong, J. Bradford. 2010a. Is Today's Unemployment Structural? *Economists' Voice* 7(3).

DeLong, J. Bradford. 2010b. *The End of Influence*. New York: Basic Books.

Deming, William Edwards. 1982. *Out of the Crisis*. Cambridge, MA: MIT Press.

Denison, Edward. 1969. *Why Growth Rates Differ*. Washington, DC: Brookings.

Denison, Edward. 1980. *Accounting for Slower Growth*. Washington, DC: Brookings.

Desai, Mihir, C. F. Foley, and James Hines. 2005. *Foreign Direct Investment and the Domestic Capital Stock*. NBER Working Paper No. 11075. http://www.nber.org/papers/w11075.

Desai, Mihir, C. F. Foley, and James Hines. 2007. *Foreign Direct Investment and Domestic Economic Activity*. NBER Working Paper No. 11717. http://www.nber.org/papers/w11717.

Donaghu, Michael, and Richard Barff. 1990. Nike Just Did It: International Subcontracting and Flexibility in Athletic Footwear Production. *Regional Studies* 24(6):537–52.

Dowd, Kevin. 2005. *Measuring of Market Risk*. New York: Wiley.

Dowd, Kevin, and Martin Hutchinson. 2010. *Alchemists of Loss*. New York: Wiley.

Duhigg, Charles, and David Kocieniewski. 2012. How Apple Side-steps Billions in Taxes. *New York Times*. April 28.

Dunmur, David, and Tim Sluckin. 2010. *Soap, Science and Flat-Screen TVs*. New York: Oxford University Press.

Dwyer, Rachel, and Erik Olin Wright. 2011. Job Growth and Job Polarization in the United States and Europe, 1995–2007. Pp. 52–74 in Enrique Fernández-Macias, John Hurley, and Donald Storrie (eds.) *Transformation of the Employment Structures in the EU and USA*. New York: Palgrave.

Eban, Katherine. 2011. Is a Doctor Reading your X-Rays? Maybe Not. *NBCNews.com*. October 26. http://www.nbcnews.com/id/44949425/ns/health-cancer.

Economist. 2006. The Container Industry: The World in a Box. *The Economist*. March 16.

Economist. 2013. Here, There and Everywhere. Special Report: Outsourcing and Offshoring. *The Economist*. January 17.

Estevão, Marcello, and Evridiki Tsounta. 2011. *Has the Great Recession Raised US Structural Unemployment?* IMF Working Paper WP/11/105.

Faggio, Giulia, Kjell Salvanes, and John van Reenen. 2010. The Evolution of Inequality in Productivity and Wages. *Industrial and Corporate Change* 19(6):1919–51.

Farber, Henry. 2008. Short(er) Shrift: The Decline in Worker–Firm Attachment in the United States. Pp. 10–37 in Katherine Newman (ed.) *Laid Off, Laid Low*. New York: Columbia University Press.

FDIC (Federal Deposit Insurance Corporation). 2013. Selected Sections of the Dodd-Frank Wall Street Reform and Consumer

Protection   Act.   http://www.fdic.gov/regulations/reform/dfa_selections.html#619.

Feagin, Joe, and Melvin Sikes. 1995. *Living with Racism: The Black Middle-Class Experience*. Boston, MA: Beacon Press.

Ferguson, Niall. 2004. *Colossus: The Rise and Fall of the American Empire*. Harmondsworth: Penguin.

Finegold, David, Mary Gatta, Hal Salzman, and Susan Schurman (eds.). 2010. *Transforming the U.S. Workforce Development System*. Urbana: ILR Press.

Finkelstein, Ellen. 2011. *AutoCAD 2012 and AutoCAD LT 2012 Bible*. New York: Wiley.

Finlay, William. 1988. *Work on the Waterfront*. Philadelphia, PA: Temple University Press.

Fishman, Charles. 2006. *The Wal-Mart Effect*. Harmondsworth: Penguin.

Fishman, Charles. 2012. The Insuring Boom. *Atlantic Magazine*. December:45–52.

Fligstein, Neil. 2001. *The Architecture of Markets*. Princeton, NJ: Princeton University Press.

Ford, Martin. 2009. *The Lights in the Tunnel*. Wayne, PA: Acculant.

Forslund, Anders, and Alan Krueger. 2008. *Did Active Labour Market Policies Help Sweden Rebound from the Depression of the Early 1990s?* CEPS Working Paper No. 158.

Fortune. 1999. GE's Jack Welch Named Manager of the Century. *Fortune*. November 1. http://www.timewarner.com/corp/newsroom/pr/0,20812,667526,00.html.

Fortune. 2012. Fortune 100. *Fortune*. http://money.cnn.com/fortune/best-companies/2012/full_list.

Fransen, Luc. 2012. *Corporate Social Responsibility and Global Labor Standards*. New York: Routledge.

Friedman, Thomas. 2005. *The World Is Flat*. New York: Farrar, Straus and Giroux.

Friedman, Thomas, and Michael Mandelbaum. 2011. *That Used to Be Us*. New York: Farrar, Straus and Giroux.

Frontline. 2005. Is Wal-Mart Good for America? PBS Video. November 16. www.shoppbs.org/product/index.jsp?productId-1889876&cp.

Frydman, Roman, and Michael Goldberg. 2011. *Beyond Mechanical Markets*. Princeton, NJ: Princeton University Press.

Geisinger, Scott. 2012. Nike as a Donut Corporation. Senior Seminar Paper, University of Kentucky, Sociology Department.

Gerard, Leo W., and Leo Hindery, Jr. 2011. *Task Force on Job Creation*. Washington, DC: New America Foundation.

Gereffi, Gary. 2005. *The New Offshoring of Jobs and Global Development*. Geneva: ILO.

Gereffi, Gary, J. Humphrey, and Timothy Sturgeon. 2005. The Governance of Global Value Chains. *Review of International Political Economy* 12(1):78–104.

German Missions in the United States. 2013. Volkswagen Trainees First in US to Receive German Apprenticeship Certificate. Germany.info. http://www.germany.info/Vertretung/usa/en/__pr /P__Wash/2013/08/13-VW-USA.html.

Gibbs, Michael. 2010. Extinction of the Middle Class. *Chronicle of Higher Education*. August 29. http://chronicle.com/article /Extinction-of-the-Middle-Class/124155.

Gibson, Donald. 2012. *Wealth, Power and the Crisis of Laissez Faire Capitalism*. New York: Palgrave Macmillan.

Gladwell, Malcolm. 2011. The Tweaker: The Real Genius of Steve Jobs. *New Yorker*. November 14.

Godofsky, Jessica, Carl van Horn, and Cliff Zukin. 2010. *The Shattered American Dream*. Rutgers University Research Institute Report.

Goeldner, Charles. 1962. Automation in Marketing. *Journal of Marketing* 26(1):53–66.

Goffman, Erving. 1952. On Cooling the Mark Out: Some Aspects of Adaptation to Failure. *Psychiatry: Journal of Interpersonal Relations* 15:451–63.

Goffman, Erving. 1963. *Stigma*. New York: Simon and Schuster.

Golden, Claudia, and Lawrence Katz. 2008. *The Race between Education and Technology*. Cambridge, MA: Belknap Press.

Goldstein, Adam. 2012. Revenge of the Managers: Labor Cost-Cutting and the Paradoxical Resurgence of Managerialism in the Shareholder Value Era, 1984 to 2001. *American Sociological Review* 77(2):268–94.

Görg, Holger. 2011. Globalization, Offshoring and Jobs. Pp. 21–47 in Marc Bacchetta and Marion Jansen (eds.) *Making Globalization Socially Sustainable*. Washington, DC: WTO; Geneva: ILO.

Goulder, Robert. 2012. US Government Indicts Swiss Bank for Aiding Tax Fraud. *Tax Notes*. 134(6):634–6. February 6.

Grobart, Sam. 2012. What Machines Can't Do. *Businessweek*. December 17.

Grove, Andy. 2010. How America Can Create Jobs. *Businessweek*. July 1.

Gruley, Bryan. 2013. How a Turkish Immigrant Made a Billion Dollars in Eight Years Selling Yogurt. *Businessweek*. February 4.

Guenther, John. 2012. Skills Gap, Real or Not, Could Put Long-Term Dent in California Economy. California Economic Summit.

October 15. http://www.caeconomy.org/reporting/entry/skills-gap
-real-or-not-could-put-long-term-dent-in-california-economy.

Hacker, Jacob. 2002. *The Divided Welfare State*. Cambridge: Cambridge University Press.

Hall, Douglas. 2001. *Careers In and Out of Organizations*. Thousand Oaks, CA: Sage.

Hall, Douglas, and Philip H. Mirvis. 1995. The New Career Contract. *Journal of Vocational Behavior* 4(7):269–89.

Halpern, Robert. 2006. *The Means to Grow Up*. New York: Routledge.

Haltiwanger, Jon, Ron Jarmin, and Javier Miranda. 2010. *Who Creates Jobs? Small vs. Large vs. Young*. NBER Working Paper No. 16300. http://www.nber.org/papers/w16300.

Hamilton, Gary. 2006. *Commerce and Capitalism in Chinese Economies*. London: Routledge.

Hamilton, Stephen. 1990. *Apprenticeship for Adulthood*. New York: Free Press.

Hamilton, Stephen. 1999. Germany and the United States in Comparative Perspective. *International Journal of Sociology* 29: 3–20.

Handel, Michael. 2003. Skills Mismatch in the Labor Market. *Annual Review of Sociology* 29:135–65.

Handel, Michael, and Maury Gittleman. 2004. Is There a Wage Payoff to Innovative Work Practices? *Industrial Relations* 43:67–97.

Hardie, Ian, and Donald MacKenzie. 2007. Assembling an Economic Actor: The Agencement of a Hedge Fund. *Sociological Review* 55:57–80.

Harney, Alexandra. 2008. *The China Price*. Harmondsworth: Penguin.

Harrigan, James. 2003. Specialization and the Volume of Trade: Do the Data Obey the Laws? Pp. 85–118 in E. Kwan Choi and James Harrigan (eds.) *Handbook of International Trade*. London: Blackwell.

Harvey, David. 1990. *The Condition of Postmodernity*. Malden, MA: Blackwell.

Harvey, David. 2007. *The Limits to Capital*. London: Verso.

Harvey, David. 2010. *The Enigma of Capital and the Crises of Capitalism*. New York: Oxford University Press.

Hicken, Melanie, and Abby Rogers. 2012. 12 Faces of the Law School Underemployment Crisis. *Business Insider*. October, 16. http://www.businessinsider.com/law-school-unemployment-crisis-2012-9?op=1.

Hira, Ron, and Anil Hira. 2005. *Outsourcing America*. New York: AMACOM.

Hoffman, Nancy. 2011. *Schooling in the Workplace*. Cambridge, MA: Harvard Education Press.

Hollister, Matissa. 2011. Employment Stability in the US Labor Market: Rhetoric versus Reality. *Annual Review of Sociology* 37:305–24.

Holmes, Stanley. 2004. The New Nike. *Businessweek*. September 19. http://www.businessweek.com/stories/2004-09-19/the-new-nike.

Holmes, Stanley. 2007. Can Nike Do It? *Businessweek*. February 7.

Holzer, Harry, and Marek Hlavac. 2011. An Uneven Road and Then a Cliff: US Labor Markets Since 2000. Pp. 1–21 in John Logan and Brian Stults (directors) *US2010 Project: Report*. Washington, DC: US Census. http://www.s4.brown.edu/us2010/Data/Report/report4.pdf.

Holzer, Harry, Julia Lane, David Rosenblum, and Fredrik Andersson. 2011. *Where Are All the Good Jobs Going?* New York: Russell Sage.

Horkheimer, Max, and Theodore Adorno. 2007 [1947]. *Dialectic of Enlightenment*. Stanford, CA: Stanford University Press.

Huber, Evelyn, and John Stephens. 2001. *Development and Crisis of the Welfare State*. Chicago: University of Chicago Press.

Hurst, Erik, and Benjamin Pugsley. 2011. What Do Small Businesses Do. NBER Working Paper No. 17041. http://www.nber.org/papers/w17041.

IBM. 2012. INNOV8-2.0. Download site. http://www-01.ibm.com/software/solutions/soa/innov8/index.html.

Ingram, Paul, Lori Qingyuan Yue, and Hayagreeva Rao. 2010. Trouble in Store: Probes, Protests and Store Openings by Wal-Mart, 1998–2007. *American Journal of Sociology* 116(1): 53–92.

Isaacson, Walter. 2011. *Steve Jobs*. New York: Simon and Schuster.

Jacobs, Jane. 1992 [1961]. *The Death and Life of Great American Cities*. New York: Vintage.

Jacobides, M. G., T. Knudsen, and M. Augier. 2006. Benefiting from Innovation. *Research Policy* 35(8):1200–21.

Jamieson, Dave. 2012. Jamie Dimon Confronted by Houston Janitor over Low Wages. *Huffington Post*. August 7. http://www.huffingtonpost.com/2012/06/19/jamie-dimon-jpmorgan-congressional-hearing-janitor_n_1610198.html.

Janoski, Thomas. 1990. *The Political Economy of Unemployment*. Berkeley: University of California Press.

Janoski, Thomas. 1994. Direct State Intervention in the Labor Market: The Explanation of Active Labor Market Policy from

1950 to 1988 in Social Democratic, Conservative, and Liberal Regimes. Pp. 54–92 in Thomas Janoski and Alexander Hicks (eds.) *The Comparative Political Economy of the Welfare State.* New York: Cambridge University Press.

Janoski, Thomas. 1998. *Citizenship and Civil Society.* New York: Cambridge.

Janoski, Thomas. 2010. *The Ironies of Citizenship.* New York: Cambridge University Press.

Janoski, Thomas. 2013. Citizenship and Civil Society in China: An Overview of Rights and the Public Sphere. Plenary paper presentation at the "Citizenship and Orientalism" conference at Sun Yat-Sen University, Guangzhou, June 15.

Janoski, Thomas and Darina Lepadatu. 2013. *Dominant Divisions of Labor.* London: Palgrave Macmillan.

Joffe-Walt, Chana. 2013. In One Alabama County, Nearly 1 in 4 Working-Age Adults Is on Disability. *NPR.* March 25. www.npr.org/2013/03/25/175293860/in-one-alabama-country-nearly-1-in-4-working-age-adults-is-on-disability.

Kalleberg, Arne. 2011. *Good Jobs, Bad Jobs.* New York: Russell Sage.

Keen, Steve. 2011. *Debunking Economics*, 2nd edn. London: Zed Books.

Kelly, Kevin. 2010. *What Technology Wants.* New York: Viking.

Keynes, John Maynard. 2000 [1923]. *A Tract on Monetary Reform.* Amherst, NY: Prometheus.

Kharif, Olga. 2007. Walmart's Latest Sale: Broadband. *Businessweek.* October 8.

Khurana, Rakesh. 2002. *Searching for a Corporate Savior.* Princeton, NJ: Princeton University Press.

Kim, Changhwan, and Arthur Sakamoto. 2007. *Declining Inter-Industry Wage Dispersion in the US.* Minnesota Population Center Working Paper, 2/27/2007.

King, Roger. 1986. *The State in Modern Society.* Chatham, NJ: Chatham House.

Kochan, Thomas. 2011. Resolving America's Human Capital Paradox: A Proposal for a Jobs Compact. http://www.employmentpolicy.org/topic/12/research/jobs-compact-america.

Krafcik, John. 1988. Triumph of the Lean Production System. *Sloan Management Review* 30(1):41–52.

Krippner, Greta. 2011. *Capitalizing on Crisis.* Cambridge, MA: Harvard University Press.

Kristal, Tali. 2010. Good Times, Bad Times: Postwar Labor's Share of National Income in Capitalist Democracies. *American Sociological Review* 75:729–63.

Kristal, Tali. 2013. The Capitalist Machine: Computerization, Workers' Power and the Decline in Labor's Share within US Industries. *American Sociological Review* 78(3):361–90.

Krugman, Paul. 1979. Increasing Returns, Monopolistic Competition, and International Trade. *Journal of International Economics* 9:469–79.

Krugman, Paul. 1980. Scale Economies, Product Differentiation, and the Pattern of Trade. *American Economic Review* 70: 950–9.

Krugman, Paul. 1981. Interindustry Specialization and the Gains from Trade. *Journal of Political Economy* 89:959–73.

Krugman, Paul. 1993. What Do Undergrads Need to Know about Trade? *American Economic Review* 83(2):23–6.

Krugman, Paul. 1996. White Collars Turn Blue. *New York Times*. September 29.

Krugman, Paul. 1999. *Return to Depression Economics*. New York: Norton.

Krugman, Paul. 2009. *The Return to Depression Economics and the Crisis of 2009*. New York: Norton.

Krugman, Paul. 2010a. Debunking the Structural Unemployment Myth. *New York Times*. September 8.

Krugman, Paul. 2010b. Structure of Excuses. *New York Times*. September 26.

Krugman, Paul. 2011. Autor, Autor. *New York Times*. March 6.

Krugman, Paul, and Maurice Obstfeld. 2009. *International Economics*. Boston, MA: Pearson.

Kurtgenbach, Elaine. 2006. Apple: No Forced Labor at iPod Plant. *Washington Post*. August 18. http://www.washingtonpost.com/wp-dyn/content/article/2006/08/18/AR2006081800230_pf.thml.

Kurzweil, Ray. 2005. *The Singularity is Near*. Harmondsworth: Penguin.

Kwon, Hyeong-ki. 2012. The Politics of Globalization and National Economy: The German Experience Compared with the United States. *Politics and Society* 40(4):581–607.

Lambert, Emily. 2010. *The Futures: The Rise of the Speculator and the Origins of the World's Biggest Markets*. New York: Basic Books.

Lane, Bill. 2007. *Jacked Up: The Inside Story of How Jack Welch Talked GE into Becoming the World's Greatest Company*. New York: McGraw-Hill.

Langille, Brian. 2005. Better Governance of the Internationalization of Employment. Pp. 143–62 in Peter Auer, Genevieve Besse, and Dominique Meda (eds.) *Offshoring and the Internationalization of Employment*. Geneva: ILO.

Lashinsky, Adam. 2012. How Tim Cook is Changing Apple. *Fortune*. May 24.

Lazonick, William. 2009. *Sustainable Prosperity in the New Economy*. Kalamazoo, MI: Upjohn Institute for Employment Research.

Lee, Ching Kwan. 2007. *Against the Law*. Berkeley: University of California Press.

Leicht, Kevin. 2012. Borrowing to the Brink: Consumer Debt in America. Pp. 195–217 in Katherine Porter (ed.) *Broke: How Debt Bankrupts the Middle Class*. Stanford, CA: Stanford University Press.

Leicht, Kevin, and Scott Fitzgerald. 2007. *Post-Industrial Peasants: The Illusion of Middle-Class Prosperity*. Belmont, CA: Worth.

Lepadatu, Darina, and Thomas Janoski. 2011. *Diversity at Kaizen Motors*. Lanham, MD: University of America Press.

Letkemann, Paul. 2002. Unemployment Professionals, Stigma Management and Derivative Stigmata. *Work, Employment and Society* 16(3):511–22.

Levine, Linda. 2009. *The Labor Market during the Great Depression and the Current Recession*. Congressional Research Service Report for Congress. June.

Levine, Linda. 2010. *Unemployment and Economic Recovery*. Congressional Research Service Report for Congress. August 20.

Levine, Linda. 2012. *Offshoring (or Offshore Outsourcing) and Job Loss Among US Workers*. Congressional Research Service Report for Congress. December 17.

Levinson, Marc. 2006. *The Box: How the Shipping Container Made the World Smaller and the World Economy Bigger*. Princeton, NJ: Princeton University Press.

Levinson, Marc. 2013. *US Manufacturing in International Perspective*. Congressional Research Service Report for Congress. February 11.

Levy, Frank. 2009. Computers, Conversation, Utilization and Commoditization. *American Journal of Roentgenology* May: 1375–81.

Levy, Frank, and Ari Goelman. 2005. Offshoring and Radiology. Pp. 411–26 in S. Collins and L. Brainard (eds.) *Brookings Trade Forum: 2005: Offshoring White-Collar Work*. Washington, DC: Brookings.

Levy, Frank, and Richard Murnane. 2004. *The New Division of Labor*. Princeton, NJ: Princeton University Press.

Levy, S. 2006. *The Perfect Thing: How the iPod Shuffles Commerce, Culture, and Coolness*. New York: Simon and Schuster.

Lichenstein, Nelson (ed.). 2006. *Wal-Mart*. New York: New Press.

Lichenstein, Nelson. 2009. *The Retail Revolution*. New York: Picador.

Liker, Jeffrey. 2004. *The Toyota Way*. New York: McGraw-Hill.

Liker, Jeffrey, and Timothy Ogden. 2011. *Toyota under Fire*. New York: McGraw-Hill.

Lin, Ken-Hou, and Donald Tomaskovic-Devey. 2013. Financialization and US Income Inequality, 1970–2008. *American Sociological Review* 118(5):1284–1329.

Linden, Greg, Jason Dedrick, and Kenneth Kraemer. 2011. Innovation and Job Creation in a Global Economy: The Case of Apple's i-Pod. *Journal of International Commerce and Economics* 3(1):223–39.

Lindsay, Colin, and Ronald W. McQuaid. 2004. Avoiding the "McJobs." *Work, Employment and Society* 18:297–319.

Litan, Robert, and Carl Schramm. 2012. *Better Capitalism*. New Haven, CT: Yale University Press.

Livingston, Robert. 2013. Looking Ahead: Opportunities for German Leadership. *AICGS Advisor*. July 25.

Lowenstein, Roger. 2004. *The Origins of the Crash*. Harmondsworth: Penguin.

Lund, Susan, James Maryika, Scott Nyquist, Lenny Mendonca, and Sreenivas Ramaswamy. 2013. *Game Changers: Five Opportunities for US Growth and Renewal*. San Francisco: McKinsey Institute.

MacKenzie, Donald. 2009. *Material Markets*. Oxford: Oxford University Press.

Magee, David. 2009. *Jeff Immelt and the New GE Way*. New York: McGraw-Hill.

Maher, Kris. 2007. Wal-Mart Seeks New Flexibility in Worker Shifts. *Wall Street Journal*. January 3. http://online.wsj.com.

Manjoo, Farhad. 2011. Will Robots Steal Your Job? http://www.slate.com/articles/technology/robot_invasion/2011/09.

Manyika, James, Jeff Sinclair, Richard Dobbs, et al.. 2012. *Manufacturing the Future: A New Era of Global Growth and Innovation*. Seoul, San Francisco, and London: McKinsey. http://www.mckinsey.com/insights/mgi/research/productivity_competitiveness_and_growth/the_future_of_manufacturing.

Markoff, John. 2011. Armies of Expensive Lawyers Replaced by Cheaper Software. *New York Times*. March 4. http://www.nytimes.com/2011/03/05/science/05legal.html?_r=0.

Martin, John, and David Grubb. 2001. What Works and for Whom: A Review of OECD Countries' Experiences with Active Labour Market Policies. *Swedish Economic Policy Review* 8(2):9–56.

Marx, Karl. 1977. *Capital*. Vol. 1. New York: Vintage.

Marx, Leo. 1983. Are Science and Society Going in the Same Direction? *Science, Technology and Human Values* 8(4):6–9.

Matthewman, Steve. 2011. *Technology and Social Theory*. New York: Palgrave Macmillan.

Micklethwait, John, and Adrian Wooldridge. 2005. *The Company: A Short History of a Revolutionary Idea*. New York: Modern Library.

Minsky, Hyman. 2008. *Stabilizing an Unstable Economy*. New York: McGraw-Hill.

Mitra, Debasis. 2005. *Industrial Mathematics at Bell Labs: Past and Present*. http://cm.bell-labs.com/who/mitra/papers/Compressed HamiltonPrsntn_100905.pdf.

Moore, Thomas S. 2010. The Locus of Racial Disadvantage in the Labor Market. *American Journal of Sociology* 116(3):909–42.

Moretti, Enrico. 2012. *The New Geography of Jobs*. New York: Houghton-Mifflin-Harcourt.

Morgan, James, and Jeffrey Liker. 2008. *The Toyota Product Development System*. New York: Productivity Press.

Moss, Phillip, and Chris Tilly. 2001. *Stories Employers Tell: Race, Skill and Hiring in America*. New York: Russell Sage.

Mourshed, Mona, Diana Farrell, and Dominic Barton. 2012. *Education to Employment*. McKinsey Center for Government. http://www.mckinsey.com/features/education_to_employment.

NAS/NSF (National Academy of Science/National Science Foundation). 2013. *National Patterns of R&D Resources* (rapporteurs Michael Cohen and Esha Sinha). Washington, DC: NAS Press.

Navarro, Peter. 2013. The Price of "Made in China." *New York Times*. August 4.

Nelson, Daniel. 1996. *Managers and Workers*. Madison, WI: University of Wisconsin Press.

Neumark, David. 2011. *Spurring Job Creation in Response to Severe Recessions: Reconsidering Hiring Credits*. NBER Working Paper No. 16866. http://www.nber.org/papers/w16866.

Neumark, David. 2012. Job Creation Policies and the Great Recession. *Federal Reserve Bank of San Francisco Economic Letter* 2012-08 March 19.

Newman, Katherine. 1999. *Falling from Grace*, 2nd edn. Berkeley: University of California Press.

Newman, Katherine. 2012. *The Accordion Family*. Boston, MA: Beacon Press.

Nie, Jun, and Ethan Struby. 2011. Would Active Labor Market Policies Help Combat High US Unemployment? *Federal Reserve Bank of Kansas City Economic Review* 3Q:35–69.

Nike. 2007. *Corporate Responsibility Report*. Beaverton, OR. http://www.nikebiz.com/crreport/content/strategy/2-1-4-a-new

-model-and-shift-to-sustainable-business-and-innovation.php?cat
=cr-strategy.

Nike. 2011. About Nike. http://nikeinc.com/pages/about-nike-inc
and http://nikeinc.com/pages/history-heritage.

Noble, David. 1984. *Forces of Production*. New York: Knopf.

Nolan, Dick. 2009. Is Boeing 787 Dreamliner a Triumph or a Folly?
Harvard Business Review. HBR Blog Network. December 23.
http://blogs.hbr.org/2009/12/is-boeings-787-dreamliner-a-triumph
-or-folly?

Obama, Barack. 2013. State of the Union Address for 2013. *New
York Times*. February 13.

OECD. 1998. *Technology, Productivity and Job Creation*. Paris:
OECD.

OECD. 2007a. *Offshoring and Employment Trends and Impacts*.
Paris: OECD.

OECD. 2007b. *Qualifications Systems: Bridges to a Better Life*.
Paris: OECD.

OECD. 2008. *Jobs for Youth: Canada*. Paris: OECD.

OECD. 2009. *Jobs for Youth: United States*. Paris: OECD.

OECD. 2011a. *Employment Outlook, 2010–11*. Paris: OECD.

OECD. 2011b. *OECD Statistics on International Trade in Services*.
Paris: OECD.

OECD. 2011c. *Globalisation, Comparative Advantage and the
Changing Dynamics of Trade*. Paris: OECD.

OECD. 2011d. *Divided We Stand: Why Inequality Keeps Rising*.
Paris: OECD.

OECD. 2011e. Labour Market Programs: Expenditures and Participants. http://dx.doi.org/10.1787/lmpxp-table-2011-1-en.

OECD. 2012a. *Employment Outlook 2012*. Paris: OECD.

OECD. 2012b. *Better Skills, Better Jobs, Better Lives*. Paris: OECD.

OECD. 2012c. *Skills Strategy*. Paris: OECD.

Ohmae, Kenichi. 1995. *The End of the Nation State*. New York:
Free Press.

OMB (Office of Management and the Budget). 2012. *Historical
Tables*. Table 9.7: Summary of Outlays for the conduct of R&D,
1949–2012. http://www.whitehouse.gov/omb/budget/historicals.

Osono, Emi, Norihiko Shizumi, and Hirotaka Takeuchi. 2008.
*Extreme Toyota: Radical Contradictions that Drive Success at the
World's Best Manufacturer*. New York: Wiley.

Osterman, Paul. 2011a. Job Training in America: Making Sense of
the System. *Work and Occupations* 38(4):500–7.

Osterman, Paul. 2011b. "Community College": Promise, Perform-
ance and Policy. Pp. 129–38 in B. Wildavsky, A. Kelly, and K.
Carey (eds.) *Reinventing Higher Education*. Cambridge, MA:
Harvard Education Press.

Osterman, Paul. 2012. Job Quality in the US: The Myths that Block Action. Pp. 78–94 in Chris Warhurst, Francoise Carré, Patricia Findlay, and Chris Tilly (eds.) *Are Bad Jobs Inevitable?* Houndmills: Palgrave Macmillan.

Palley, Thomas I. 2007. Jack Welch's Barge: The New Economics of Trade. *Economics for Democratic and Open Societies.* http://www.thomaspalley.com/?p=87

Patel, Nilay. 2012. Vizio Reboots the PC: A Quiet American Success Story takes on Sleeping Giants. *Verge.* June 15. www.theverge.com/2012/6/15/3076519/visio-reboot-pc-american-hdtv-sucess-do-it-again.

Peck, Don. 2011. *Pinched: How the Great Recession Has Narrowed Our Futures and What We Can Do About It.* New York: Crown Publishers.

Pension Benefit Guaranty Corporation. 1998–2012. *Annual Report of the Pension Benefit Guarantee Corporation.* Washington, DC. http://www/pbgc.gov/res/annual-reports.html.

Perot, Ross. 1992. Transcript of the Second Presidential Debate, October 16, 1992. *New York Times.* http://www.nytimes.com/1992/10/16/us/the-1992-campaign-transcript-of-2d-tv-debate-between-bush-clinton-and-perot.html.

Perrow, Charles. 1984. *Normal Accidents.* New York: Basic Books.

Pew (Pew Research Center). 2012. *The Lost Decade of the Middle Class: Fewer, Poorer, Gloomier.* August 22. Washington, DC: Pew Social and Demographic Trends.

Pfaffenberger, Bryan. 1992. Technological Dramas. *Science, Technology and Human Values* 17(3):282–312.

Phelps, Edward. 1994. *Structural Slumps.* Cambridge, MA: Harvard University Press.

Pierson, Paul, and Jacob Hacker. 2010. *Winner Take All Politics.* New York: Simon and Schuster.

Pollack, Andrew. 2003. Who's Reading Your X-Ray? *New York Times.* November 16.

Portelligent. 2003. *Apple-iPod 30GB Digital Music Player: Report #152-031110-1c.* Austin, TX: Portelligent.

Portelligent. 2005a. *Lenovo ThinkPad T43 1.86GHz Notebook PC: Report #120.051103-D Hg.* Austin, TX: Portelligent.

Portelligent. 2005b. *HPnc6230 1.86GHz Pentium M Notebook Computer: Report #120-051111-TMe.* Austin, TX: Portelligent.

Porter, Katherine. 2012. *Broke: How Debt Bankrupts the Middle Class.* Stanford, CA: Stanford University Press.

Prasad, Monica. 2006. *The Politics of Free Markets.* Chicago: University of Chicago Press.

Preda, Alexandru. 2009. *Framing Finance.* Chicago: University of Chicago Press.

Prince, Marcelo, and Willa Plank. 2012. A Short History of Apple's Manufacturing in the US. *Wall Street Journal*. December 6.

Quijano, Elaine. 2012. Apprenticeships Better than College for Some. CBS News Text and video. http://www.cbsnews.com/2102 -18563_162-57399640.html?tag=contentMain; contentBody.

Raworth, Kate, and Thalia Kidder. 2009. Mimicking "Lean" in Global Value Chains: It's the Workers Who Get Leaned On. Pp. 165–89 in Jennifer Bair (ed.) *Frontiers of Commodity Chain Research*. Stanford, CA: Stanford University Press.

Reisenbichler, Alexander, and Kimberly Morgan. 2012. From "Sick Man" to "Miracle": Explaining the Robustness of the German Labour Market During and After the Financial Crisis of 2008–09. *Politics and Society* 40(4):549–79.

Ricardo, David. 1821 [2001]. *On the Principles of Political Economy and Taxation*. Kitchener, ONT: Batoche Books.

Rifkin, Jeremy. 1995. *The End of Work*. New York: Putnam's Sons.

Rivera, Lauren A. 2012. Hiring as Cultural Matching: The Case of Elite Professional Service Firms. *American Sociological Review* 77(6):999–1022.

Romer, David. 1990. Endogenous Technical Change. *Journal of Political Economy* 98:71–102.

Romer, David. 2012. *Advanced Macroeconomics*, 4th edn. New York: McGraw-Hill Irwin.

Rothkopf, David. 2012. *Power, Inc: The Epic Rivalry between Big Business and Government*. New York: Farrar, Straus and Giroux.

Rothstein, Jesse. 2012. *The Labor Market Four Years into the Crisis: Assessing Structural Explanations*. NBER Working Paper No. 17966. http://www.nber.org/papers/w17966.

Rubin, Beth. 1996. *Shifts in the Social Contract*. Thousand Oaks, CA: Sage.

Rubin, Richard. 2012. Cash Hoard Grows by $187 Billion in Untaxed Overseas Profits. *Bloomberg*. March 2. http://www .bloomberg.com/news/2012-03-02/cash-horde-expands-by-187 -billion-inuntaxed-offshore-accounts.html.

Rugman, Alan, and Gavin Boyd. 2003. *Alliance Capitalism for the New American Economy*. London: Edward Elgar.

Rybczynski, Witold. 1985. *Taming the Tiger: The Struggle to Control Technology*. New York: Viking/Penguin.

Şahin, Ayşegül, Joseph Song, Giorgio Topa, and Giovanni L. Violante. 2011. Measuring Mismatch in the US Labor Market. Presentation at the NBER Economic Fluctuations and Growth Research Meeting, October 21. http://users.nber.org/~confer/2011 /EFGf11/Sahin_Song_Topa_Violante.pdf..

Sale, Kirkpatrick. 1996. *Rebels Against the Future*. New York: Basic Books.

Sarbaugh-Thompson, Marjorie, Lyke Thompson, Harold Wolman, and Marie Olson. 1999. Organizational Mismatch in Urban Labor Markets: The Detroit Case. *Social Science Quarterly* 80:19–36.

Sassen, Saskia. 2000. Territory and Territoriality in the Global Economy. *International Sociology* 15(2):372–93.

Satariano, Adam, and Peter Burrows. 2011. Apple's Supply-Chain Secret? Hoard Lasers. *Businessweek*. November 11.

Satariano, Adam, and Josh Tyrangiel. 2012. Apple to Invest in Manufacturing Macs in the US, Cook Says. *Businessweek*. December 6.

Scheer, August-William. 2011. *Computer Integrated Manufacturing*. New York: Springer.

Schilling, Melissa, and H. Kevin Steensma. 2001. The Use of Modular Organizational Forms: An Industry-Level Analysis. *Academy of Management Journal* 44(6):1149–68.

Schlozman, Kay, and Sidney Verba. 1979. *Injury to Insult: Unemployment, Class and Political Response*. Cambridge, MA: Harvard University Press.

Schott, Ben. 2010. Generation R. *New York Times*. April 10.

Schumpeter, Joseph. 1950. *Capitalism, Socialism and Democracy*, 3rd edn. New York: Harper.

Shapiro, C., and Varian, H. R. 1999. *Information Rules*. Boston, MA: Harvard Business School Press.

Sharone, Ofer. 2013. Why Do Unemployed Americans Blame Themselves While Israelis Blame the System? *Social Forces* 91(4):1429–550.

Silver, Beverly. 2003. *Forces of Labor*. New York: Cambridge University Press.

Slater, Robert. 1999. *Jack Welch and the GE Way*. New York: McGraw-Hill.

Smil, Vaclav. 2010. *Prime Movers in Globalization: The History and Impact of Diesel Engines and Gas Turbines*. Cambridge, MA: MIT Press.

Smil, Vaclav. 2013. *Made in the USA: The Rise and Retreat of American Manufacturing*. Cambridge, MA: MIT Press.

Smith, Adam. 1776 [2007]. *An Inquiry into the Nature and Causes of the Wealth of Nations*. Ed. Jonathan Wight. Petersfield: Harriman House.

Staddon, John. 2012. *The Malign Hand of the Markets*. New York: McGraw-Hill.

Stevenson, Richard. 1992. GE Guilty Plea in US Aid to Israel. *New York Times*. July 23.

Stiglitz, Joseph. 2010. *Freefall*. New York: Norton.

Stone, Chad. 2013. NPR Misses the Mark with Flawed Piece on Disability. *US News and World Report*. March 29. www.usnews .com/opinion/blogs/economic-intelligence/2013/03/29/nprs -misses-the-mark-with-flawed-piece-on-disablity.

Strang, David, and Young-mi Kim. 2005. The Diffusion and Intensification of Managerial Innovations. Pp. 178–99 in S. Ackroyd, R. Batt, P. Thompson, and P. Tolbert (eds.) *The Oxford Handbook of Work and Organizations*. New York: Oxford University Press.

Streeck, Wolfgang. 2009. *Re-Forming Capitalism*. New York: Oxford University Press.

Sturgeon, Timothy. 2002. Modular Production Networks: A New American Model of Industrial Organization. *Industrial and Corporate Change* 11(3):451–96.

Surana, Suresh. 2011. *Talking Points: India as the Global Technology Hub*. RSMI International. http://www.rsmi.com /attachments/approved/india-as-the-global-technology-hub/en /Indiaasaglobaltechnologyhub_june2011.pdf.

Tasci, Murat, and John Lindner. 2010. Has the Beveridge Curve Shifted? Federal Reserve Bank of Cleveland. http://www .clevelandfed.org/research/trends/2010/0810/02labmar.cfm.

Tenner, Edward. 1997. *Why Things Bite Back*. New York: Vintage.

Thelen, Kathleen. 1999. Historical Institutionalism in Comparative Politics. *Annual Review of Political Science* 2:369–404.

Thelen, Kathleen. 2004. *How Institutions Evolve*. New York: Cambridge University Press.

Thibodeau, Patrick. 2010. Ohio Bans Offshoring as It Gives Tax Relief to Outsourcing Firm. *Computer World*. September 17. http://www.computerworld.com/s/article/9183570/Ohio_bans _offshoring_as_it_gives_tax_relieft_to_outsourcing_firm.

Thompson, E. P. 1966. *The Making of the English Working Class*. New York: Vintage.

Thompson, Paul. 1989. *The Nature of Work*, 2nd edn. London: Palgrave Macmillan.

Todd, L., T. Sitthichok, K. Mottus, G. Mihlan, and S. Wing. 2008. Health Survey of Workers Exposed to Mixed Solvent and Ergonomic Hazards in Footwear and Equipment Factory Workers in Thailand. *Annals of Occupational Hygiene* 52(3):195–205.

Tomaskovic-Devey, Donald, and Ken-Hou Lin. 2011. Economic Rents and the Financialization of the US Economy. *American Sociological Review* 76:538–59.

Townsend, Matt. 2011. Nike's Profit Tops Analysts' Estimates as US Sales Gain. *Businessweek*. June 27.

Toyota. 2004. *Employees Handbook*. Georgetown, KY: TMMK.

Turco, Catherine J. 2010. Cultural Foundations of Tokenism: Evidence from the Leveraged Buyout Industry. *American Sociological Review* 75(6):894–913.

Tybout, James. 2003. Plant- and Firm-Level Evidence on "New" Trade Theories. Pp. 388–415 in E. Choi and James Harrigan (eds.) *Handbook of International Trade*. New York: Blackwell.

Tyrangiel, Josh. 2012. Tim Cook's Freshman Year. *Businessweek*. December 6.

Uchitelle, Louis. 2006. *The Disposable American: Layoffs and their Consequences*. New York: Knopf.

Uchitelle, Louis. 2011. Working for Less: Factory Jobs Gain, but Wages Retreat. *New York Times*. December 29.

UNCTAD (UN Conference on Trade and Development). 2010a. *UNCTAD Handbook of Statistics, 2010*. Geneva: UN.

UNCTAD (UN Conference on Trade and Development). 2010b. *World Investment Report, 2010*. Geneva: UN.

US-GAO (US Government Accountability Office). 2006. *Offshoring in Six Human Services Programs*. GAO-06-342. March. Report to Congressional Committees. Washington, DC: GAO.

US-JEC (US Congress, Joint Economic Committee). 2011. *Addressing Long-Term Unemployment after the Great Recession*. Washington, DC: US Congress. August. http://www.jec.senate.gov/public/?a=Files.Serve&File_id=97c2e98e-a791-47fc-a324-6b407948e083.

Van Horn, Carl, Cliff Zukin, Mark Szeltner, and Charlie Stone. 2012. *Left Out. Forgotten? Recent High School Graduates and the Great Recession*. Work Trends. New Brunswick, NJ: Rutgers.

Vernon, Raymond. 2001. *In the Hurricane's Eye: The Troubled Prospects of Multinational Enterprises*. New York: Harvard University Press.

Vidal, Matt. 2010. *On the Persistence of Labor Market Insecurity and Slow Growth in the US: Reckoning with the Waltonist Growth Regime*. IRLE Working Paper 2010–16. www.irle.ucla.edu.

Vidal, Matt, and Leann Tigges. 2007. Temporary Employment and Strategic Staffing in the Manufacturing Sector. *Industrial Relations* 48(1):55–72.

Volscho, Thomas, and Nathan Kelly. 2012. The Rise of the Super-Rich: Power Resources, Taxes, Financial Markets and the Dynamics of the Top 1 Percent, 1949 to 2008. *American Sociological Review* 106:303–49.

Volti, Rudi. 2010. *Society and Technological Change*. New York: Worth.

Wallerstein, Immanuel. 1974. *The Modern World System*. New York: Academic Press.

Walters, Helen. 2007. Nike's New Down-Market Strategy. *Businessweek*. February 27.

Walton, Sam, and John Huey. 1993. *Sam Walton*. New York: Bantam.

Watson, Matthew. 2005. *Foundations of International Political Economy*. New York: Palgrave Macmillan.

WCC Smart Search and Match. 2011. *Case Study: Bundesagentur fur Arbeit*. Utrecht and Washington, DC: Division of Accenture. www.wcc-group.com/document.aspx?menu=products_006&page=download_dcoument&id=95364701.

Weber, Max. 1958. *The Protestant Ethnic and the Spirit of Capitalism*. New York: Scribners.

Webster, Edward, Rob Lambert, and Andries Bezuidenhout. 2008. *Grounding Globalization: Labor in an Age of Insecurity*. Oxford: Blackwell.

Weisbord, Marvin. 2004. *Productive Workplaces*, rev. edn. San Francisco: Jossey-Bass.

Weisenthal, Joe. 2013. America Is Not Drowning in Debt. *Business Insider*. April 9.

Weiss, Linda. 1998. *The Myth of the Powerless State*. Ithaca, NY: Cornell University Press.

Weissmann, Jordan. 2013. The Grad School Bubble is Set to Burst. *Atlantic*. June 19.

Wilson, William Julius. 2012. *The Truly Disadvantaged*, 2nd edn. Chicago: University of Chicago Press.

Wolter, Stefan, Samuel Mühlemann, and Jürg Schweri. 2003. *Why Some Firms Train Apprentices and Many Others Do Not*. IZA Discussion Paper 916.

Womack, James, Daniel Jones, and Daniel Roos. 1990. *The Machine that Changed the World*. New York: HarperCollins.

Wood, Robert. 2013. Amazon No Longer Tax Free. *Forbes*. August 22. http://www.forbes.com/sites/robertwood/2013/08/22/amazon-no-longer-tax-free-10-surprising-facts-as-giant-loses-ground.

World Bank. 2013. *World Development Indicators: Distribution of Income or Consumption*. Washington, DC: World Bank. http://databank.worldbank.org/data/download/WDI-2013-ebook.pdf.

Wright, Erik Olin, and Rachel Dwyer. 2003. The Patterns of Job Expansions in the USA: A Comparison of the 1960s and 1980s. *Socio-Economic Review* 1:289–325.

WSJ (*Wall Street Journal*). 2013. A Revolution in the Making. *Wall Street Journal*. June 11.

Yardley, Jim. 2013. Justice Still Elusive in Factory Disasters in Bangladesh. *New York Times*. June 29.

Yergin, Daniel, and Joseph Stanislaw. 2002. *The Commanding Heights*. New York: Simon and Schuster.

Yu, Kyoung-Hee, and Frank Levy. 2010. Offshoring Professional Services: Institutions and Professional Control. *British Journal of Industrial Relations* 48(4):858–83.

Yung, Katherine. 2011. Jobs in Michigan: Hunt for Work is an Endurance Test. *Detroit Free Press*. March 27.

Zuboff, Shoshana. 1984. *In the Age of Smart Machines*. New York: Basic Books.

Subject Index

Name Index